SACRAMENTO PUBLIC LIBRARY

3 3029 04609 1120

CENTRAL LIBRARY
828 "I" STREET
SACRAMENTO, CA 95814
JAN   2002

T0699861

Bloody Saturday in the Soviet Union

Novocherkassk, 1962

Samuel H. Baron

Bloody Saturday in the Soviet Union

Soviet Union

Novocherkassk, 1962

STANFORD UNIVERSITY PRESS

STANFORD, CALIFORNIA 2001

Stanford University Press
Stanford, California

© 2001 by the Board of Trustees of the
Leland Stanford Junior University

Printed in the United States of America
on acid-free, archival-quality paper

Library of Congress Cataloging-in-Publication Data

Baron, Samuel H.
    Bloody Saturday in the Soviet Union :
Novocherkassk 1962 / Samuel H. Baron.
        p.   cm.
    Includes bibliographical references and index.
    ISBN 0-8047-4093-3 (alk. paper)
        1. Novocherkasskiæ çlektrovozostroitel§'yæ zavod
Strike, Novocherkassk, Russia, 1962.   2. Strikes and
lockouts—Locomotive industry—Russia (Federation)
I. Title.

HD5397.2.R12 1962 B37 2001
331.892'82526'094749—dc21

                                    2001020023

Designed by Janet Wood
Typeset by G&S Typesetters, Inc., in 10.5/14 Adobe
Garamond

Original Printing 2001

Last figure below indicates year of this printing:
10   09   08   07   06   05   04   03   02   01

Contents

Illustrations

Seventeen pages of photos follow page 92

Preface and Acknowledgments

The title of this book is a transparent allusion to Bloody Sunday, the infamous massacre of peaceful demonstrators in St. Petersburg by the tsar's soldiers that touched off the Russian revolution of 1905. In Soviet Russia, the event was held up in schools and in historical and popular writings as one of the most abominable acts of the reactionary imperial regime, and was so regarded by the population at large. It was unnecessary to state what was considered obvious, that nothing of the kind could possibly happen in the "workers' state." But on June 2, 1962, what had been deemed impossible occurred in the south Russian town of Novocherkassk. There demonstrators taking part in a great strike were subjected to an attack that killed twenty-four people and seriously wounded sixty-nine others. Immediately reminded of the episode of January 9, 1905, persons on the scene dubbed what they had just experienced "Bloody Saturday." [1]

The strike had erupted on June 1 at the Novocherkassk Electric Locomotive Works (NEVZ), which employed 13,000 workers. The workers had several grievances, but most immediately the strike was triggered by the Khrushchev government's announcement on May 31 of a steep rise in the prices of meat and butter. The stoppage rapidly spread to other plants in the city's industrial zone, bringing out many thousands of workers. Activists in the party and Komsomol (Communist Youth League) who attempted to justify the government policy and dissuade the workers from striking were hooted down and sometimes roughed up. Some of the strikers blocked a train on the nearby Saratov–Rostov line, bringing the traffic on much of the line to a halt. Others invaded the factory administration building and for a while held hostage the first secretary of the Rostov oblast (province) party organization, who had tried in vain to persuade the workers to return to work. Efforts of local police and military garrison forces to bring the disorder to an end proved fruitless. With lightning speed, the vaunted Communist apparatus lost the control that it customarily exercised. Heartened by their successes, the strikers resolved to march the following day, Saturday, to the *gorkom*, the headquarters of the local party organization, to press their demands for a reduction in food prices and an increase in pay.

The Kremlin learned of the strike and some of the workers' collateral actions by midday of June 1. So alarmed was the leadership that a top-flight team headed by F. R. Kozlov, Khrushchev's heir apparent, and the venerable Anastas Mikoyan was dispatched to deal with the situation. Although the possibility of a peaceful resolution of the conflict was envisaged, the military option was not excluded, and several thousand troops as well as tank units were hastily deployed into the city. It was considered mandatory to keep the strike from spreading, and to that end the roads into and out of Novocherkassk were sealed off and telephone communication with the outside world was interrupted. Lacking a tradition of collective action and having taken no steps to create a strike committee, the workers were ill prepared to negotiate. The elite leaders who came to Novocherkassk disagreed on the course to take and proved inept at exploring the possibility of a negotiated settlement. An agreement might have been worked out, however, had the contest not come to a head so speedily—only twenty-eight hours after it had begun.

On June 2, thousands of strikers, some accompanied by wives and children and their ranks soon swelled by supporters and curious onlookers, marched nine kilometers to the gorkom. Led by Father G. A. Gapon, the demonstrators in St. Petersburg in 1905 had carried religious icons, uttered prayers, and sung the national anthem, "God Save the Tsar." The Novocherkassk demonstrators affirmed their devotion to the ideals of the revolution by holding aloft red banners and portraits of Lenin and singing revolutionary songs. The authorities planned to block the procession at the one bridge over the Tuzlov River that connected the industrial zone with the town proper. In the event, the tanks arrayed there neither intimidated the marchers nor attempted to stop them. As the marchers approached the gorkom, they generally shunned disorderly conduct; but the Moscow leaders assembled there perceived them as a vicious mob and fled ignominiously to the security of a military compound.

The demonstrators took possession of the square before the gorkom. Then, exasperated by the unwillingness of the leaders to confer with them, elements of the crowd rioted. They seized the building, vandalized some of the rooms, and harangued the throng from the balcony. When a female speaker contended that some fellow strikers arrested the night before were being abused at the police station, a contingent hastened there and forced their way in. In the skirmish that ensued, the soldiers on guard killed five persons and wounded others. About half an hour later, military forces cleared the gorkom of the intruders, who offered no resistance. Although the crowd refrained from other aggressive acts, the patience of the Moscow leaders was running out, and they determined to disperse the throng one way or another. When a general's warning over a loudspeaker went unheeded, firing began, first into the crowd and then at men, women, and youths fleeing the area. Sixteen persons were killed and dozens wounded. Strange as it may seem, to this day there is uncertainty as to who precisely ordered the fusillade, who carried it out, and whence it came. A hypothesis on these matters is offered in the body of the text.

Mass arrests followed the shootings, and 114 persons were tried in a series of court proceedings. In the most important trial, conducted before a panel of the Supreme Court of the Russian Soviet Federated Socialist Republic (RSFSR), seven persons were convicted of fomenting mass disorders and banditry, sentenced to death, and executed. The courts sentenced scores of others to long terms in "severe regime" correctional labor camps.

Because the Novocherkassk massacre so flagrantly contradicted the Soviet regime's ideology and rhetoric, it was inevitable that it would be covered up. The bodies of those slain on Bloody Saturday were secretly buried at places some distance from Novocherkassk. Not a word about what had occurred on June 2 or of the trials held in August and September appeared in the Soviet press. Fragments of information did seep out of the USSR and were published abroad but, understandably, for a long time what the outside world knew of the Novocherkassk events was both extremely limited and flawed in many respects. In the mid-1970s, Aleksandr Solzhenitsyn produced much the best account to that point in his searing indictment of the Soviet regime, *The Gulag Archipelago*.[2] Unfortunately, his rendition also perpetuated a good many errors and myths about the events of 1962. When such dissidents as General Petr Grigorenko, Andrei Sakharov, and his wife, Elena Bonner, gained an inkling of the Novocherkassk story, they clandestinely sought to publicize it.

It was not until the advent of glasnost, however, that the Soviet people had occasion to learn of "the Novocherkassk tragedy," as it came to be called. From obscurity it then achieved the status of a cause célèbre, in good part because of the unremitting agitation of P. P. Siuda, one of the strikers who had been imprisoned for several years. Beginning in mid-1988 and continuing for the next four years, investigative reporters zealously ferreted out and published bits and pieces of the shocking story in dozens of newspaper articles. Public revulsion was magnified by Yevgeny Yevtushenko, who vented his outrage at the government's handling of the matter in a poem conspicuously featured in *Literaturnaia gazeta*.[3]

Parallel with these revelations, a campaign was launched in Novocherkassk to secure a reconsideration of what had occurred and of the trial verdicts as well. The campaign gained momentum when reformist deputies elected to the First Congress of People's Deputies (May 1989), led by the dean of Leningrad University's law school, A. A. Sobchak, demanded an independent review of the matter and the rehabilitation of people wrongfully slain or convicted. For many months the KGB, the USSR Procuracy, and the military high command did everything they could to obstruct efforts to disclose the embarrassing truths. When it was no longer possible to deny that people had been shot, the authorities justified the action as the appropriate response to "mass disorders" instigated by criminals and hooligans who had attacked soldiers and state institutions. Ultimately, as the Soviet regime went through its death throes, the Supreme Court of the USSR exonerated the victims, and the Procuracy followed suit. In a final act to the protracted drama, the bodies of those murdered on Bloody Saturday were located, disinterred, and, exactly thirty years after the day of the massacre, given a decent burial in a Novocherkassk cemetery.[4]

Solzhenitsyn surely exaggerated in characterizing the Novocherkassk upheaval as "a turning point in the modern history of Russia."[5] But it would be equally misleading to assert that it did not have significant consequences. Corrective actions instituted by the party-state in the short term included such measures as the provision of more adequate food supplies to the city, the sacking of political and industrial personnel, and the tightening of security measures. More important were certain long-term results. To make some headway against the shortages of meat and dairy products, the regime began to import large amounts of feed grain. Yet so shaken was the Soviet leadership by what had transpired at Novocherkassk that it never dared to increase food prices again. Accordingly, agricultural subsidies grew apace, consumed ever larger shares of the state's budget, and necessitated cuts in the budgets for other economic sectors. The resulting unbalancing of the economy contributed more than a little to the steady decline in the overall growth rate, rightly considered a key factor in the collapse of the Soviet regime. The Novocherkassk eruption was an early signal that the Soviet economy had begun to lose its dynamism, that it would prove impossible for the USSR to continue its early rate of growth and simultaneously modernize its industry, raise living standards, and maintain its status as a superpower.

The economic factor was not the only cause of the regime's decline and fall, and the Novocherkassk events figured in another way in that saga. In the glasnost era, the revelation week in and week out of happenings discreditable to the party-state obviously eroded its legitimacy. Surely one of the most devastating blows was the disclosure that the "workers' state" had perpetrated a massacre of workers who had been struggling to better their conditions.

This study tells two stories, one about the 1962 events—the strike, the massacre, and the trial; the second about how knowledge of those events, quite effectively concealed for a long time, was progressively brought to light. Included also is a chapter on General M. K. Shaposhnikov and P. P. Siuda, two interesting characters whose names are closely identified with the events. A social democrat by conviction and a long-time member of the American Civil Liberties Union, I approached the Novocherkassk happenings with a distinctive mind-set. No doubt my values have colored my treatment in some measure, but I have endeavored to understand as objectively as possible the motives and behavior of the contending groups. Having studied the evidence, I incline to think that the brutal suppression of the strike was not inevitable, other outcomes were possible, and miscalculation and error on one side and the other figured importantly in determining what happened.

I first heard something of the massacre in 1963–64, when I was engaged in research in Moscow. A student at the university residence hall where I was housed told me in a hushed voice that something awful had happened in Novocherkassk. The student was vague about the circumstances, and my research at the time was focused on seventeenth-century Russia, so the rumor made little impression on me. So far as I can remember, I never encountered anything in print on the Novocherkassk affair until about thirty years later. At a conference in St. Petersburg in 1993, A. A. Chernobaev, the editor of the journal *Istoricheskii arkhiv*, handed me a copy of the most recent issue. The journal contained the first installment of a two-part collection of secret KGB documents produced contemporaneously with the events of mid-1962. I read the documents on the flight back home, and so engrossing and revealing did the materials appear to me that I resolved then and there to explore the events further. This was undoubtedly an impulsive decision, inasmuch as I had been mainly concerned with Russia's history in the sixteenth and seventeenth centuries in the preceding twenty years or so. Other commitments prevented me from investigating the story in a sustained way until 1997, although in the intervening years I managed to locate and read much of the relevant published material—dozens of newspaper articles, several pieces that appeared in journals, and a singular pamphlet by Irina Mardar'.

In 1997 I spent a fruitful six weeks, and in 1998 a month, researching the subject in Novocherkassk, Rostov-on-Don, and Moscow. In Novocherkassk and Rostov I interviewed a number of persons (some of them repeatedly) who either had been involved somehow in the events or had written about them. Two of the latter called to my attention important unpublished material of whose existence I had been unaware. I had an opportunity to examine closely the terrain in Novocherkassk on which the events unfolded. The oblast library in Rostov yielded supplementary information in provincial and local newspapers. I gained admission to and gathered precious data in archives in Rostov and Moscow. But it was by no means smooth sailing all the way.

I had learned of an eight-volume record of the principal trial and, believing it to be a cardinal source, did all I could in both 1997 and 1998 to track it down and secure access to it. My effort foundered, even though an influential jurist intervened on my behalf. Fortunately, in the State Archive of the Russian Federation (Gosudarstvennyi Arkhiv Rossiiskoi Federatsii [GARF]) I came upon the lengthy record of the preliminary investigation that preceded the trial, a document that surely prefigured, as was generally true, the course that the trial ran. I had also noted a reference to a thirty-one-volume collection of testimony on the Novocherkassk story amassed by the Chief Military Procuracy (Glavnaia Voennaia Prokuratura) in 1990–91. Although I was denied an opportunity to examine these materials, located in Moscow, a rich 170-page summary of this compilation came to my attention. Those in authority have evidently considered it imprudent to publish this summary, but it turned out to be the single most important source for my reconstruction of the strike and massacre. In hopes of acquiring a feel for the setting of the drama, I carefully observed the exterior of the NEVZ administration building and the adjacent area in which much of the action occurred on the first day of the strike. But the officious staff member of the plant with whom I managed to secure an interview belittled the significance of the strike and massacre, and stubbornly refused me permission to have a look inside the works. Obviously, persons committed to the practice of secrecy and cover-up remain ensconced in many important positions in post-Soviet Russia.

Having focused on a topic in recent history, relied to a fair degree on interviews and newspaper reportage, and been stonewalled from time to time in my quest for information, I feel somewhat like a journalist. Yet I have not, of course, abandoned the historian's craft that I've plied for fifty years. So perhaps my current work may be considered a cross between history and journalism. A byword has it that journalism is "a rough draft of history," but I believe that my endeavor is something more than that. It is one of the first attempts at a scholarly study of the Novocherkassk affair; the only other one is a fine, extended chapter in a volume by V. A. Kozlov that appeared after I had completed my work.[6] The two treatments overlap to some extent, but Kozlov concentrates on the strike and devotes little or no attention to other dimensions of the story that figure prominently in my study. Besides, although both of us have depended on some of the same sources in dealing with the strike, each has also drawn upon materials that the other has not, so the two renditions of the strike are complementary. It is a safe bet that as previously inaccessible sources are made available and others come to light, new and more comprehensive studies of this critical episode will join our pioneer endeavors.

I wish to express my deep appreciation to the many institutions and individuals who have generously assisted me in bringing this work to fruition. Grants from the University of North Carolina, Chapel Hill, and the International Research and Exchanges Board enabled me to do indispensable investigatory work in Russia. V. A. Kozlov, deputy director of GARF, whose writing on the Novocherkassk upheaval was then in press, graciously guided me to several key sources. Director N. Ia. Emel'ianenko kindly permitted me to consult relevant materials in the Contemporary History Documentation Center (Tsentr Dokumentatsii Noveishii Istorii [TsDNI]) in Rostov-on-Don. It would be difficult to overestimate the importance of the aid rendered me in Rostov by the knowledgeable journalists Ol'ga Nikitina and Iurii Bespalov, who had published the first articles on Novocherkassk in the Soviet press and continued to bring forth illuminating evidence in further articles. Viktor and Alla Panchenko made me feel at home in Rostov through their friendship, endless hospitality, and support. My work in Novocherkassk was signally assisted by the local archaeologist M. I. Kraisvetnyi, who escorted me to the key sites and provided information about them and arranged interviews with persons I wished to meet. Other leaders of the Novocherkassk Tragedy Foundation, the former striker Valentina Vodianitskaia, and the journalists Irina Mardar' and Tat'iana Bocharova willingly received me, answered my questions, and shared with me their knowledge and insights. Milton O. Gustafson, of the U.S. National Archives, and Jennie Levine, former librarian at the Open Society Archive in Budapest, kindly found relevant materials in their repositories for me. My long-time friend Vladimir Treml made numerous helpful suggestions and comments on the work in progress. Bruce Menning and Peter Solomon gave me the benefit of their expertise on a number of points. Tatiana Cherednik and Lawrence Feinberg kindly translated some difficult passages for me. Barbara Salazar edited the manuscript meticulously. I am especially indebted to Steven I. Levine, who volunteered to read a part and then the completed manuscript, and whose incisive comments prompted me to reconsider many matters and make constructive revisions. Of course, I alone am responsible for remaining errors.

Abbreviations

FNT	Fond Novocherkasskoi Tragedii (Novocherkassk Tragedy Foundation), Novocherkassk
GARF	Gosudarstvennyi Arkhiv Rossiiskoi Federatsii (State Archive of the Russian Federation), Moscow
GVP	Glavnaia Voennaia Prokuratura, "O Novocherkasskikh sobytiiakh 1962 goda"
IA	*Istoricheskii arkhiv*
KD	*Krytyi dvor*, 1990, no. 2.
KP	*Komsomol'skaia pravda*
LG	*Literaturnaia gazeta*
MVD	Ministerstvo Vnutrennikh Del (Ministry of Internal Affairs)
NA	National Archives, Washington, D.C.
NCMO	North Caucasus Military Organization
NEVZ	Novocherkasskii Elektrovozostroitel'nyi Zavod (Novocherkassk Electric Locomotive Works)
NR	"Ob'ediniaites' vokrug Khrista–Bol'sheviki povysli tseny," *Neizvestnaia Rossiia XX vek*, vol. 3 (Moscow, 1993)
TsDNI	Tsentr Dokumentatsii Noveishei Istorii (Contemporary History Documentation Center), Rostov-on-Don

A Note on Transliteration

I have followed the system established by the Library of Congress for the transliteration of Russian words and names, omitting the ligatures. I have made exceptions for well-known persons and places whose names are more familiar to readers in other spellings: Gorky, Herzen, Kazan, Mayakovsky, Trotsky, Vyshinsky, Yeltsin, Yevtushenko.

Bloody Saturday in the Soviet Union

Novocherkassk, 1962

Chapter 1   A Fateful Announcement

An article in *Pravda*, May 31, 1962, was headlined: "New tremors in capitalist economy. Sharp drop in price of stocks in USA. Alarm in stock markets of West European capitals. Monopolists seek way out by intensifying exploitation of workers." Beneath the article were other eye-catching reports with ominous headings: "Shock in Washington"; from London: "Dramatic drop"; "Anxiety in Japanese business circles." The news from abroad may have comforted Soviet true believers, suggesting that the long-predicted crisis of capitalism, portending its collapse, might at last be on the horizon. Contrariwise, the same issue of the newspaper reported Nikita Khrushchev's celebratory remarks on the state of the Soviet Union to a visiting delegation from Mali. His was the first country to make a socialist revolution, he boasted; it had established socialism and was on the way to building communism. "Even our enemies now acknowledge our successes . . . they see that no barriers can stop our development." He urged the visitors "to get acquainted with our achievements in the development of the economy, culture, and science. . . . You will see with what enthusiasm the Soviet people work to bring our great program into being."

Khrushchev was engaging in double-speak. The next day the entire front page of *Pravda*—an identical spread appeared in *Izvestiia* as well—conveyed a message to the Soviet people from the Central Committee of the Communist Party of the Soviet Union (CPSU) and the Council of Ministers of the USSR (read: Khrushchev and his colleagues) about serious economic difficulties that necessitated the tightening of belts, and solicited their understanding. The government had resolved to increase the prices of meat, meat products, and butter rather steeply. The blow, although slightly cushioned by the accompanying news of reductions of 5 percent in the price of sugar and 20 percent in the price of rayon yarn and cloth, produced decided tremors in the USSR.

The message presented an elaborate rationale for the decision, focused primarily on difficulties in the agricultural sector of the economy. Significant gains achieved since 1953 in the production of grain now provided harvests adequate for the country's requirements, but increases in the production of meat and milk were not nearly enough to meet the growing needs of a rapidly increasing population. Between 1953 and 1961, the urban population had grown by 29 million and incomes had increased by 89 percent. But, unfortunately, labor productivity in Soviet agriculture lagged behind that in capitalist countries. Often the price the state paid farmers for meat they had produced was less than the cost of production. It was imperative to increase productivity on the collective and state farms; this goal would be achieved, on the one hand, by investing in the essential infrastructure of cattle raising (buildings, mechanization, electrification), and on the other, by granting farmers higher prices—an incentive to produce more—for what they sold to the state. The wherewithal to do so would come from the higher prices to be charged at the retail shops.

Khrushchev gave his readers to understand that every conceivable way to cope with the problem other than raising prices had been canvassed but found unacceptable. There could be no reduction in expenditures for defense when the imperialists, led by the United States, constituted a persistent threat to the socialist motherland. (As a matter of fact, Khrushchev had significantly cut the military budget twice since coming to power. He favored further cuts in the spring of 1962, but had to back down in the face of stiff opposition from the military establishment.)[1] Cutting the budgets of the metallurgical, chemical, and machine-building industries would unforgivably undermine the country's economic base. Reducing outlays for housing construction was ruled out by the crying need to provide the people with more adequate living space. Nor was it permissible for the government to curtail the array of costly social benefits it provided to the populace: inexpensive housing, free medical care, free education. . . . Accordingly, the leadership had concluded that their only option was to increase the price of meat and meat products (sausage and the like) by 30 percent and butter by 25 percent.[2] The measures decreed would be temporary, making it possible to increase outputs, close the gap, and enable the authorities to lower prices again. The leadership expressed confidence that the people would understand and endorse the economic necessity of a painful decision.

The decision announced on June 1 had been made on May 17, but it was communicated to party organizations throughout the country only on May 31. It was evidently assumed that the explanation for the price rises would be accepted with resignation by a populace accustomed to going along with whatever had been decided on high, that there was no particular need to alert the local authorities well in advance to a possible backlash. Complacent leaders overlooked the fact that for the first time their subjects were being confronted with a jarring increase in food prices, a reversal of the repeated reductions since the end of the war that they had come to consider the norm. Did the leadership consider it irrelevant that in 1953 in East Germany and in 1956 in Poland food supply problems had triggered very serious riots?[3] As for the allegedly temporary nature of the price rises, a byword among the people had it that there was nothing so permanent as the temporary. Contrary to expectations, the May 31 announcement called forth a reaction whose intensity would be incomprehensible without reference to the agricultural policies Khrushchev had pursued in the nine years since he had been elevated to the pinnacle of leadership as first secretary of the CPSU.

Overall, he had a number of goals: maintaining the authority of the CPSU and his supremacy within it while loosening controls on society and culture that Stalin had imposed; increasing the efficiency and productivity of the economy by a variety of measures, improving the living standards of the long-suffering population, and maintaining the Soviet Union's position as one of the two superpowers, while abandoning the idea of inevitable conflict in favor of peaceful coexistence with the capitalist world. Some genuine efforts had been made to improve living standards: Khrushchev's references to earlier price reductions on foods, expanded housing construction, and free education and health care had a basis in fact. Together with security of employment, these elements constituted one side of a tacit social contract that had taken shape between the regime and the populace in the post-Stalin years. In exchange for these benefits, the contract required popular acceptance of the party's authority to manage the political and social order. Government measures had certainly improved the standard of living, but the standard was still abysmally low. Neither Khrushchev nor anyone else in the leadership then realized that it would prove impossible to continue the regime's earlier rate of growth and simultaneously to modernize its industry, continue raising living standards, and maintain its status as a military superpower.[4]

Khrushchev proclaimed himself an advocate, in his words, of "goulash socialism"—a socialist order could not be justified if it did not feed its people decently. He was chagrined by the all too common food shortages—and the correspondingly long queues—in his supposedly superpower realm. Of course, the agricultural sector had the primary role in fulfilling this task, but it had been an intractable problem ever since the extraordinarily rapid and forceful implementation of collectivization in 1929–32. This counterrevolutionary measure had nullified what was for the peasants the historic achievement of the Bolshevik Revolution. Not without reason, a great many of them viewed the system imposed upon them as a new serfdom.[5] Subject to exorbitant demands and yet treated in many respects as second-class citizens, the peasants applied themselves indifferently to their tasks. The correspondingly low level of productivity rendered Soviet agriculture incapable of provisioning the growing population adequately. The solution to the agricultural problem was a high-priority matter for Khrushchev, and he addressed it repeatedly. The measures he put into effect were well intentioned, but they were characteristically impulsive, at times contradictory, and on the whole unsuccessful.

Beginning shortly after Stalin's death, the leadership eased the condition of the peasants by reducing taxes and increasing the prices paid for their products. Khrushchev resorted to such measures more than once in the next nine years, and he steeply increased expenditures for machinery in agriculture as well. Such moves improved the conditions of the agricultural population to a certain extent, but did not go far enough to produce the desired results. The leader also took what appears to be a contradictory tack—seemingly designed to reduce the peasants to something like factory workers—in consolidating 87,500 collective farms into 36,500 between 1955 and 1964 and doubling the number of state farms in roughly the same period.

Perhaps dissatisfied with the results of some of these early measures, or disbelieving they would fulfill acutely felt needs, in 1954, with considerable fanfare, Khrushchev initiated an audacious campaign to bring under cultivation a huge and constantly increasing area of virgin land in Siberia and Kazakhstan. A very successful harvest there in 1956 evidently led him to suppose that more of the same could be counted on regularly thereafter. In 1957, without consultation with his Presidium colleagues, he rashly announced that by 1963 the USSR would surpass the United States in per capita production of meat, milk, and butter. To do so would require more than a tripling of production in six years.[6] Others in the leadership must have persuaded him afterward that his stated objective was excessively ambitious, for the seven-year plan adopted in 1959 called only for a doubling of production of those commodities.[7] Time would show that even the adjusted figure was well beyond the attainable. The successful harvest of 1956 in the virgin lands was followed by another in 1958, but the successes were not sustained in subsequent years, and indeed, harvests were poor in the country as a whole in 1959 and 1960. Nevertheless, yields from the virgin lands did provide the country with a secure supply of grain for bread, although much less than the very large quantities of feed grain that would be necessary for a major increase in meat production.

Meanwhile other agricultural policies Khrushchev decreed had distinctly deleterious effects. In February 1958 he pushed through the dismantling of the machine-tractor stations that had serviced the collective farms; the machinery was to be sold to the farms. The intention was to give the collectives greater control over their operations, but because the change was carried through without adequate forethought and preparation, it produced great disarray and declines in productivity. Ever seeking a panacea, Khrushchev became a zealous proponent of maize cultivation—his impulse along this line powerfully stimulated by the bumper crops of hybrid corn he saw in Iowa during his visit to the United States in 1958. Contending that "maize and maize alone is capable of resolving the problem of increasing the production of meat, milk, and other dairy products," he demanded that it be planted everywhere.[8] Such considerations as soil and weather conditions were overlooked, with predictably unfortunate results.

Perhaps even more hurtful was his assault on the private plots that Stalin had permitted the peasants to cultivate when the dimensions of resistance to collectivization had become manifest. The peasants tended to invest more energy in the plots, which rewarded their labor much more generously than did labor on the collective land. On these diminutive plots, averaging about one acre, the peasants produced almost 45 percent of the meat and dairy products available to the population as a whole.[9] To reduce their size would cut down on the distrusted private sector, it was thought, and presumably favor more intensive work and higher yields on the collectively held land. Instead, these measures aroused bitter resentment among the peasants, and a dramatic reduction in the production of meat and dairy products. As if that were not enough, another perverse decree in 1959 further aggravated the situation. Many residents of suburbs and worker villages kept a cow, and collectively their animals made a not inconsiderable contribution to available stocks of meat, milk, and butter. Now this practice was prohibited, putting yet another crimp in the supply of these products.

In 1964 the Hungarian-born Eugen Varga, who had become an eminent

Soviet economist, confided to his diary a mordant analysis of the Soviet system and its troubled agricultural component:

> Instead of the "workers' state" of the 1920s there emerged in the 1960s a bureaucratic state with Khrushchev as dictator at its summit. In lieu of the socialist society in which, according to the official ideology, "the people and party are united" and "there are no social contradictions," [the society] is actually split into classes and strata with sharply differentiated incomes, and the lower strata oppose the ruling bureaucracy and engage in class struggle against it by such means as are available: the collective farm peasants sabotage work on the collective land and before all else cultivate their small plots. The peasants steal everything they can from the kolkhoz for their private economies: feed, firewood, fertilizer. They deliberately leave a part of the kolkhoz harvest of grain, potatoes, beets, and corn in the fields in the hope that later they can use it for their own cattle. It is a system in which the workers have no material or moral interest in the growth of productivity of the social economy.[10]

By 1962, Khrushchev's brave promises notwithstanding, the USSR still lagged embarrassingly behind the United States in agricultural production and indeed had made very little progress in closing the gap. Soviet statistics indicated that the increase in animal products over the preceding five-year period came to just a bit more than 20 percent.[11] To repeat, the steep rise in food prices decreed on May 31, 1962, was conceived as a corrective action, designed to cover the cost of a large increase in payments to collective farmers for their products.

The announcement of the price rises provoked an outburst of indignation, myriad details of which the KGB regularly reported to party and government leaders. Invariably the reports stated reassuringly that the overwhelming majority of the population appreciated the leadership's wisdom in discerning what needed to be done, and was prepared to shoulder the hardships they entailed uncomplainingly. Statements along these lines were adduced in support of these propositions—it was a simple matter to garner positive comments from the party and Komsomol faithful. As for the overwhelming majority, how its purportedly positive attitude had been determined was not addressed. The writers of the reports surely engaged in wishful thinking. Then, too, the absence of overt opposition of one kind or another by the silent majority could be taken to mean acquiescence—and, with a rhetorical stretch, approval.

Overt opposition was in fact reported, but it was said to represent the views of an insignificant clutch of malcontents, criminals, hooligans, and the like.

There is no way of knowing for certain how most people reacted to the price increases; but absent the most exceptional circumstances, has anything of the kind ever elicited anything but a negative response? On that score, those who overcame their understandable fear of going public and somehow managed to express their dissatisfaction were, arguably, more truly representative of popular opinion than those cited in favor. As a perspicacious brigade leader at Riga commented: "They will say in the newspaper that the people approved the decision of the party and the government. But that's not so. Many do not approve. They should have managed it differently." [12] The KGB summarized as follows the "hostile manifestations" observed by the security organs: "They were expressed in the distribution of anti-Soviet placards and leaflets, the inscription of graffiti on sidewalks, walls of buildings, gates, and other places, [and] malicious speech by individuals who appeal for protests in the form of strikes and demonstrations." [13] The numerous specifics referred to in a series of dispatches composed on June 2, 3, and 4 indicate that the eyes and ears of the security organs were totally engaged. They also make plain how widespread were expressions of dissatisfaction and opposition, both geographically and socially, and how varicolored as well. Conspicuous is the couching of dissatisfaction in terms of "us against them," a matter that has been elucidated for the years 1934–41, and it certainly persisted into 1962. [14]

At the most basic level, individuals complained about the hardships in store. Said a female worker in Dushanbe: "I've lived with insufficiency all my life, and only began to eat enough in the past two or three years. Now our leaders have raised prices. So workers with low pay will have to do without meat and butter." A resident of Piatigorsk lamented: "It's impossible to live this way any longer. There isn't enough food, and we're raising prices." An army lieutenant in Turkestan asserted: "The workers and their children will suffer." Said a carpenter in Penza: "The head understands but not the stomach." On a telephone pole in Perm appeared a placard with the sardonic advice: "Eat soup with sawdust, snack on coal." Someone in Tallinn posted a placard with another dietary suggestion: "Eat grass, meat's not necessary." [15]

Many an individual diagnosed reasons for the troubling situation, and some put forward solutions. Especially prominent was the belief voiced by, among others, a machinist in Azov: "Our government distributes gifts, feeds others, and now we ourselves have nothing to eat." Now, at the expense of the workers, they seek a way out of the situation they created. Overheard in a Kishinev store: "We're feeding our 'friends,' selling, giving without charge, and we can't provide ourselves with the essentials. We're even feeding the Iranians, and their shah works with the Americans." It followed that cutting off aid to "the weakly developed socialist countries" was a preferable solution. Another remedy advanced was to reduce the pay of highly placed officials. Instead of raising the prices of food, suggested another, they should increase the prices of television sets, refrigerators, alcohol, and tobacco. Complaints were heard against the government decree forbidding residents of suburbs and worker villages to keep cattle. If they were permitted to do so, there would be ample supplies of meat. A canny engineer in Mestechkin remarked: "They blame everything bad on Stalin, say that his policy brought agriculture down. But has it really not been possible to restore agriculture since his death? No . . . there are deeper roots about which one apparently must not speak." [16]

In view of the rarity of strikes in the USSR, calls for strike action were surprisingly frequent. In Novosibirsk a worker asserted: "The workers have to be stirred up to protest against the new prices." Someone addressing a group of his fellow workers in Nizhnii said: "Nothing good can be expected of the present government. We must have a strike and demand improvement of living conditions." Said a miner: "If we had the right to strike, we wouldn't fail to organize a strike in response [to the price increases]." A metalworker remarked disdainfully: "If the workers weren't stupid and organized a strike in the factories, as workers abroad do, the government would take the working class into account." Ten leaflets found in the Cheliabinsk railroad station declared: "Down with this disgraceful government decision. Strike to begin the 4th." A female inspector of cadres in Moscow who asserted that "the state fleeces the people" anticipated strikes "at the great enterprises in Leningrad and Moscow." An anonymous protester struck a solitary religious note: "Unite around Christ—the Bolsheviks have raised prices." [17]

Some individuals, evidently considering a strike too mild a response, called for more violent action. At a metallurgical plant in Petrovsk-Zabaikal'skii, in the midst of a discussion about the Central Committee and the Council of Ministers, one worker among a group of 100 exploded: "We need a submachine gun to shoot them all." A machinist in Dnepropetrovsk said to his department head: "We must shoot the whole contingent, beginning with you and going on up from there." A joiner in Minsk had another idea: "We must beat the Communists. They've brought things to such a pass that they've begun to raise food prices." A metalworker in Novoviatsk made terrorist threats against the leaders. A kiosk attendant at the Khabarovsk railroad station berated a Communist within earshot and declared: "People power. Let's make a revolution." One individual who either was misquoted or had taken leave of his senses asserted that Kennedy had a right to drop an atomic bomb on the Soviet Union.[18]

Although the KGB sought to shield them from the specifics, it reported intense hostility to and a good deal of abuse of party and government leaders, with Khrushchev the principal target. Leaflets attacking the government were found in Pavlovo-Posad and Zagorsk in Moscow Province, in Leningrad, Tambov, Cheliabinsk, and Chita Province, in Kemerovo Province and Khmel'nitskii; and slanderous graffiti in Kiev, Minsk, and Moscow. Clearly the leadership had suffered a considerable loss of trust. In Donetsk a leaflet attached to a telephone pole declared: "They have deceived us and they are deceiving us. We will fight for justice." In Kalinin a female worker who was also a deputy in the town soviet remarked: "There is no truthfulness. None of the leaders can be believed."[19]

Some loyalists were embarrassed and dismayed by the announcement of price increases. Said an English teacher: "I don't know what the members of the circle where I do [educational] work will say to me. I always stressed our wonderful program, spoke of the uninterrupted growth of the workers' welfare. What can I say now? They'll simply stop believing me." The commanding officer of a company of engineers, figuratively wringing his hands, complained: "What will we tell the soldiers in our political discussions now? We've told them the opposite. . . . The price increases are a step backward in party and government policy. . . . How will our ideology be able to fight against capitalist ideology?" A senior technician in Moscow asked: "How can we believe our official pronouncements?" A lecturer on international affairs had branded rumors of impending price rises spread by the BBC as "enemy propaganda," and "it turns out that the BBC is right."[20]

Not surprisingly, distrust spilled over into skepticism about the goals the leadership had projected at the 22nd Congress of the CPSU in October 1961. In Tbilisi, a number of people were reported as believing that the price rises signaled "the breakdown of the Soviet economy." The head of a construction unit in Tula stated: "The program of the CPSU looks to the improvement of the Soviet people's well-being, but in reality they have begun to retreat." A party member in the Stavropol area lamented: "Although we are building communism, the shops won't soon be full of goods and bought for very little, as in America." A doctor in Kishinev observed: "The price increases confirm again that communism will not be built, and talk of communism is only words." A lieutenant in the Black Sea fleet said he did not support the measures the party had announced and would not attempt to justify them to the sailors.[21]

Especially striking are the references to the United States in disparagement of the Soviet Union. An RSFSR Honored Artist commented: "We won't die as a result of the measure, but it's shameful in relation to the outside world. If only we'd keep quiet about already overtaking America. It's disgusting to hear our loudspeaker [going on] every day about we, we, we. All this endless boasting." According to an engineer in a Penza factory, "in America there are two million hungry, and we'll have two hundred million." A Piatigorsk resident said: "I heard on a radio program from England that in America seventy percent of the national income goes to the population. People there live at the highest level, and we at the lowest. We only shout a lot that all's well with us, better than anywhere." A Leningrad electrician remarked ironically: "They were overtaking America long ago, [but] they won't build communism for us." Perhaps complaints about the absence of democracy implicitly involved comparisons between the two superpowers, but in any case are noteworthy. One metalworker observed: "We don't have democracy in the USSR. So the government introduces harmful measures even for the workers." And in Minsk a party member asserted: "I'm a Communist, but no one asked me and no one consulted me [about the price increases]; they did everything on high, and they want me to be contented." Before prices were raised, a party secretary in Vilnius reflected, "They ought to have consulted the whole people." Two whose remarks were recorded praised Stalin, who, in contrast to the present leaders, so they said, had repeatedly lowered prices.[22]

Although one person, expressing the sentiments of many, urged: "We've had enough talk, we must organize and establish machinery for action,"[23] the "hostile manifestations" remained almost entirely verbal. In Vyborg-Karpov, a worker with a sign on his chest reading "Down with the new price rises!" was quickly arrested. In Kalinin, some workers incited others not to go to work on Sunday; and a Minsk hand tried to persuade an incoming shift to walk out.[24] The KGB dispatches indicated that persons who made inflammatory statements were often rebuffed by others—undoubtedly party and Komsomol members. The agency's people worked diligently to contain and stamp out sparks of opposition. A lone strike that erupted June 17 in a factory in Mirnyi was hastily brought under control by the local party cohort. Everywhere the kind of "prophylactic" measures the party organizations and the

KGB employed to maintain order sufficed, with one exception. As the KGB chief, V. E. Semichastnyi, (wishfully) reported to his superiors, an absolute majority of the population correctly understood the measure everywhere but in Novocherkassk.[25]

Novocherkassk

Novocherkassk was the capital of the Don Cossacks from its founding in 1805 until the Bolshevik Revolution of 1917.[26] The town was established by their ataman (chieftain) at the time, the military hero Matvei Ivanovich Platov (1751–1818). He was determined to replace the old administrative capital of the host, Cherkassk, which was subject to frequent spring flooding when the Don River overflowed its banks. Understandably, the site chosen for the new town was an eminence, about thirteen miles from the Don. Located 600 miles south of Moscow and 23 northeast of Rostov-on-Don, Novocherkassk is surrounded on three sides by two tributaries of the Don, the Aksai and the Tuzlov. As a new city, it was to be built according to a plan, with broad streets radiating from spacious squares laid out on a generous allotment of almost 10,000 acres of land. Evidently projecting a glorious future for his town, Platov designated a site for a cathedral (it was not completed until 1905), and in 1817 he erected a grandiose triumphal arch near the Tuzlov River at the entrance to the infant town, to celebrate Russia's victory over Napoleon.

The town grew slowly, as the Cossacks were reluctant to abandon their old homes and the river that sustained them as both a choice fishery and an artery of trade for a rather remote place with ill-tasting water. Still, by 1854 it boasted a population of 18,000, which included officials of the Cossack administration, military men, clergy, and merchants in what had become a market town of some consequence. The most notable building was the ataman's palace, sited on a square at the town's center. In 1851 a statue of Novocherkassk's founding father was installed opposite the palace. (After the revolution, the palace became the headquarters of the local Communist Party organization, and Platov's monument was replaced by one of Lenin.)

A new stage in the town's development began in 1864, with the opening of a railroad line and the inauguration of a water conduit that made palatable water available. Thereafter, industrial enterprises such as iron foundries and brick and tobacco plants sprang up, many of them owned by foreign, especially German, entrepreneurs. By 1896, the population had increased almost fourfold to 67,000, a large minority of whom were Cossacks. The Cossacks generally were not city dwellers, but Novocherkassk was an exception, the one city with a substantial Cossack population. Even so, over time the influx of outsiders progressively reduced their weight as a percentage of the whole. Moreover, the distinctive character of the Cossacks as a military caste was gradually eroded. In 1897, 17 percent of Cossack heads of households worked in industrial trades, and the numbers continued to grow down to the outbreak of World War I. More generally, as Robert McNeal observed, the Cossacks were becoming something of an anachronism in a modernizing Russia. While "legal social classes devoted to soldiering were common in many cultures in bygone days, the form had vanished in modern countries." [27]

The advent of radical and revolutionary activity in the country was echoed modestly in Novocherkassk. The Cossacks, once a freebooting, freedom-loving, rebellious people, had been an intractable problem for the autocratic tsarist regime. They had long since been brought to heel, however, and transformed into bulwarks of that regime. The process was undergirded in the nineteenth century by the majority's attainment of a relatively high level of well-being. But the Don region was no longer the abode of Cossacks alone. There was also a substantial population of peasants, mostly poor; and the territory also embraced the important non-Cossack industrial town of Rostov. This city's residents included a significant proletarian population, whose militance was advertised in a celebrated general strike in 1902, in which 10,000 to 15,000 workers were joined by nonfactory segments of the population. [28]

During the revolution of 1905 the Don Cossacks proved their value as a counterrevolutionary force, but it would be a mistake to think of them as an undifferentiated monolith. Labor stoppages, in which Cossack workers undoubtedly played a part, occurred in Novocherkassk in 1905–6; and in September 1905 a Cossack Union was formed to seek redress of perceived economic grievances. On one notable occasion, a platoon of Novocherkassk Cossacks refused a police officer's order to attack a worker demonstration, flinging at him: "Now we're not your servants, we'll serve the black hats [the workers]." [29] When the First Duma was dissolved, several Cossack deputies signed the Vyborg Manifesto. A healthy majority of the Cossack representatives in the Second Duma aligned themselves with the Kadets and the Trudoviks, and endeavored to replace the Ministry of War's arbitrary authority over them with a form of self-government. [30]

Oppositional tendencies reappeared during World War I as material conditions worsened. When the imperial regime was overthrown, Don Cossack leaders threw their support to the Provisional Government. Wary of those who strove to push the revolution onward, they began as early as May–June 1917 to rally their forces to hold back the tide. A regional Cossack convention elected General A. A. Kaledin their ataman, and he in turn secured the support of the Kuban and Terek atamans. The Don region was destined to become the Cossack Vendée, and Novocherkassk the capital of counterrevolution in southern Russia. This was the case, two Soviet historians explained, because some 64 percent of the Don area's population were either Cossacks or kulaks. Besides, its location close to the Azov and Black seas facilitated the rendering of foreign aid, first German and then Entente, to the anti-Bolshevik forces.[31] Kaledin denounced the October Revolution and vowed to assume all power in the Don region. In November, General M. V. Alekseev, former commander in chief of the Russian armies, arrived in Novocherkassk and began to form a White Volunteer Army to overthrow the Soviet regime. Other generals, among them A. I. Denikin (later the head of the Volunteer Army) and Lars Kornilov shortly joined his crusade. In February 1918 Bolshevik forces, aided by a schism in the Cossack population, managed to drive the Whites from the city, but their victory was short-lived. In May the Whites regained control, and it was not until January 1920, as the Civil War was winding down, that Novocherkassk definitively fell into Bolshevik hands.

The "White Terror" inflicted on the not inconsiderable number of people in the Don region who had opposed the return to power of those dedicated to the preservation of wealth and privilege was now succeeded by the Red Terror. The Soviet government was determined to stamp out this "nest of reaction," and it mercilessly pushed along the process of de-Cossackization, which had proceeded a considerable distance by the outbreak of World War I.[32] The Cossack military caste was abolished; there were to be no more atamans, no separate Cossack regiments, no separate province in which the Cossacks' demands were given preference over those of the peasants. Indeed, to their chagrin the Cossacks were now classified, in accordance with Leninist ideology, as peasants, rich, middle, or poor.[33] The decimation of the Cossacks was abetted by the emigration of 50,000 of their number who were unwilling to submit to the new regime.

The final blow to the Don Cossacks was administered during the campaign to collectivize agriculture. Until 1933, a relatively large proportion of Cossack farms in the Don region remained under private ownership, in spite of particularly harsh measures. As elsewhere, anyone who opposed the government's policy was portrayed as a kulak, and masses of landholders became candidates for dekulakization. The authorities rightly regarded the Cossack regions as the most dangerous and difficult to collectivize, so in late 1929 additional army units were deployed to the Don and the North Caucasus Military District. In late 1932, the Don and Kuban were declared to be under military emergency on the pretext of a cholera epidemic. Mikhail Sholokhov, the famous author of *The Silent Don*, published a novel on collectivization in the Don region. Although his presentation is ultimately triumphalist, it truthfully portrays the bitter resistance to the policy and the violence directed against those who would not submit.[34] Indeed, Sholokhov was moved to write a letter of protest to Stalin about what was occurring in his native hearth. A Soviet article that portrays collectivization as a fundamentally benign policy nevertheless reports that 19–20,000 "kulak" households in the region were uprooted and exiled.[35] "In the Kuban and the Don," according to Robert Conquest, "the collectivization struggle never ceased, and merged directly into the terror famine of 1932–3."[36] In 1962 the population of Novocherkassk included a good many de-Cossackized and dekulakized people, but whether they figured prominently in the upheaval there is uncertain.

In the Soviet era and since, Novocherkassk has been a constituent part of Rostov oblast, whose administrative capital is the city of Rostov-on-Don. In the decades after the revolution, Novocherkassk became an important industrial city and a major educational center, its population by 1962 numbering 130,000. Its government was centered in the former ataman's palace, now dubbed the gorkom, the headquarters of the town's Communist Party organization. The party had a strong presence in Novocherkassk, counting 8,699 members, 52 percent of them in industrial enterprises. With its 190 primary cells, 156 departments, and 209 party groups and its Komsomol complement of 21,633 members, it thoroughly permeated the social order, relentlessly striving to mold, motivate, and control it. Its endeavors were abetted by some fifty-six People's Militia squads (*druzhiny*), with more than 4,000 members (*druzhinniki*), who served as auxiliaries to police and judicial organizations in safeguarding public order and security.[37]

The city's first institution of higher education, the Don (later Novocherkassk) Polytechnical Institute, had been founded in 1907. It expanded over time until in the 1960s it enrolled some 13,500 students in forty areas of specialization. It ranked as one of the most important institutions of its kind in southern Russia, indeed in the Soviet Union. Two other institutions of higher education had been established more recently, and the town boasted seven scientific research institutes and many technical schools as well. In all, Novocherkassk had over 30,000 students in upper schools of one kind or another. Approximately 16,000 university students and young workers lived in forty-two dormitories in and around the city. Their living conditions, particularly the meals in their dining halls, were miserable. V. M. Zakharov, who had been a student at the Polytechnical Institute in the 1950s, recalled decades later "the squalid conditions in the student dining room. Day in and day out, we ate pea soup, cutlets composed of gristle and macaroni (of a dirty-gray color), and plum juice made from concentrate." After *Pravda* published a letter of complaint from him, the food service management, anticipating a visit by a Moscow inspection team, initiated major improvements. When the team had departed, the dining hall reverted to the pre-inspection standard and Zakharov was expelled from the Institute.[38] Another former student, S. Podol'skii, wrote of "living from hand to mouth" in 1962.[39] Both contended that food was hard to come by in the town as well: white bread was a thing of the past, meat and sausage were rare, and one had to wait on long lines to buy milk. A month after the June 1962 strike, a meeting of the Executive Committee of the Rostov Province party organization noted that only 30 percent of the food slated for the Polytechnical Institute students had been provided, and acknowledged that the dining facilities in the student dormitories were generally "unsatisfactory."[40] Little wonder that ideological work among the 16,000 dormitory residents was poor enough to be reported in the local newspaper *Znamia kommuny* on June 19.

The record of a conference of the city's party leaders on February 1, 1962, devoted to a consideration of the Komsomol, is relevant here. It began with a statistical inventory, revealing that there were 21,633 members in all, 12,219 (a smaller number than one would expect) in schools of various levels, 7,250 in industry and transportation, 2,007 in "other." Of the total, 14,802 were either enrolled in or had graduated from a university or a middle school, 6,066 had not managed to complete middle school, and 584 had only an elementary education. Like party members, Komsomol members were expected to demonstrate the highest level of conduct. But, as a work on the youth organization published in 1965 noted, the coercive factor—"the relentless pressure of recruitment" and the obligatory membership for those who hoped to enter the universities—produced effects of a "negative" kind. An additional factor was the bureaucratization of the organization, which had produced a "stultifying atmosphere" of "deadening formalism." Komsomol undoubtedly had a core of convinced activists, but a large majority had joined reluctantly and participated perfunctorily; some even displayed "nihilistic attitudes." [41]

Conditions in Novocherkassk's Komsomol were evidently no better than those elsewhere. Despite the organization's extensive educational work, the report relates, the level of hooliganism, drunkenness, and negative attitudes among its members was alarming. When some individuals' drunkenness and brawling were publicized in the local humor magazine *Krokodil*, they destroyed the output of the magazine. They and another member, who had engaged in thievery, were expelled. A member who worked at the electric locomotive factory was attracted to "reactionary" nineteenth-century literature, denied the creativity of Maxim Gorky and Vladimir Mayakovsky, and attacked "party-mindedness" in literature. Still another threw away his membership card and was arrested while trying to leave the country. Some had gone so far as to embrace religion and were proselytizing among their fellows.

More important, it would seem, there was considerable evidence of a passive attitude, even among some leaders, toward the task of energizing students for the "struggle for communist labor." If some departments of the electric locomotive works deserved commendation on this score, a supposed Komsomol brigade in another plant had but one member. And 50 percent of the members in two industrial enterprises were not engaged, as good Communist youths ought to have been, in study of one kind or another. The party's never-ending call for selfless dedication to the building of a communist society as often as not, it would appear, was answered with slackness and indifference. [42] Some of these problems were attributable to a recent educational reform, which had mandated two years of industrial labor for graduates of secondary schools before they could be admitted to universities or other institutions of higher education. Young people who aspired to be engineers, scientists, or cosmonauts often resented this interruption of progress toward their goals, and some were apt to engage in antisocial behavior and exhibit a poor attitude toward their work. [43] An indeterminate number of these people worked in the Novocherkassk factories and lived in the dormitories, no doubt producing a leavening effect on their discontented fellows. Young people were to be disproportionately involved in the turbulence of the early June days in 1962.

Far and away the most important industrial enterprise in Novocherkassk was the Budenny Electric Locomotive Construction Factory (NEVZ). The first plant of its kind in Russia, it was established during the second five-year plan, and in 1962 employed 13,000 workers. Other significant plants included the Nikol'skii Machine-Building Factory (called Gormash), the oldest of its kind in the city, where 1,000 workers produced mining and geological equipment; an electrode factory, employing 3,000 workers, which made equipment for metallurgical and chemical enterprises; a relatively new synthetic products factory, with several thousand workers, which turned out synthetic materials for the chemical and pharmaceutical industries; a machine-tool plant, with around 1,000 workers, which produced metal-cutting machines as well as articles for popular use; and the only permanent-magnet factory in the Soviet Union, employing 1,000 workers who made magnetic alloys and magnets for industrial use. The most important electrical power station in southern Russia—it furnished power to a wide area—was also located in Novocherkassk.

Most of the factories were sited in an industrial district some six miles north of the city proper. A railroad station named Lokomotivstroi was located just across a square from NEVZ. On the other side of the tracks was a large settlement called Oktiabr' (October), one of several in the neighborhood of the plants, where factory workers and their families, some 40,000 people, resided. Many lived in barracks that had been built only for temporary use, and some were obliged to live in tents. Because housing of any kind was in short supply, in 1962 as many as 1,700 persons were waiting to be assigned living quarters.[44]

Working conditions at the factory also left a great deal to be desired. Because of inadequate safety conditions, 200 workers in one of the departments had recently been poisoned. Laborers in another department had refused to work for three days, demanding improvement of their working conditions.[45] There were three work shifts, one commencing at 8:00 A.M., the second at 4:00 P.M., the last at midnight. Lacking a place to change their clothing, the laborers had to replace their clean garments with their work clothes at their machines. To accommodate the workforce during meal breaks, there were only eight dining rooms with a total of 600 seats. Many of these mess halls were in need of repairs, and one had been closed for six months. Accordingly, many workers were unable to get hot meals—and none at all were available to the night shifts. In any event, the food was meager—peas and kasha were constant, variety was nonexistent, and coffee was often not available. There was insufficient drinking water. The standard of cleanliness was low and the serving people were rude. Meanwhile a new administration building with a good

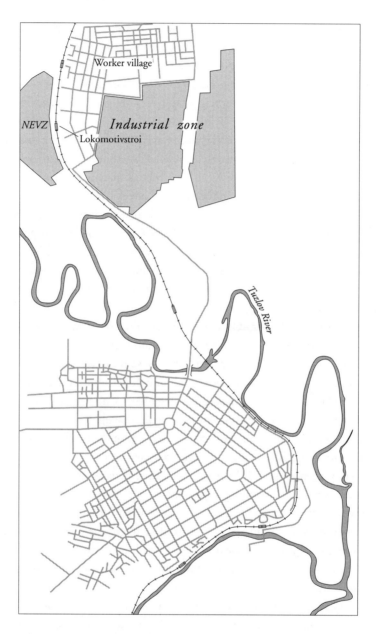

The town of Novocherkassk. The industrial zone, represented in gray, is separated from the town center by the Tuzlov River. The railroad line divides the industrial zone and skirts the town center on the east. (Original map by G. R. Dobbs)

dining room for the managerial staff had been constructed. These data are unimpeachable, reported as they were for the most part by the man who became director of NEVZ shortly after the great strike. He discovered that only 25 percent of the funds budgeted for improvements had been spent.[46]

Workers had other grounds for dissatisfaction. The wages paid were not uniform, not objectively based, not related to the importance or difficulty of the work performed. Individuals who went to the trouble of upgrading their skills were not necessarily rewarded with pay increases. And when wage rates were altered, the only criterion that was said to count was party membership. Given all these circumstances, there was bound to be a good deal of labor dissatisfaction. Moreover, the Khrushchev government had repealed the ban on quitting one job and taking another. According to one report, in the preceding three years 19,000 persons had worked in the plant, indicating an average annual labor turnover of more than 15 percent. Under the circumstances, the factory administration could not be too fastidious about whom it hired, and numerous people who had been convicted of one crime or another were present in the workforce. Such persons were forbidden by law to live in the main cities, but, according to a KGB report, 1,585 were then residing in Novocherkassk.[47]

Another pair of circumstances in the NEVZ-Novocherkassk nexus demands attention. On April 6, 1962, the editors of *Znamia kommuny*, the daily newspaper of the Novocherkassk party organization, initiated a campaign to mark the fiftieth anniversary of the founding of *Pravda*. The venerable newspaper should be honored in the Don region, it was suggested, by an exceptional effort to effect savings in the industrial economy, and thus advance the well-being of the country as a whole. The initial impetus for the campaign had come in the form of a challenge thrown down by Rostselmash, the massive agricultural machinery plant in neighboring Rostov. The regional party organization, with headquarters in Rostov, had undoubtedly prompted its Rostselmash subdivision to initiate a socialist competition, a long-standing feature of the Soviet economy, calculated to stimulate enthusiasm and give an extra push to economic development. The workers in one department of the Nikol'skii plant quickly rose to the challenge, pledging to do seven hours of work in six hours for an indeterminate period of time. With the campaign picking up steam, in mid-April the Komsomol organization at NEVZ promised its support, and the plant administration soon followed suit. NEVZ was undoubtedly the industrial enterprise with the greatest concentration of party strength; in mid-1962 it boasted 1,400 party members and 2,400 Komsomols, according to a former KGB agent.[48] On May 11, NEVZ leaders signed on to the campaign, pledging that each worker would achieve savings of 100 rubles in a year. This could have amounted to a contribution of a month's labor for a good many people, inasmuch as the average wage was 90–100 rubles a month.[49]

Whereas the party leadership in Rostov and Novocherkassk, the party press, and the party and Komsomol organizations in the factories had initiated and were propelling the campaign, it is not unreasonable to suppose that the non-party rank and file were not consulted, or were consulted perfunctorily, and were less than enthusiastic if not downright resentful. This supposition is powerfully reinforced when another matter is brought into focus. In the course of 1962, the management of the works had imposed on one factory department after another a revision upward of the work norms—that is, the amount of output a worker had to produce in order to receive a certain level of pay. The revised norms—workers in other countries call this a "stretchout"—amounted to a pay cut of as much as 30 percent. To require greater effort from the workers to celebrate the *Pravda* anniversary on top of the pay cuts was shortsighted, to say the least. For the workers the situation was aggravated by another circumstance, noted long after the events by the plant's chief engineer, S. N. Elkin: the work norms were supposed to be revised upward at NEVZ only when technological improvements increased labor productivity.[50]

The management was just getting around to implementing a reform in the wage structure that Khrushchev had initiated as long ago as 1955 and was supposed to be completed by 1962.[51] Behind the facade of an ostensibly rational, planned economy there had developed a plethora of practices relating to wage-setting, and to many other aspects of the production process as well, that were inconsistent, mutually contradictory, and counterproductive.[52] Khrushchev hoped to systematize wage payments in ways that would promote efficiency and increase productivity. A student of the effort concluded that it proved well nigh impossible to devise the "stable and predictable incentives" essential to achieve the goal.[53] Why the management of NEVZ waited so long to institute the wage reform is unclear. But it may be inferred that its introduction sequentially in the various departments was planned in expectation that its announcement would fuel discontent. The risk would be diminished if it were introduced piecemeal rather than throughout the plant at once.

Most of the data just recorded have been extracted from KGB or local party documents drawn up in 1962, some of them reported before the June eruption, some afterward. The impression they convey is that of a penurious population ruled by a bureaucratic element, whether party, economic, or educational, that paid scant attention to the welfare of those they were in principle supposed to serve. Yet Soviet society purportedly had already attained socialism and was projected to attain the ultimate goal of communism in twenty years. This was the theme of the 22nd Congress of the CPSU, held in October 1961, which also trumpeted the end of the dictatorship of the proletariat and the advent of the "state of the whole people."[54] The contrast between the rhetoric and the reality could not have been more striking. Still, bad as they were, the conditions prevailing in Novocherkassk were probably not exceptional.[55] The announcement of the price increases on meat, meat products, and butter soon after the revision of the work norms was, in Irina Mardar''s apt phrase, the "fateful coincidence" that produced the explosion on June 1.

Chapter 2   June 1: The Strike Begins

The Sources

The reader should be apprised of the sources on which the following account of the strike is based, beginning with one of a series of KGB documents published in 1993.[1] Very soon after the strike began, 140 KGB operatives were dispatched to Novocherkassk, along with the agency's vice president, P. I. Ivashutin, to monitor what was happening.[2] On June 7, Ivashutin drew up a rather lengthy, absorbing narrative, grounded on the observations made virtually around the clock by agents on duty throughout the area during the three days of the strike. A precious source because of its contemporaneity, it is written of course from the perspective of the guardians of order, for whom a work stoppage and accompanying acts of defiance of authority were anathema. Accordingly, the strikers are generally referred to as "hooligans," "bandits," "criminals," "extremists," "anti-Soviet elements," and the like. Besides, a perusal of other sources alerts us to the omission of significant facts, probably for self-serving purposes. Nevertheless, in contrast to a brief report Ivashutin composed on the day the strike began, which registers the immediate, unrelievedly abusive reaction to the eruption, the one produced six days later, based on effective intelligence gathering in the interim, explains the outbreak of the strike rather well, while still condemning it.[3] Making due allowance for its understandable bias, one may extract from this KGB document a multitude of details and a usable outline of the events, set forth with a surprising degree of objectivity.

22   Almost all the other testimony we have, whether from the workers or others who were involved, was recorded twenty-six years or more after the events, and is therefore subject to the vagaries of memory. Among these reminiscences, the one composed by P. P. Siuda in 1989 stands out. A striker who was arrested,

tried, and sentenced to twelve years in prison, Siuda from the time of his arrest was keenly interested in reconstructing and understanding the train of events in the early June days. In prison he interviewed many of the others who had been detained and, combining their information with what he had personally witnessed and experienced, cobbled together an informative and reasonably coherent narrative. He seems not to have committed it to paper at the time, but, intensely focused on the matter as he was, through the years he kept in mind much of what he had constructed. What he later presented in a number of newspaper articles, therefore, is a valuable telling of the story from below. His memory was not flawless, it must be added, and close study reveals some confusion about the timing and sequence of events and other matters. Moreover, if Ivashutin's account portrays the events from the perspective of the guardians of order, of course Siuda's has a particular slant too. His father, an Old Bolshevik who lost his life during the purges, had instilled in his son an identification with the radical movement that culminated in the October Revolution. Siuda views the NEVZ strike through the prism of an idealized Leninism. Projecting his own sense of things onto the strikers generally, he contends that they were "educated in the ideology of the revolution," and their tactics were well suited to the ends they wished to achieve. They were disciplined, maintained solidarity, understood that resort to mindless violence would be self-defeating, and rejected the counsel of those who called for extreme measures.

A third source derives from the efforts of an organization called the Novocherkassk Tragedy Foundation, formed in the glasnost era, specifically in 1989. One of its primary aims was to determine the truth about what had occurred in June 1962. Its moving spirit was Irina Mardar', a local journalist. She assiduously sought to find and publicize every scrap of relevant information. One result of her efforts was a collection of reminiscences by individuals who had participated in, witnessed, or been affected by the events. A second was a sixty-page pamphlet, the most considerable recital of the story to appear down to 1999.[4] It is based on information painstakingly gathered from many more persons than the number represented in the collection of reminiscences. The pamphlet contains many nuggets not to be found elsewhere, but because it was modestly conceived as a journalistic endeavor, unfortunately, it lacks footnotes. Although her sympathies are clearly with the workers, Mardar' presents testimony from the other side as well. Hers is a notable endeavor to portray what happened evenhandedly.

The newspaper and magazine articles produced by investigative reporters in the glasnost era constitute a fourth important body of source material. Between 1988 and 1992, a dozen or more writers made contributions in such organs as *Komsomol'skaia pravda, Literaturnaia gazeta, Izvestiia,* and *Trud.* Especially valuable is the testimony they collected from participants in and eyewitnesses to the events. The work of two journalists, Ol'ga Nikitina and Iurii Bespalov, deserve particular mention. Both were based in Rostov-on-Don, close to the scene and many of the dramatis personae; each played a major role in bringing the massacre to light; and both maintained a continuing interest in discovering all they could about the Novocherkassk story. Bespalov's reports appeared mainly in *Komsomol'skaia pravda,* Nikitina's in the regional press, and also in television broadcasts.

The last of the sources came into being in the early 1990s as a consequence of the then reformist government's charge to the Chief Military Procuracy to make a thorough investigation of the strike and the shooting associated with it. The intention was to transcend the government versions to date, which were rightly considered tendentious. The charge was taken seriously: the investigation lasted a year and half and produced thirty-one volumes of documentary material. They included testimony of many scores of people, not only party and government officials, military, police, and KGB personnel, both high level and rank and file, but many workers and bystanders. These volumes were not available for study, but an extended summary of 176 pages, featuring the testimony of 120 individuals, did come to my attention. One cannot help wondering how the immense collection was boiled down to fewer than 200 pages; in particular, how accurately the edited material reflects the foundation on which it is based. At present there can be no absolute certainty on this score, but the compilation inspires confidence in that it includes plenty of testimony given by army, KGB, and police officials who, thirty years after the events, felt free to provide evidence strikingly at odds with the official version. Offering a wealth of detail and the diverse perspectives of a wide assortment of people, this is the most important source for my account.

Close study of all these materials brings home a sense of how chaotic those days were, the fallibility of memory, the proliferation of mythology, the contradictory perceptions of the witnesses, and the impossibility of ever establishing what occurred more than approximately. If there is and will always be uncertainty about many details, the principal episodes in the strike are presented with the conviction that they are on the whole reasonably accurate.

Turbulence at NEVZ

The electric locomotive construction works is fronted by a five-story building, with four-story wings to the left and right. The administration offices were located in the right wing. An arched entryway led to a large inside court, whence, extending outward, were numerous buildings and yards. On the facade of the main building there were two balcony-like platforms at the second-floor level. Suspended some distance above the entryway was an expanse of red cloth on which was inscribed in white letters: "Loyalty to Leninism—the Source of All Our Party's Successes." A railroad line ran parallel to the factory, and directly opposite the administration building was the Lokomotivstroi station. Between the two lay a wide open space. This was where much of the action took place on the first day of the strike.

The first shift at NEVZ normally began work at 8:00 A.M. On June 1, however, eight or ten workers of the steel foundry division arrived at the factory half an hour early, a likely indication that they were upset by the preceding day's news.[5] They began discussing the food price rises, which they must have regarded as an intolerable assault on their already meager living conditions. When Ia. K. Buzaev, a high-ranking party member in the division, undertook to explain and justify the new policy, another dozen or so workers left their stations and entered the discussion. The workers were not mollified, and a protracted wrangle ensued. Presently the head of the foundry, a man named Chernyshkov, approached and admonished his subordinates to quit chattering during work hours and get back to their jobs. Instead of obeying his order, the now excited workers left their division for the square outside, where they continued increasingly heated conversations, which KGB observers characterized as "provocative."

The pleas of Buzaev and Chernyshkov having been ignored, a higher power, the plant director, B. N. Kurochkin, together with members of the factory's party committee, came to the square. Kurochkin, who had served as chief engineer and deputy director until his recent promotion to the highest post, hoped to pressure the recalcitrant workers to disperse. Instead, upon hearing that the director had come out, workers from other factory divisions poured into the square. The crowd angrily deluged Kurochkin with complaints about working conditions, the absence of protective equipment, poor living conditions, and low wages, and they demanded a pay increase. Taken aback by such brazen conduct and probably believing that he was bound by a party directive to stand his ground, the director conceded nothing. Still worse, when a distraught female worker asked Kurochkin how he expected them to get along with the prices steeply raised, he flippantly replied: "If there isn't enough money for meat and sausage, let them eat *pirozhki* [pasties] with liver."[6] His insensitivity infuriated his listeners and unleashed a storm of catcalls and insults. "The scoundrels are mocking us," one worker was overheard yelling. Having intended to face down the workers, Kurochkin was now compelled to retreat to the factory administration building. Siuda later contended that Kurochkin's boorishness was the spark that touched off the powder keg.[7] Arguably, the turmoil would have continued anyway, but the director's remark surely inflamed the situation. It was then, around mid-morning, that the strike began in earnest.

The strike was certainly spontaneous, its course reminiscent of the dynamics of the February Revolution in 1917 as Trotsky described it.[8] Certainly, no group planned or directed either that revolution or the Novocherkassk strike. But in the one case as in the other, now and again individuals came to the fore who initiated some action that moved the process forward, and then faded back into the crowd.[9] Trotsky claimed that the active individuals in 1917 were "conscious and tempered workers educated for the most part by the party of Lenin." In fact, Menshevik-schooled workers were active as well in the February eruption, both groups benefiting from participation in or knowledge of labor initiatives in the revolution of 1905. Of course, none of the Novocherkassk strikers had directly participated in either the 1905 or the 1917 revolution. However, they were certain to have been exposed to the endless celebration of those events in Soviet schools and films, had thereby participated vicariously, and so had clues as to how they should act. The idea underpinning many of their endeavors was to expand the strike movement and thereby compel the authorities to heed their demands and give ground.[10] But there was an incongruity between the resort to quasi-revolutionary methods in order to achieve narrowly limited goals.

Shortly after the confrontation with Kurochkin, two militants burst into the factory boiler room, ousted the man in charge, and set off the siren used to signal the beginning and end of the workday. The blast, sounding continuously at an unusual time of day, brought out a great many additional workers, and people from the surrounding villages as well.[11] Sharing as they did the grievances of those who had already quit work, a healthy portion of them required little agitation to make common cause with the strikers. Militants bent on spreading the strike by other means made the rounds of the many NEVZ divisions—and, presently, other plants in the industrial area as well—calling upon their fellows to lay down their tools.[12] Before long, 2,500 to 3,000 workers were out, and by noon 6,000 to 7,000 workers and others had gathered.[13]

At some point, in a daring effort to shut down NEVZ's production completely, several strikers entered the area's gas depot and tried to cut off the flow of fuel. They were repelled. Others went to the electrode factory to bring out its workers. That initiative misfired, at least temporarily, when a Communist worker named Viunen'ko warned that if they did not leave his sector, he was prepared to sacrifice himself along with them by blowing up the place. They left.[14] Two factory officials told of warding off other intruders who tried to close down their shops.[15] These gains for the forces opposing the strike were more the exception than the rule.

Around eleven o'clock, a large group of workers marched by the administration building, where they were joined by people from other departments who were on their meal break. One of them began chanting what was to become the strike's signature slogan: "Meat, butter, a pay raise." Others picked it up. Soon afterward a placard bearing those words was affixed to the top of a nearby electric transmission tower, where it conspicuously remained for the duration of the strike.

Shortly after noon, the insurgents seized part of a barricade that fenced the square off from the railroad line adjacent to the factory, placed it across the tracks, and, having adorned it with red streamers, blocked an oncoming passenger train en route from Saratov to Rostov. (A more radical proposal, to tear up the tracks, had been rejected.)[16] This maneuver, which brought traffic on one of southern Russia's major lines to a standstill for more than fourteen hours, was calculated to publicize far and wide what was occurring in Novocherkassk, garner wider support, and intensify pressure on the authorities. (Needless to say, it greatly inconvenienced the passengers, who were without water and much else.) Several strikers invaded the driver's cabin and set the train's whistle blowing, adding to the din. The blast brought out workers of the second and third shifts, among others. The strikers inscribed on the sides of the railroad cars their demand for meat, butter, and a pay raise. In anticipation of the impending meat shortage, another slogan—"Make sausage out of Khrushchev"—appeared on the locomotive, and was repeated elsewhere.

The authorities at the local and province levels had been alerted soon after the troubles began, and each in turn endeavored to arrest the strike. By late morning the head of the city's party organization and local KGB officials had already joined the factory's party committee in the director's office, which served as a command post. Their task was to work through the factory Communists and "leading workers" to keep the strike from spreading and to persuade those already on strike to get back to work. Their line of argument may be readily surmised: The price increases were temporary, and they were essential to boost production of meat and dairy products for the Soviet people. It therefore made no sense for the workers to strike. By doing so they set themselves against the party and the government, which had their interests at heart. Rather than disrupt production, their self-interest demanded that they rebuff those who urged them to support and continue the strike. For the activists on the front lines, this was an unenviable assignment, the equivalent of trying to stop a river in its course.

Many a verbal battle was waged in NEVZ workshops, spilling over into outdoor spaces and neighboring plants, between workers bent on convincing their fellows to lay down their tools and party stalwarts and their supporters who opposed them. One Communist worker, exclaiming that he did not want to remain in such an organization, is said to have ostentatiously torn up his party card.[17] Those promoting the strike damned those who refused to join them as "strikebreakers," "traitors," even "fascists." Ivashutin conceded that the party, factory, and KGB officials "had no success" in their efforts to influence the strikers.[18] Astonishingly, with almost lightning speed the vaunted party apparatus lost the control it customarily exercised.

Two close-ups of the raging battles deserve attention. One episode occurred on the second rather than the first day of the strike. Although manifesting some special features, it is undoubtedly representative in many ways of the kinds of conflict that repeatedly occurred in the workshops. It involves Andrei Korkach, the most remarkable of the strikers about whom we have information. He had a day off from the electrode factory on June 1, and left town before the strike began. When he turned up at his workplace early the next day, he heard that NEVZ strikers had come the day before to ask for support. He joined his fellow workers in the off-duty room, where they were discussing the events of the preceding day generally and the bid for their support in particular. Korkach's co-workers respected him because of his technical know-how and upright character. He asked the others whether they should go along with the request, but it was plain that he had already decided the matter for himself. Every minuscule invasion of workers' living standards in foreign countries, he pointed out, was made much of in the Soviet press. Yet "our" people are expected meekly to accept a 30 percent increase in the price of meat and butter. When the chief engineer put in an appearance and justified the price hikes, Korkach asked him how much he earned. After the engineer indicated that he was paid 300 rubles a month, his well-informed questioner remarked that that sum was supplemented by a bonus of 300. "Where," he then pointedly asked, "is your communist consciousness?" Not content with convincing his own cohort to quit work, Korkach began urging workers in other departments of his factory to come out. One department head who attempted to counter his pleas quoted him as saying: "We've been deceived for forty-five years, not allowed to speak, our patience is exhausted. . . . The policy of the party and the Soviet government on provisioning the workers is false." Korkach would pay with his life for his audacity.[19]

The other incident occurred in the early afternoon of June 1. Stormy discussions continued alongside the halted train, where many strikers were concentrated. Talk at times gave way to aggressive actions. A portrait of Khrushchev was ripped from the facade of the factory—and others later from the interior—and destroyed. Communist workers and druzhinniki who called for an end to the disorders were shoved aside and roughed up. An effort by the plant's chief engineer, S. N. Elkin, to cut off the train's whistle blast was frustrated, and he was abused. A vivid depiction of the chaotic situation was recalled by V. Vodianitskaia, a young factory worker.

> I went along with all the others toward NEVZ. A train was standing by, and many people were in the square. Immediately I saw a woman being beaten. . . . When I asked why, it turned out that her name was Khrushcheva. I remember well how they were dragging the chief engineer, Elkin, from somewhere near the train. Someone said he should be helped, that the fire gates were open, and he should be told to run behind them. I pushed closer to Elkin and whispered: "Run to the gates, they're waiting for you there." Whether he didn't hear or because his supporters were fewer [than the attackers], our effort didn't succeed. I was hit on the head with a brick. Someone may have heard my whispering to Elkin, and perhaps in assaulting him fell upon me [as well].
>
> In the crowd I saw the party organizer of our division, Alekseenko. He approached and said: "Go home, little daughter." I headed for home but

saw Aleksandr Iosifovich Braginskii [another factory official and a party member] standing on an embankment, surrounded by a crowd. I wanted to listen to what he was saying, and drew closer. He [was trying to] reply to [their] questions, but they didn't want to hear the answers. Braginskii's calm tone irritated [them], and they harassed him in every way. I noticed a group of young people surrounding him, drowning him out with whistling and looking [knowingly] at one another as if to say, "We've heard enough, let's push him over." They obviously wanted to shove him off the embankment. I knew Braginskii well, had studied under him. I cried: "Boys, don't do it. He's a good man." A woman standing alongside grabbed me and began to strangle me. While she choked me, she said: "What are you doing defending a Jew? They've drunk our blood, and you defend [them]. See what they've done to you, how you're dressed," and began to pull on my dress. I don't know how this might have ended if another woman hadn't seized my hand, taken me aside, [and said]: "What are you getting into! They'll kill you. Go home." [20]

This rather terrifying reminiscence is notable on several scores. It carries conviction because it was recalled not by a partisan of the guardians of order but by a woman who was arrested for participation in the strike and sentenced to ten years' imprisonment; moreover, she would become one of the most outspoken critics of the regime's behavior at Novocherkassk. Anything but black and white, her depiction hints at the complexity of the situation: There were good men as well as the likes of Kurochkin among the factory officials, Communists who spoke respectfully to and sympathized with the plight of the workers. They were appreciated by that large majority of the workforce who, as will be shown farther along, were disciplined and conducted themselves peacefully. On the other hand, among the workers there were men and women—undoubtedly a minority—who were oblivious of such distinctions, whose powerful feelings overrode rational considerations. They could behave mindlessly—the assault on the woman who, unfortunately for her, had the same name as the reigning Soviet leader. They displayed a penchant for violence and racism—Elkin was a Jew—all too reminiscent of the behavior of the Black Hundreds. Siuda elaborates on the role of Elkin, who, as chief engineer, was the second highest NEVZ official: He came out to speak to the workers not as a spokesman for the administration but on his own initiative. He advised the strikers to return to work, but some of the more agitated dragged him into the cab of a truck, plied him with angry questions, and demanded concrete solutions from him. "Nevertheless, I and my comrades always valued Elkin's civic feeling and courage," Siuda comments. "For both him and the strikers, the trouble was that the chief engineer had no authority to negotiate."[21]

According to Siuda, with efforts at persuasion failing, the authorities attempted a provocation. It was a sultry, breezeless day. A truck loaded with bottled drinks was sent into the troubled area. It was expected that an unorganized mob would fall upon it, seeking to assuage their thirst, and provide a pretext for forceful intervention. Indeed, some were inclined to grab bottles, but the strikers overwhelmingly declined to do so; instead they formed a corridor through which the truck could drive unmolested.[22] The authorities were certainly capable of concocting such a provocation, but one wonders whether there may have been a less sinister motive: the truckload of drinks might have been sent to bring relief to the passengers on the halted train.

Responding to the tumultuous situation developing in Novocherkassk, around 12:30 A. V. Basov, the first secretary of the Rostov Province party organization, called upon Gen. I. I. Pliev, commander of the North Caucasus Military Organization, to bring military forces into the city.[23] He also dispatched almost all the leaders of the provincial party organization—the second secretary, L. I. Maiakov; the president of the Executive Committee, I. I. Zametin; the president of the Economic Council (Sovnarkhoz), V. A. Ivanov—and a group of KGB officials headed by the deputy director of the provincial organization, I. I. Lazarev, to Novocherkassk and thence to the plant. He himself appeared there only later. Work having stopped in most of the plant's divisions, a great crowd had by then gathered just outside the factory, immediately adjacent to the railroad station. What had begun as a discussion among fewer than a dozen foundry workers had within hours ballooned into a throng embracing a large part of the workforce. A spontaneous work stoppage had spread like wildfire, mobilizing a mass of people with a focus on very specific demands. The task now confronting the authorities assembled in the director's office was to disperse the crowd so that the halted train could proceed. So long as the crowd adamantly refused to leave—that is, until late in the night—the authorities were stymied.

Around 2:00 P.M. the chief of the provincial KGB, Iu. P. Tupchenko, and his agents arrived on the scene, together with diverse Communists, Komsomols, druzhiniki, and policemen in plain clothes, intending to divide the crowd, force it from the railroad siding, and enable the train to move on. Failing in that endeavor, they attached a steam engine to the rear of the train and managed to move it backward three kilometers, but it was then blocked again. It was four o'clock before the train was freed sufficiently to allow it to move forward, but only back to the Lokomotivstroi station.

One kind of activity, however, was not frustrated: everywhere KGB agents were busily at work. One group, sent from Rostov, went to NEVZ after dressing in worker clothing, divesting themselves of documents and weapons, and furnishing themselves with cover identities. They circulated among clusters of workers, listening to conversations, and some silently photographed the most prominent activists. These individuals would be arrested sooner or later, and some of them paid the supreme penalty for their actions. At some point, rumors spread that agents were about, and calls went up to find and beat them.[24]

Around four o'clock the highest ranking official in the province, A. V. Basov, arrived from Rostov, joined the others in the director's office, and took charge. Basov was first secretary of the Rostov Province party organization, a member of both the Central Committee of the CPSU and the Supreme Soviet. He appears to have been the first official to call for the army to restore order. For hours the crowd had milled about in the square outside the administration building. Some of the most bellicose now barged into the building and on into the director's office, where they demanded that the leaders speak to the crowd on the square. The besieged authorities had no choice but to yield. Around 4:30 a loudspeaker was set up on a balcony, and Basov, Zametin, and T. S. Loginov, first secretary of the Novocherkassk party committee, came up to the microphone. Tupchenko claims to have advised Basov to defuse the situation by announcing that Kurochkin would be dismissed, but Basov stubbornly declined.[25] The crowd quieted down as Basov began to speak.

To curry favor, he started out by declaring that he had been an orphaned and homeless child, and had known a hard life.[26] Rather than address the workers' concerns, however, he then expounded the substance of the announcement made the day before. He was interrupted by cries : "We're literate, we've read the appeal, but tell us how we're to live with a cut in wages and higher prices." When he held out no hope that the policy announced the day before would be reversed, the exasperated audience rained stones, metal objects, and bottles onto the balcony.[27] Some strikers attempted to seize the microphone, but in the scuffle they were thwarted when the wire was severed. Basov and other leaders fled into a room in the building's interior, which was then barricaded.

The province's leading official had become a hostage, and so he remained until well into the night, reportedly furious that nobody rescued him.

Exhortations having failed, in the evening authorities who remained at liberty attempted to squelch the strike by a show of force. Between six and seven o'clock, 200 uniformed policemen in a dozen or so vehicles were sent to restore order. They left their cars, formed into two ranks, and advanced toward the workers in the square. Stamping and whooping, the far more numerous workers moved in a wave toward the policemen, causing them to retreat to their vehicles and drive away. According to the KGB document, three of those who lagged behind were beaten, but Siuda claims that two who were slow to flee were in fact escorted under guard to a house to protect them from possible harm by the kind of "extremists inevitably present in any mass of people caught up in an emotional situation." [28]

Two hours later, military elements, who were expected to be more effective, were brought into play. Five autos filled with soldiers and three armored troop carriers arrived at the square. The crowd ran to meet them, blocked the road, and compelled them to stop. The strikers added insult to injury, according to the KGB account, by taunting the soldiers. The latter were roundly rebuked for interfering in a dispute between the workers and the administration, which was none of their business. [29] Then, to the accompaniment of whistles, catcalls, and laughter, the cars turned about and departed.

A different reading of this episode is suggested by other details. The KGB document comments that the officers and soldiers involved lacked determination, and stood as if paralyzed. There are indications that some strikers, seemingly recalling the famously successful tactic employed by demonstrators during the February Revolution in 1917, urged the soldiers to join their protest. Was it on this score that the soldiers evinced a "lack of determination"? It is said that when one of the strikers, "without hindrance," climbed atop an armored troop carrier and urged a continuation of the action, at least one soldier joined him. Is it fanciful to suggest that the local law enforcement personnel, whether policemen or garrison soldiers, were unreliable, could not be depended upon to suppress the strike? Siuda flatly states that the strikers and the soldiers fraternized, and the officers were hard put to disengage their men and lead them away. [30]

A mass meeting began in the square and continued far into the night. The strikers had reason to be self-satisfied: they had defied and put to flight the local authorities and taken the leading provincial official hostage; they had succeeded in warding off the police and the garrison soldiers sent to rout them; they controlled the NEVZ district. The workers were exhilarated, according to Siuda, by the heady experience of liberty. The next move was the question they now had to resolve. Using the top of the entrance to the railroad underpass facing the square as their platform, many speakers passionately addressed the throng. For a while the area was illuminated by a bonfire made of portraits of Khrushchev.[31] Speakers urged the crowd not to disperse, but to continue their triumphant activity. A variety of tactics was advanced.

To expand the strike, delegates should be sent to other enterprises in Novocherkassk and elsewhere. A delegation should also be dispatched to the organs of power to demand price cuts and pay hikes. (Word must have gotten out that party leaders from Moscow had arrived in Novocherkassk.) One of the more radical participants, a Polytechnical student named Iu. Dement'ev who had joined the strikers, urged them to head for the town, to seize the post and telegraph offices. Of course, the Bolsheviks had taken this route in 1917, but circumstances in Novocherkassk in 1962 were hardly comparable. Still, the idea made some sense, once the strikers learned that all roads out of the city had been blockaded, so that no delegates could be sent to other towns.[32] Fearing that such a move would call down forceful retaliation by the authorities, Siuda and others urged instead a mass parade into the city to demonstrate the numbers and solidarity of the strikers, make their grievances known to the authorities, and demand redress—and this view prevailed.[33]

In a move no doubt inspired by remembrance of the origins of the soviets in 1905, it was suggested that workers from the various factories elect delegates to present their demands to the authorities. It would also have made sense to draw up a written statement of the demands. But in the prevailing confusion, neither the one idea nor the other was acted upon. The strike had erupted suddenly, and what had been achieved on the first day was remarkable. But one could hardly expect an effective organization to spring out of this turbulence immediately, especially from a mass of people with no experience of self-initiated collective action. Yet, without such an organization, the prospects for further success were problematic. The strikers at least agreed that they should reassemble at 5:00 A.M. on June 2. Around 1:00 A.M. Dement'ev mounted his bicycle and headed for his dormitory, where he agitated for a student turnout to support the strikers in the morning.[34] While the strikers were celebrating what they had accomplished and attempting to define their next move, the instruments of the Soviet state were mobilized to deal with the mutinous population.

Hooliganism and Criminal Behavior

It behooves us to assess the charge that the strike action on June 1 was replete with hooliganism and criminal behavior. The KGB summary reads: "On the first day of the disorders, Communists, police, and officers and soldiers of the Soviet army were beaten. Hooligans attacked tanks, ruined instruments, and threw stones, which resulted in the wounding of two tank personnel."[35] The authorities contended that many strikers were inebriated, and that whether inebriated or not, they engaged in violent activity directed against both persons and property. There can be no doubt that many of the strikers were drinking, some of them to the point of sottedness. Drinking was an integral part of worker culture, and it was not uncommon for workers to drink on the job. Drunkenness during working hours was certainly known at NEVZ. Many people regularly celebrated the end of the workweek with a binge.[36] With the strike beginning on Friday, the weekend was starting a day early, and it would be surprising if a good deal of drinking had not gone on. Besides, the strikers were transgressing, they had to know that their activity might cause them serious trouble, and the consumption of alcohol could have diminished anxiety, dissolved inhibitions, and emboldened them to continue on their perilous path. According to an old Russian proverb, "What the sober person thinks, he blurts out when drunk." Significantly, more than one observer noted that those who addressed the crowds were especially likely to have been drinking, but it strains credulity that a mass of people, the great majority of whom were said to be well disciplined, would have heeded speakers who were far gone.[37] As in much else about the strike, the evidence is ambiguous.

After lunch on June 1, the deputy police chief of Novocherkassk, A. I. Vereshchagin, was sent by his superior to NEVZ and the adjacent worker village to check up on laborers who were reportedly wrecking shops, getting drunk, and in general behaving like hooligans. Salespeople in the village, however, told him that less liquor than usual had been sold that day so far. Nevertheless, to be on the safe side, he ordered sales to be discontinued. He then proceeded to NEVZ, where, instead of wrecking, quiet reigned. He remained on duty there continuously through June 4, organizing security of state property—

warehouses, snack bars, dining halls, and the rest. During this time, he reported in 1990, there was not a single case of destruction or theft in the factory. He personally inspected all the divisions, and the only property damage he had found was some broken windows in a snack bar; nothing had been stolen.[38] M. A. Makiev, who as police chief in the workers' village was acquainted with many of them, reported that when he appeared at the factory, the strikers treated him respectfully. He checked all the stores and institutions in the village and found everything undisturbed—in other words, no looting had occurred.[39] Coming from police officials, this testimony is certainly impressive, but it concerns particular times and places, and certainly cannot be considered an exhaustive description of the situation.

Contrariwise, a master craftsman in the instrument division at NEVZ, Iu. V. Gusev, said he had been told by other workmen that vodka had been distributed along the railroad siding, without charge, to anyone who wanted it.[40] This is uncorroborated hearsay. If true, it might have been the work of provocateurs.

As for violence, the incidents reported leave no room for doubt that it did occur, Siuda's contention to the contrary notwithstanding. Even he inadvertently expressed awareness that "extremists are inevitably present in any mass of people caught up in an emotional situation." Vodianitskaia's recollection provides powerful evidence, and there is more. Mardar', despite her partiality to the strikers, writes candidly about the "pogrom" (riotous) activity of some of them.[41] Numerous assertions that individuals who tried to persuade the workers to return to work were roughed up are certainly believable. One worker recalled long after the events that he had been mistaken for a strikebreaker and beaten by a "workers' patrol."[42] Mention has been made of stones and other missiles thrown at Basov. An inspection of Kurochkin's office on June 6 revealed that strikers who had invaded the place had wrecked the door's transom, broken windows, torn the telephone from its housing, littered the place with broken bottles, and scattered documents about. One of the perpetrators vented his feelings on a magazine cover, where he wrote: "Work hard and you get nothing in return."[43] When tanks rolled toward NEVZ that evening, individual strikers attempted to disable them, reportedly clambering aboard one or more, smashing their periscopes and headlights, covering the turrets with tarpaulins, and in some cases inserting metal objects into the tank treads. At another time and place, at least one motor vehicle, and perhaps more than one, was overturned; one of the occupants suffered a broken leg. An irate worker assaulted one of a group of soldiers who came to the square to restore order, breaking his rib.[44]

On the other hand, many witnesses remarked that there were frequent appeals for discipline, that the strikers should refrain from threats, getting drunk, and beating those on the other side. No few observers noted that only a small minority was guilty of breaches of order, and, not surprisingly, such "outrages" as occurred were committed mostly by persons under thirty years of age.[45] The overwhelming majority behaved peacefully, if not in conformity with the law. It must be kept in mind that the workers possessed no means of self-defense: no real trade unions but only the supine, officially sanctioned ones; no independent political organization but a ruling party purportedly governing in their behalf while in fact upholding their interests mostly rhetorically; and, of course, they possessed no legal right to strike. Their material conditions were miserable even before their wages were cut and food prices increased. Understandably, then, they were driven by desperation to extraordinary measures.[46] When they destroyed portraits of Khrushchev, they were attacking symbols of authority. However, they did not dream of overthrowing the government—their explicit objectives were much more modest. They did not tear down portraits of Lenin;[47] it was Khrushchev they reviled. Khrushchev had betrayed the ideals of the founder, to whom they remained steadfastly loyal. When the next day they marched with portraits of Lenin and red banners, they were implicitly asserting that they and not the established authorities were the true legatees of the revolution.

The Response from on High

Khrushchev's background and life experience conditioned him to empathize with working people. Born in 1894 into a family of miners in the Donbass, he himself began work in factories and mines at the age of fourteen. By the time he joined the Bolshevik Party in 1918, he was undoubtedly aware of the shootings of unarmed workers in St. Petersburg on January 1905, and of a similar event in the Lena gold fields in 1912. Indeed, he may have been predisposed to labor radicalism by a smaller-scale episode of the kind in 1916 in the region where he worked. According to an account published in 1961, in the third year of the Great War a massive strike broke out in the Donbass, aimed against the war and the tsar and for bread and freedom. It is remarked in passing—an obligatory gesture?—that Khrushchev was one of the organizers of the strike. In April the miners in one district gathered to demand an increase in pay and improvement in working conditions. The mine owners refused to negotiate and instead strengthened the police forces and called in the army. On April 19 they opened fire on the unarmed workers, killing four and wounding two. Afterward many strikers were arrested and exiled.[48]

As a young member of the Bolshevik Party, Khrushchev would probably have had trouble imagining himself as the executioner of worker-protesters who sprang from the same class as he. As he rose rapidly in the party hierarchy, however, his identification with the regime's goals necessitated a shift in his relation to the workers. With economic growth and productivity increases becoming a priority in the 1920s and given increasing emphasis with the inauguration of the five-year plans, the welfare of the workers became a secondary consideration. In the words of one of his recent biographers, "Strikes were common [in the 1920s] and [within the area under his supervision] it often fell to Khrushchev to break them." In the 1930s he demanded that enterprise managers "take a hard line toward workers," and denounced those who advocated easing workers' output norms.[49] His knowledge of the terrible suffering and privation that the population endured during World War II—he had been the party boss in Ukraine—led him in 1947 to favor some reordering of priorities "to the expansion of consumer goods production and the raising of the living standards of the working people."[50] But Stalin had to die before it became possible to make good in some measure on this promise.

Khrushchev was one of the triumvirate, along with G. M. Malenkov and V. M. Molotov, that assumed power after Stalin's death, and ordered the use of Soviet tanks to smash the East German workers' eruption in June 1953. This brutal Stalin like act did not keep Khrushchev from denouncing Stalin three years later in the famous speech he delivered to the 20th Congress of the CPSU in 1956. It would be a mistake to suppose that with this speech Khrushchev was breaking totally and irrevocably with the Stalinist past. (Had he done so, he could not have survived as long as he did.) Like Goethe's Faust, he was impelled by two contradictory tendencies. As Fedor Burlatskii, who was close to him from 1960 to 1965, has observed, although he dealt "a crushing blow to the cult of Stalin," he had been "formed under the influence of Stalinist thinking" and "was still captivated by many of Stalin's concepts of socialism." True, "he was drawn toward the idea of diversity and pluralism," but he also had a "dogmatic belief in the superiority of the state system."[51] Later Khrushchev's son-in-law,

Aleksei Adzhubei, represented the matter somewhat differently: Khrushchev, he wrote, took a dim view of the bureaucracy, the apparatchiks who had lost contact with the rank and file, yet he was ever more obligated to those elements to cover up unpleasant incidents.[52]

Decidedly germane to the Novocherkassk story for what it reveals of their modus operandi for dealing with insurgencies is the reaction of Khrushchev and his colleagues to the Hungarian uprising in 1956, which his epoch-making speech did much to trigger. The complicated story, presented here in bare outline, is based on an excellent reconstruction grounded in the recently declassified notes of contemporary Presidium meetings.[53] The crisis began when on October 23 a mass demonstration in Budapest turned into a popular uprising. Iurii Andropov, the Soviet ambassador in Budapest, immediately contacted the commander of Soviet troops in Hungary, General Lashchenko. The general indicated that he could do nothing without explicit authorization from the political leaders. Rather cautiously, Khrushchev asked Erno Gerö, who had recently replaced Mátyás Rákosi as chief of the Hungarian Communist Party, to submit a written request for help to the CPSU Presidium, but the Soviet leader soon realized that events were moving too quickly to wait. When the Presidium urgently met that night, Khrushchev and all but one of the other members supported the introduction of military forces to Budapest. The lone dissenter was Anastas Mikoyan, who argued that "the Hungarians themselves will restore order. We should try political measures, and only then send in troops."

With the leadership divided, Khrushchev chose a two-track strategy, both to try political measures and to send in troops. He dispatched Mikoyan and M. A. Suslov, another member of the Presidium, to Budapest to explore the possibility of a political solution. At the same time, Khrushchev authorized Marshal G. K. Zhukov, the minister of defense, to deploy Soviet units to the Hungarian capital. A massive force of over 30,000 troops, more than 1,000 tanks, and 159 planes was rushed in. The designated commander, Gen. M. Malinin—he had accompanied Mikoyan and Suslov from Moscow to Budapest—speedily created an "operational group" of high-ranking officers. Contrary to expectations, the introduction of the armored forces proved ineffective in the clogged streets of Budapest—and also counterproductive, in that it further inflamed the resistance. Alarming reports from Mikoyan and Suslov led the hard-line opponents of Khrushchev—Molotov, Kliment Voroshilov, and Lazar Kaganovich—to object that Mikoyan was "acting improperly and pushing us toward capitulation." The split deepened as other figures, Zhukov and Malenkov and even Khrushchev, defended Mikoyan, although they disagreed with his noninterventionist stance.

As the situation deteriorated in Hungary, with hundreds of Soviet soldiers and Hungarian civilians having lost their lives and the government of Imre Nagy calling for the withdrawal of Soviet troops, the Moscow leadership had great difficulty in deciding how to respond. The situation is "complicated," Khrushchev twice remarked on October 28: "the workers are supporting the uprising," and, as opposed to the Kremlin's definition of the situation, the insurgents "want to reclassify what is occurring as something other than a counter-revolutionary uprising." Faced with the prospect of putting down a movement in which workers figured prominently, the Presidium wavered. By October 30, all the members, even Molotov and Voroshilov, had resolved that the USSR should forgo large-scale military intervention. Even more surprising, the Presidium members unanimously agreed to go along with the option Khrushchev now favored: "the peaceful path—the path of troop withdrawals and negotiations"—rather than "the military path, the path of occupation." As Mark Kramer has suggested, "the Soviet Presidium actually may have been willing to accept the collapse of Communism in Hungary," but this position would prove ephemeral, because many of the insurgents were unwilling to settle for "ill-defined negotiations that, once under way, would be subject to delay or derailment."[54]

With this consideration coming home to those on the ground, simultaneously with the Moscow leadership's move toward a soft line, the Mikoyan-Suslov communications took on a more pessimistic cast with respect to the prospects for a satisfactory peaceful solution. The uprising could be terminated only by force, they warned, and it would have to be Soviet force, for the Hungarian army appeared to be unreliable. Their ideas were buttressed almost immediately by reports of a bloody attack made by a mob on the Budapest party headquarters. In response, just one day after the Presidium had opted for the "peaceful path," it reversed itself and decided unanimously for the military path.

Mikoyan and Suslov were not in Moscow when the vote was taken; they arrived there only that evening. Contrary to the views he had expressed the day before, Mikoyan now strongly opposed the decision to use force and pleaded for negotiations, arguing that armed intervention "would undermine the reputation of the Soviet government and party."[55] The most arresting feature of this fascinating story is the leadership's difficulty in responding to the crisis: its wavering between a political and a military approach, the division in the collective, and its willingness, however briefly, to accept a humiliating defeat.

The course of discussions and events relating to the Hungarian revolution are germane to the Novocherkassk story. In the one case as in the other, the Soviet regime was faced with a serious challenge and ultimately resorted to force to deal with it. The Hungarian uprising was certainly more serious, for it threatened the USSR's position not only within Hungary but, because of its potential ripple effect, throughout its East European bloc. For that matter, it gave rise to pro-Hungarian activity in the Soviet Union itself, bringing to the surface opposition to the regime, which the government firmly suppressed. It was easier to contain the eruption in Novocherkassk than the one in Hungary, but it too was ultimately envisaged as a threat that had to be dealt with forcefully.

Thanks to the notes compiled by Vladimir Malin, head of the General Department of the Central Committee, we know a good deal about the leadership's thinking with regard to the Hungarian problem, but we have nothing comparable for the Novocherkassk events. Additionally, when in the early 1990s a serious reexamination of the Novocherkassk occurrences was undertaken, no testimony could be secured from most of the principals, because they were no longer among the living. Gone were both Khrushchev and Kozlov, his principal agent at Novocherkassk; the minister of defense, A. R. Malinovskii; the two military men most actively involved, Generals I. A. Pliev and Oleshko; and the other Presidium members—Mikoyan, A. P. Kirilenko, and D. S. Polianskii—whom Khrushchev had dispatched to Novocherkassk along with Kozlov. Then, too, Khrushchev wrote a good deal about the Hungarian crisis in his memoirs, but he studiously avoided any reference to the Novocherkassk events. Therefore, we are seemingly obliged to make do with scraps of information from the published sources and available archival material (notably the testimony of V. E. Semichastnyi and A. N. Shelepin), which provide no more than a fragmentary and rather puzzling picture. To the extent that available information permits comparison, however, the evidence on the Hungarian uprising, which occurred less than six years before the Novocherkassk events, may serve as a template of sorts for understanding high-level thinking and action regarding Novocherkassk. Of course, such an approach requires caution: Malin's notes directly indicate the leaders' responses to the developing situation, while the recollections of those who testified almost thirty years later were apt to be fuzzy, and besides, they may have been doctored in self-serving ways.

Mikoyan has been quoted as saying that Moscow was informed of the troubles in Novocherkassk twenty minutes after the train had been halted; that is, about 12:30.[56] Apparently Khrushchev first learned of the matter from the Rostov Province party leadership, and then again from Semichastnyi, his KGB chief. He must have been shocked to hear that several thousand workers were on strike and out of control, engaging in activities that he considered detrimental to their genuine interests, personified in the Soviet state. During the Hungarian crisis he had badgered Malenkov, who had gone to Budapest, for his failure to explain the true state of things to the new leadership in Hungary. Malenkov insisted that he had explained things but the other side would not agree with him. If that was the case, Khrushchev retorted, then "it is clear that they simply don't understand, even though it is very simple"; and he then undertook to explain the situation, which in truth was inexplicable from his ideological standpoint—and to no avail, of course.[57]

Similarly, when the trouble began at Novocherkassk, he of course considered his just-announced policy to be correct; and he also believed, not without reason, that he was able to communicate effectively with common people. According to Adzhubei, when Khrushchev first heard of the strike in Novocherkassk, "he wanted to go there immediately, wanted to explain himself to the citizens, to calm passions," and was barely talked out of doing so.[58] Interestingly, Gen. M. K. Shaposhnikov, who took charge of the military forces at NEVZ sometime on June 1, advised the strikers to send a delegation to state their grievances and wants to Khrushchev. They declined his counsel for fear, as they said, that instead of being permitted to go to Moscow and meet Khrushchev, they would wind up in prison.[59] In principle, a meeting between Khrushchev and striker delegates might have produced a settlement. There was certainly no possibility that he could or would have reversed the decision on food price increases, but other concessions could have been made—as indeed they were after the strike had ended.

Having convinced themselves that socialism was already a reality and, ipso facto, the well-being of the workers assured, some of the top officials were inclined to blame foreign agents or domestic foes for what was occurring. The head of the Rostov Province KGB, Iu. P. Tupchenko, noted retrospectively that it had been deemed necessary to look into the possible participation of "foreign special services" in the strike. Party officials on the scene may have propagated the idea that agents of hostile foreign powers were to blame for the eruption. At any rate, I. Fesenko, a docent at the Polytechnic Institute, recalled a widespread rumor to that effect. Another rumor had it (contrary to the truth) that the "imperialist" press had published accounts of the shooting at Novocherkassk the very next day, indisputable evidence of the presence of foreign agents on the ground. This was not the only purported root of the troubles. Arriving in Novocherkassk early on June 2, the Central Committee secretary, L. F. Ilychev, kept reciting like a mantra: "The religious sectarians [and/or the Cossacks] have instigated the mutiny." When on June 1 General Pliev, commander of the North Caucasus Military District, was ordered, with no explanation, to proceed to Novocherkassk, he too supposed, according to one of his subordinates, that the Cossacks were up in arms.[60]

Khrushchev himself remained in Moscow, but we may gauge his alarm by the makeup of the team he dispatched to Novocherkassk to deal with the situation. The group was headed by F. P. Kozlov, secretary of the party's Central Committee and Khrushchev's heir apparent, and Mikoyan, first vice president of the Council of Ministers. Both were members of the eleven-person Presidium, as were two others who flew to the troubled area, A. P. Kirilenko and D. S. Polianskii. In addition, two prominent secretaries of the party's Central Committee, A. N. Shelepin (a former KGB head) and L. F. Ilichev (a former editor of *Pravda*), went along. There is reason to believe that Khrushchev initially entrusted the task to Kirilenko and Shepilov. The latter later claimed that when the two approached Novocherkassk, they were met by an angry crowd who cursed and threatened to beat and kill them.[61] There is no independent support for this assertion, but it may at least be inferred that the two advised Moscow that the situation was more grave than it was initially believed to be, and the other four were sent immediately to join them. Paralleling what had occurred in Budapest in 1956, Kozlov organized an operations group, which met regularly to discuss conditions and formulate proposals. He also arranged for a direct telephone connection between the operations center and the Kremlin, enabling Khrushchev to keep in close touch with developments and proposals.[62]

As in the Hungarian case, a two-pronged strategy was to be implemented. Hopeful but uncertain that efforts to resolve the strike peacefully would succeed, the leadership alerted regional military units of the Ministry of Internal Affairs (MVD)—the 505th Regiment of the 89th Division, stationed in Rostov—and the Soviet army's North Caucasus Military Organization (NCMO), which included a complement of tank forces. Gen. I. A. Pliev was commander of the NCMO, Gen. M. K. Shaposhnikov the second in command. Both had been named Hero of the Soviet Union for their exceptional valor during World War II. Pliev and his staff, who had been engaged in a training exercise in the Krasnodar area, flew to Rostov, where they were met by vehicles that took them to Novocherkassk.

During the night, 3,000 NCMO troops and 300 MVD troops were concentrated in Novocherkassk. General Shaposhnikov placed the factory under military guard and imposed a curfew on the town. He had a group of tanks at his disposal, and another fifteen tanks took up positions on the Tuzlov River bridge. Military units were posted to critical points, among them the gas depot, the party headquarters, the building housing the police station and the KGB offices, the bank, the post and telegraph offices, and the radio station, while other forces were held in reserve. In what was clearly an all-out effort, policemen from other towns, Komsomol leaders, druzhinniki from inside and outside the factories, and cadets of area military schools were mobilized as well. Komsomol and People's Militia personnel spent the night guarding the party headquarters.[63] Strikers who wished to enlist the support of students were barred from entering the dormitories; and, to prevent young people from joining the demonstrators on June 2, brigade officers at the dormitories were instructed to make sure that the residents stayed in their rooms.[64]

The balance of power, which only yesterday had lain with the insurgent strikers, had shifted to the side of the party-government forces. In strategic terms, the stage was now set for a possibly peaceful resolution of the crisis. Persons close to Khrushchev affirmed that he favored a peaceful settlement. Long after the events, Semichastnyi, the KGB chief, stated that his superior had hoped to bring the strike to an end by finding a common language with the people. Shepilov reported that when Khrushchev assigned him and Kirilenko to Novocherkassk, he had warned them to avoid impulsiveness and panic, and not to resort to arms.[65] The available sources say nothing about how they were expected to bring the disorders to a peaceful conclusion. If they were simply supposed to rehearse and justify the message announced the day before, they were bound to fail, as the experience of the local and provincial party leaders demonstrated. There is no evidence that those sent from Moscow were authorized to negotiate with representatives of the strikers, unless that is the import of Semichastnyi's assertion that a common language with the people should be found. It is conceivable that once they had determined the causes of the eruption, Khrushchev's emissaries might have ended the work stoppage by making concessions. We have no indications, however, that anyone sought a meeting with representatives of the workers, either at NEVZ or in the town.

An approach more in line with police methods was suggested, appropriately enough, by Semichastnyi: it was imperative to keep the strike from spreading and to isolate the most active participants and thus avoid the need to resort to force.[66] The authorities were successful on the first count—the strike was contained. (A KGB report filed on June 12 refers to "mass disorders" in the nearby towns of Rostov, Taganrog, and Shakhty, but no further information about them or indication that they were sparked by the Novocherkassk strike has come to light.)[67] The outcome on the second count would prove disastrous. Whether at the KGB chief's urging or not, twenty-two persons, including many who had come to the fore on June 1, were taken into custody that night. In a surprising display of leniency, twenty of them were freed after questioning, assertedly "to avoid unnecessary complications."[68] The decision makers anticipated that the arrests would anger the strikers, that they would seek to liberate their fellows, and an unwanted clash would ensue. Correspondingly, instead of being jailed in the building that housed both the Novocherkassk police station and the local KGB headquarters, the two who were not released, presumably because they were considered most disruptive, were transported out of town. This seemingly sensible calculation went awry. The freeing of most of those who had been arrested was a fateful blunder, for several of them subsequently behaved as firebrands, and the violent clash that was to have been avoided by spiriting away the others came to pass.

Semichastnyi had foreseen the termination of the disorders in a few days, and the way of negotiation, if it were to be pursued in earnest, would also have required some days. But one of the decisive features of the Novocherkassk story was the lightning speed with which the crisis came to a head, thereby foreclosing various theoretically possible solutions. Between the first stirrings at Novocherkassk and the shooting on the square, a mere twenty-eight hours elapsed, twenty-four hours from the point when the Kremlin learned what was afoot, no more than nineteen hours from the arrival of Kirilenko and Shepilov, and a still shorter time from the appearance of Kozlov, Mikoyan, and the others.

Kirilenko and Shelepin arrived in Novocherkassk toward evening on June 1, the others during the night.[69] Aghast to learn how far out of hand things had gotten, Kirilenko, the senior delegate from Moscow, determined to take firmer measures than Khrushchev had advised. This was more easily said than done, he discovered, when he summoned Pliev to a conference. Both Pliev and his deputy bridled at being called upon to intervene in the disturbances on the ground that the army's mission was to defend the country against foreign foes; it was the responsibility of the police and the MVD's internal security forces to deal with civil disorders. According to M. A. Derkachev, a staff officer who was present, a dramatic exchange between Kirilenko and Pliev on this score occurred around 5:00 P.M. (it must surely have occurred later) in the office of a tank regiment commander. To Kirilenko's query as to what he should do to keep the strikers from coming into the city, Pliev indicated his intention to set up a barrier of tanks on the bridge over the Tuzlov River, which separated the industrial area from the town. Not getting the reply he apparently desired, Kirilenko repeated his question, and received the same answer. His temper rising, Kirilenko put the question a third time. Pliev doggedly repeated his response and added: "I do not plan to take other measures against the workers. The maintenance of order in the city is the duty of the local authorities and the police organs, not the commander of the military district." At that Kirilenko indignantly declared: "I have nothing more to say to you. Leave!"[70]

Shelepin seems not to have been present at the time; at any rate, he reported nothing of the sort in the testimony he gave in the early 1990s. D. A. Ivashchenko, another NCMO officer who was present, gave no such details, but recalled that Kirilenko was "very rude . . . blamed everything on the army . . . [and] responded [to Pliev's objections] with gross obscenities."[71] A. S. Davydov, still another officer who was present, gave a rather different account, which indirectly calls into question the accuracy of Derkachev's intriguing and widely credited testimony.[72] Kirilenko was evidently upset by the NCMO chief's inaction thus far, for he assigned Pliev the task of liberating Basov within the next hours; "Otherwise you are [no longer] a commander."

Resentful though he may have been, Pliev immediately ordered Davydov and the commander of the 406th Tank Regiment, Colonel M. P. Mikheev, to proceed with thirty to forty troops to NEVZ, reconnoiter the situation, and bring Basov out. Advancing toward the factory in armored cars, they met with no aggressive action, no efforts to overturn vehicles; but they were not permitted to approach and enter the administration building, so they left. On the way back to town they encountered a column of 800 men under the command of General Oleshko headed for NEVZ. Apparently considering Pliev's response to his order inadequate, without waiting for the return of the Davydov-Mikheev detachment Kirilenko had categorically ordered Oleshko to accomplish the task. Now the two groups proceeded together to the factory, where they discovered that Basov had already been liberated.[73]

Some hours later, the group headed by Kozlov and Mikoyan arrived in Novocherkassk. According to Semichastnyi, Kozlov was a tough character, the most extreme of the lot, impatient with talk, preferring action. The implicit contrast is with Mikoyan, whom Semichastnyi perceived—and this view corresponds with Mikoyan's role in the Hungarian crisis—as a more flexible person, indeed "a great diplomat."[74] Khrushchev doubtless viewed Mikoyan—his "closest associate," according to Burlatskii[75]—as a counterpoise to the hard-line Kozlov. While the one could explore the chances for a peaceful solution, the other could be relied upon to crack down should the situation warrant.

According to Shelepin, when he and Kirilenko informed the newly arrived Kozlov of where things stood, Kozlov immediately replied (in a vein much like that of Kirilenko a bit earlier): "We'll have to resort to arms." Shelepin vehemently objected, pointing to Khrushchev's instruction to avoid what Kozlov now was calling for. In words reminiscent of Mikoyan's argument against military intervention in Hungary, he claims to have said that "our people" would see such an action as tantamount to the shooting of the workers in 1905 and the Lena gold field massacre. "We would be condemned not only in our country but throughout the entire world."[76] Kozlov brusquely reminded his critic that it was he, the higher-ranked party person, who was in charge. Kirilenko remained silent, and Mikoyan predictably argued that there was no need to hurry or get unduly excited: it was essential first of all to get a full and clear picture.

At some point in the argument, Kozlov suggested that Shelepin phone their leader, and he did so, explaining his view of the situation. Then Khrushchev asked to speak to Kozlov, but unfortunately Shelepin didn't hear what was said. As in the Hungarian crisis, the leadership was divided, had difficulty in responding to an unexpected and especially troubling situation, a massive worker insurgency against the "socialist" state's policy. The split between Kozlov-Kirilenko and Mikoyan-Shepilov almost certainly mirrored Khrushchev's own ambivalence: Yes, it was necessary to liberate Basov and the halted train. But these ends should be accomplished by means other than shooting, and in fact they were in the course of the night. Men of the army's special forces (*Spetsnaz*), dressed in workingmen's clothing, managed to penetrate the NEVZ administration building and succeeded in getting Basov and his colleagues out. Well along into the night, when most of the crowd at NEVZ had dispersed, troops posted nearby easily cleared the tracks so that the train could proceed. After a day in which everything had gone the strikers' way, some of the lost ground had been regained; some immediate objectives had been achieved, and without bloodshed. And by the morning of June 2, to repeat, the investment of the town with a mighty military force gave the guardians of order the wherewithal to negotiate from a position of strength or to force the strikers to submit.

That Kozlov was at the helm was a fact to be reckoned with in the developing situation. Semichastnyi contended that his high rank bestowed upon Kozlov the power to make any decision, to give binding orders to the ministers of defense and internal affairs and the commander of the NCMO. He might be constrained by Khrushchev's emphasis on the desirability of resolving things by peaceful means. But if he had been served notice that caution was obligatory, he may also have been given leave to do what was necessary should the situation become critical. In other words, he could have had the discretion whether or not to recommend the use of arms. Shelepin's view of Kozlov was implicitly at odds with Semichatnyi's. With no elaboration of the point, he contended that Kozlov, far from being a tough operator, was cowardly by nature. For that reason, Shelepin declared, Kozlov would never dare to order a resort to arms without Khrushchev's authorization.[77] Still, Kozlov was the key person on the ground, so his perception of the evolving situation and what he conveyed to Khrushchev could be decisive in determining what action should be taken. Although much remains unclear, it seems certain that any decision to bring force into play would derive from the interplay between Kozlov and Khrushchev.

Thanks to *Pravda's* publication the next day of a long, rambling speech Khrushchev delivered to a delegation of Cuban youths then visiting Moscow, we may gain insight into his thinking on June 2. It is inconceivable that the leader would have expended so much time and verbiage on a rather unimportant delegation in ordinary circumstances, much less in the midst of a crisis. Ostensibly speaking to the Cuban delegation, however, he was really addressing his own people about matters that deeply disturbed him.[78] His remarks about Cuba's achievements and problems were interwoven with an extensive discussion of the Soviet regime's past struggles and present difficulties.

When he spoke of the Castro government's inability to meet the needs of the Cuban people, the shortages of meat, rice, and milk, and the consequent inclination of some people to question the value of the revolution, Khrushchev clearly had his own people in mind. He obviously knew of the protests against the increase in food prices and the Novocherkassk strike, although he did not mention it by name. What was new in his long-winded justification of the measures just announced was his effort to put the matter into historical perspective and his invocation of Lenin. Rather hyperbolically, he likened the regime's current difficulty to the one it had faced at the end of the Civil War, when Lenin chose to inaugurate the New Economic Policy and even gave concessions to foreign capitalists. That was a hard decision, and some comrades who found it incomprehensible withdrew from the party. But Lenin stood by a program that realistically responded to the needs of the time; the party fought against the unbelievers and went on to glorious triumphs.

Khrushchev dubbed the "antisocial" opponents of the present policy "grabbers, slackers, and criminals," and hinted at the correct approach to such elements in his delineation of stages in the Cuban revolutionary process. The first featured an armed struggle against the enemy, but once the revolutionary forces took power, new and in some ways more difficult problems had to be faced. With a portion of the population not comprehending the impossibility of rapid improvement in living standards, the enemy no longer appears before you with a rifle in his hands; instead "he may be dressed in the same worker shirt as you." Under these conditions, "it is not shooting that is needed" but a sustained repulse of the opposition and a determined effort to build up the economy. Toward the end of his oration, Khrushchev returned explicitly to the situation in the Soviet Union. Speaking again of grabbers, slackers, and criminals, he insisted that it was necessary to explain and enlighten, but also absolutely necessary "to bring into line [*odergyvat'*] "those who don't understand and don't wish to understand."[79] Khrushchev appears to be saying that, like Lenin, he would not yield to pressure to reverse his policy, and if necessary would resort to coercive measures. What these measures should be remained undefined, so Khrushchev's counsel was ambiguous, and therefore open to interpretation. It is a matter of interest that individuals at the top reflected their ambivalence by adducing diverse historical references to buttress their positions: on one side, Lenin's decision to do what was necessary to overcome opposition; on the other, the consequences of intransigence, as in 1905 and 1912.

At the beginning of Day 2 of the strike, Khrushchev's agents in Novocherkassk seemed also to be uncertain as to how to deal with the demonstration scheduled to come into the city. From what followed, it appears that they were sitting between two stools, unprepared to negotiate and also loath to resort to force.

Chapter 3   June 2: Bloody Saturday

The workers generally conceived of their strike as a dispute between themselves and the factory management, and bitterly resented the introduction of military forces. They seemingly had failed to assimilate one of the ABCs of the official Marxist philosophy: that the state is an instrument of the ruling group, whose function is to perpetuate its dominance. Or perhaps they had not imagined that this dictum, which their tutors invariably associated with capitalist regimes, might apply to the Soviet state as well. Not surprisingly, then, when at 8:00 A.M. the workers of the first shift discovered that the plant was under military occupation, they were enraged. They refused to work at gunpoint, and the effort to make them do so ensured a massive turnout for the march into the city. After discussing the events of the previous night, strikers within the factory grounds tore down the gate separating the administration building from the square and poured outside.

Their indignation was fed by the discovery that the military intrusion had facilitated the arrest of a number of strikers. It had also enabled the train that had been halted the preceding day to move onward; and to prevent another such incident, a contingent of soldiers had been posted at the railroad station. Impelled to retaliate, when a passenger train came along, a mass of strikers broke through the perimeter of troops on guard, bringing the train—and hence all traffic on the line—to a halt. As on the day before, some invaded the engine car, expelled the driver, and blew the whistle. The soldiers, who then piled into trucks and were driven away, had been equipped with weapons but no ammunition, an indication that the authorities hoped to avoid violence. As for the strikers, they had vented their anger without assaulting the soldiers. General Shaposhnikov, the commander of the forces at NEVZ, chose not to intervene either when the gate was torn down or when the train was stopped.

Both sides were showing restraint—but, at Kozlov's command, ammunition was distributed to troops posted elsewhere around 8:00 A.M.[1]

The NEVZ strikers sent delegates to other factories in the industrial zone, seeking to draw as many workers as possible into the planned demonstration. They succeeded in rounding up many supporters, who formed into columns on side streets and awaited the entrance of the principal column from NEVZ on the main thoroughfare. Meanwhile the manager of the electrode factory, also known as Plant No. 17, pleaded with the operatives not to leave, because the plant was engaged in round-the-clock production. The consequences of an interruption in production would be serious, possibly even an explosion. Understanding the seriousness of the situation, the workers behaved responsibly: although hundreds joined the demonstration, those absolutely essential to keep the plant operating remained at their posts.[2]

According to one active participant, as many as 2,000 workers from various enterprises congregated at a fork in the road and fell in behind the throng that came along from NEVZ. Many workers joined out of curiosity, or simply because their friends were in the column. One such worker recalled much later: "Personally I had no definite intentions. I quit work because other workers in the department did. . . . I was moved by curiosity. I neither hated nor was dissatisfied with the state . . . indeed, I respected Soviet power, as I had been brought up to do. My grandfather defended this power, fighting in Budenny's First Cavalry Army; my father, an officer, died at the front defending this power. But neither did I condemn those who wanted to improve their lives, and that's why I went to the gorkom."[3]

Not "provocateurs," as the KGB reported, but anonymous, clever persons among the strikers conceived the idea of equipping some of the demonstrators with portraits of Lenin, red banners, and placards with the slogan "Bread, Meat, and Butter" or "Bread, Meat, and a Pay Raise." Another sign proclaimed: "We need apartments." Other workers carried placards identifying the divisions in which they labored. Shrewd individuals also contrived to include wives and children in the procession, perhaps to bring home the difficulties the price rises created for families, and certainly to emphasize the demonstration's peaceful intentions. The column filled the road from side to side and extended hundreds of meters in length. As it moved toward the town, many onlookers, whether sympathetic or simply curious, fell in as well. The marchers were calm, orderly, and resolute. Everything seemed to proceed spontaneously rather than under the direction of any leadership group. Now and then someone would step out of the column and admonish the marchers to refrain from unruly conduct. As the procession drew near the Tuzlov River bridge, tension mounted.

When Shaposhnikov had asked one of the NEVZ workers where he was going, he replied: "If the mountain won't come to Mohammed, Mohammed will go to the mountain."[4] The mountain in this case was the elite group that had descended from Moscow upon Novocherkassk. Why, one wonders, did the "mountain" not endeavor to thwart the demonstration before it got under way? Reflection suggests a number of answers. For one, Shaposhnikov had been given no orders to disperse the workers if and when they should begin to congregate. A senior commander sympathetic to the workers' cause, he regarded what was taking shape as a peaceful demonstration and did not feel called upon to interfere with it. By the time on Saturday morning that Pliev commanded him to stop the procession, the NEVZ contingent had already departed. It should not be ruled out that the responsible persons, political and military, were at something of a loss as to what steps they should take and so failed to take timely action. But these matters aside, a strategic consideration was surely decisive.

The repulse of police and military units the day before could have suggested the inadvisability of engaging the strikers on their home ground. To be sure, the military forces now available were formidable. But to squelch the demonstration in the industrial zone, to confront and face down many thousands of workers in a wide-open space, would have been difficult to carry off and might easily have provoked a bloody clash. Very likely for this reason, no attempt was made to break up the column as it marched the first five of the nine kilometers between NEVZ and the city center. But to reach the town, the procession would have to cross the bridge over the Tuzlov, a narrow pass where armed forces could most effectively block the march. From the military perspective, that was plainly the point at which to take a stand.

Pliev ordered Colonel Mikheev to deploy fifteen tanks and a number of armored cars on the bridge, but that was by no means all. Hoping to stop the procession just before it reached the bridge, he had another one of his officers position troops at the northern approach, by the village of Khotunok. Besides, detachments of cadets from a military school who had been mobilized to assist were stationed on the bridge and at both approaches to it. The leaders in the operations center thought it well to have someone in authority meet the col-

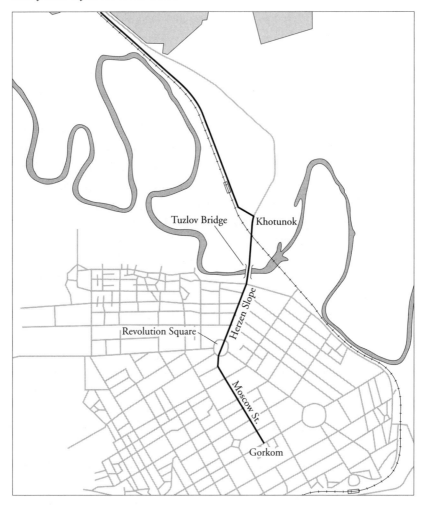

The demonstrators' line of march to the city center on the morning of June 2, 1962. (Original map by G. R. Dobbs)

umn at the bridge and dissuade the demonstrators from proceeding. According to Gen. D. A. Ivashchenko, a staff officer, both Kozlov and Mikoyan flatly refused the part, and Pliev declined as well.[5]

Ivashchenko claims to have undertaken the task himself, driving from town to the far side of the bridge, where he awaited the procession's arrival. The soldiers positioned there were greatly outnumbered, and the marchers surged onward relentlessly. When they reached the bridge and stopped in front of the tanks, Ivashchenko mounted one of them and asked for an opportunity to speak. Unwilling to listen or to halt their advance, the crowd called for the way to be cleared. The demonstrators then divided into two parts. One group bypassed the bridge by scrambling down to the river's edge and crossing through the water, which was only knee-deep at the time. The others jostled the cadets aside and passed over and around the closely arrayed tanks and vehicles to the other side of the bridge.[6] An officer from the military school who attempted to stop the demonstrators was thrown off the bridge into the water below, but he was not hurt. According to one observer, some of the demonstrators sought to disable the tanks by breaking off their antennas and damaging their periscopes. Such efforts were needless, for the tanks merely remained in place and offered no resistance. They had been provided with ammunition that morning, but not with orders to use it. It must have been anticipated, erroneously as it turned out, that a concentration of military armor would be sufficient to intimidate the demonstrators, and no provision had been made for resort to force. Pliev evidently stuck to the tactic he had reportedly enunciated to Kirilenko the day before, and it proved ineffective.

But a second line of defense had been put in place. Fire engines had been posted at the south side of the bridge, near the triumphal arch, and at the next several street corners adjoining Herzen Slope, the main thoroughfare. In the event that the demonstrators somehow managed to cross the Tuzlov—so went the reasoning—the crowd could be dispersed by powerful jets of water. The throng continued to advance and the fire hoses were at the ready but, rather incomprehensibly, none of them were turned on.[7] Those in charge may have been paralyzed by the sight of the oncoming thousands and decided that discretion was the better part of valor.

Having traversed a major barrier, the marchers became more confident and their demonstration assumed a festive air. They lustily sang the "Internationale" and other revolutionary and Civil War songs, accompanied by harmonicas. On the way to the town center, the procession was joined by a large number of mostly young people, a population destined to have a disproportionately large part in the ensuing events. The multitude now numbered anywhere from 5,000 to 12,000 (estimates varied). Numerous witnesses, both demonstrators and police and military men deployed along the line of march, later testified that the procession moving through Revolution Square and down Moscow Street to the party headquarters on Lenin Square was peaceful and orderly. Their numbers and solidarity may have infused them with a sense that they would prevail. Marching under portraits of Lenin and red banners, they symbolically advertised their loyalty to the ideals of the revolution. It was unthinkable that the authorities of Soviet Socialist Russia could replicate the atrocious deed of the tsarist executioners in 1905.

The deputy chief of the Rostov Province KGB organization, who was assigned to provide for the security of the Moscow leaders, had installed them in a military compound, which then served as the staff headquarters.[8] Around eight o'clock they were joined by Major General Chugunov, head of the Ministry of Internal Affairs' security forces, who took charge of his units present. In the morning they congregated in the local party center, together with the town leaders. It would be instructive to know what they were thinking and saying, although they were probably uncertain as to what to do, had no precise scenario to follow. Not surprisingly, therefore, they maintained contact with Khrushchev.

An operations officer of the NCMO, I. P. Snezhkov, reported long after the events a conversation he overheard between Kozlov and Khrushchev at nine or ten o'clock on June 2. Kozlov assured the leader that the tanks on the bridge would halt the demonstration, and spoke of a projected meeting (which never took place) between party activists and representatives of the workers. Khrushchev warned that there was to be no backing away from the food price increases, but also instructed Kozlov to act in the spirit he had advanced in his speech to the Cubans.[9] This was ambiguous advice, as the speech was hardly unequivocal. Whether to meet, speak, and possibly negotiate with the demonstrators was one critical question. It became more acute once the leaders received the shocking news that the procession had not been blocked at the Tuzlov and was coming their way.

Mikoyan is said to have wished to speak to the demonstrators from the balcony of the party headquarters, but was dissuaded from doing so for security reasons. Not only was he more inclined than Kozlov to be flexible, but earlier in his career he had served as head of the Rostov Province party organization. Semichastnyi considered him a respected figure in the North Caucasus region, an opinion borne out in some measure by calls from some in the crowd in Lenin Square for Mikoyan to speak.[10] Apart from Mikoyan, no one was willing to face the approaching marchers, and when the procession drew uncomfortably close, the entire group fled from the party center by a back door for the safety of the military compound.

The decision to flee from the gorkom, it may be reasonably assumed, was preeminently Kozlov's call; and we are reminded of Shelepin's characterization of Kozlov as a coward. But the conduct of his entire group was no doubt conditioned by their knowledge of the reception given Basov the day before and Ivashchenko's inability to make any impression on the surging crowd at the bridge. They could hardly be faulted for believing that it would be impossible to negotiate with the vast crowd streaming into Lenin Square. There could be no negotiating in the absence of a negotiating partner. The failure of the strikers to elect leaders and to draw up a slate of demands was a serious blunder. Its significance was heightened by the ignominious flight of Kozlov and his associates from the gorkom, an embarrassment that could only diminish any inclination on their part to negotiate. Kozlov's hard line was gaining the upper hand over Mikoyan's approach. The Moscow group was tilting away from a quest for a peaceful solution toward a military resolution of the troublesome situation.

Military units had invested the city, including such key points as the gorkom, where more than 100 MVD troops were stationed, and the police station (which also housed the local offices of the KGB), where 85 MVD soldiers were posted. The forces at the gorkom were supplemented by other military units positioned nearby, as well as by Komsomols, druzhinniki, and cadets from the Artillery School. Moreover, once the demonstrators had crossed the bridge, a battalion of tanks and other armored vehicles were sent to reinforce those guarding the gorkom.[11]

The procession moved through Moscow Street to the square, the leading ranks arriving there around 10:30. Two tanks stood at each side of the square. The demonstrators filled the rest of the square, the large public garden immediately behind it with its statue of Lenin, and neighboring streets. Two lines of armed MVD troops stood before the former ataman's palace, a line of druzhinniki with red armbands in front of them. Other troops were positioned at windows and on the roof.[12] The marchers moved to within a short distance of the guards, halted, and demanded that the leaders come out to hear their heartfelt grievances and address them. The chairman of the city's party committee tried to speak to the crowd but was pelted with sticks and stones, and he and some aides then either fled the building or hid within it.[13]

Because none of the Moscow leaders deigned to listen to the demonstrators, disappointment was rife, and more aggressive elements now took the lead. Persons in the rear ranks pressed those in front forward through the defensive lines, which gave way without a struggle. Upon reaching the main entrance, some of the more furious, disbelieving assurances that no one was in the building, broke through the door and scattered throughout the interior. Soldiers who had been deployed within the building offered little more than token resistance, leaving the city's key building in the hands of the insurgents. Of course the Moscow leaders were nowhere to be found, all but one having fled. Shelepin had somehow remained behind, and the former head of the KGB was discovered hiding in one of the rooms. Those who had invaded the gorkom allegedly tried to force Shelepin to speak, but he refused.[14] Consumed by rage, some of the intruders broke furniture, rummaged through cabinets and strewed their contents over the floors, ripped portraits of Khrushchev from the walls and flung them down into the square. Meanwhile, others came onto the balcony, elevated a portrait of Lenin, unfurled a red banner, and addressed the crowd.[15]

There was much complaining about poor working and living conditions, with special emphasis on the new hardships the price increases would impose. Some persons spoke two or three times. One individual appeared on the balcony holding up a partially emptied bottle of Stolichnaia vodka and a dish of expensive sliced sausage he had found in an inside room. "See the fine things they have," he shouted "while we have nothing." Another brought out and indignantly read to the throng a communication from the local Communists to the Central Committee of the party, approving Khrushchev's just-announced policy. Still another proposed sending a delegation to Moscow to meet with Marshal Voroshilov, who was thought to be an opponent of Khrushchev and might help the workers.[16] Reflecting confusion among the strikers, some orators heaped abuse on the soldiers while others appealed to the officers and their men to join the insurgency. One speaker allegedly pronounced "slanderous" aspersions on Lenin, and (more believably) denounced the Soviet state's policies. A well-dressed man encountered in the building—he was an aide to the Novocherkassk procurator—was compelled to speak. He told the people they were behaving improperly, and was shouted down.[17] It was a vociferous throng, reacting to speakers with applause or whistles and shouts of disapproval. It was also a mix of diverse elements.

While some had engaged in mindless vandalism, others punctuated their speeches with exhortations to avoid hooliganism. V. A. Demin, the commander of a battalion of the 406th Tank Regiment, affirms that "none of the orators called [upon the people] to engage in pogroms and other illegal activities."[18] Indeed, a worker and fervent young Communist, V. V. Kovtunov, who was dismayed by evidence of destructive activity and sought to counter it, was supported by many in the crowd. Thousands of good Soviet people were asking for dialogue, he considered, and no more than a hundred were hooligans. A believer in benevolence and justice, he thought that the leaders had an obligation to speak to the demonstrators in a comradely way. He entered the building, came out on the balcony, announced that he was a Young Communist, and asked for help in ousting the hooligans and restoring order. He received a favorable response, but was interrupted before he could proceed.[19]

E. P. Levchenko, an agitated dark-haired woman in a sleeveless sweater, appeared on the balcony and delivered a rabble-rousing speech. One of those who had been arrested the night before and released at 6:00 A.M., she urged that a detachment go to liberate the workers still in police custody, who, she reportedly cried in anguish, had been beaten.[20] A group estimated at about fifty, with Levchenko and another woman in the lead, hurried from the square to the police station, a half kilometer away, whose security had been entrusted to the commanding officer of the 505th MVD Regiment, N. S. Maliutin. A handful of people had stopped there earlier, seeking the release of their comrades. V. V. Sagin, the company commander they encountered, told them that no prisoners were there, and invited any one of them to look through the rooms to ascertain the truth of what he said. The group was convinced and departed.[21]

When Levchenko and her followers arrived, she served notice that they had come to liberate the prisoners. An officer told the excited group that no one was being detained in the building. In fact the authorities, foreseeing a possible attack on the police station, had spirited the two arrested men out of town during the night.[22] The officer warned that if the intruders did not leave, they would be shot. Levchenko brazenly replied: "There are a lot of us, you can't shoot us all." A soldier then fired a warning shot into the air, causing many to flee.[23] Supposing that they were being deceived, others tore the outer door from its hinges and used it as a battering ram to crash through a second door. Soldiers deployed within the building were pressed back through a long vestibule toward a staircase leading upward. Soldiers on the landing between the first and second floors then fired a warning volley over the heads of the intruders. In close contact with those pressing them, the troops used the butts of their guns to repel the invaders. One of the latter attempted to seize the gun of a soldier, N. V. Repkin, who removed the magazine an instant before it was wrested from him. Another soldier, Sh. Iu. Azizov, unaware that the gun had been unloaded, fired a warning shot into the air and then shot and killed the worker.

Immediately some of the invaders retreated toward the entrance, while others fled into a room to the left of the vestibule and from there jumped out of windows into an inner courtyard. Soldiers stationed there, who had heard the shooting within, fired and killed or wounded several of them. Some thirty managed to escape into a room that the police used as a temporary holding place for arrestees. Someone slammed the door after them and locked it. Thirty of the demonstrators who had come to liberate two arrested men were now themselves arrested and, in the bargain, five others lay dead. Two sixteen-year-old onlookers presently died of their wounds.[24]

The authorities justified the killings as an appropriate response to an attack on a government institution. There was certainly provocation—Levchenko's manipulative rhetoric to the demonstrators on the square and the action it inspired deserve condemnation—but the response was wildly disproportionate. The people who broke into the police station had no weapons, and were certainly not a mortal threat to the eighty-five heavily armed soldiers posted in the building and the adjacent courtyard. A small group that had tried to approach the building through the courtyard had been repelled by a warning volley, suggesting that the crowd was controllable.[25] Given the chaotic and taut circumstances then prevailing, Azizov's shooting of the man who had seized Repkin's weapon is perhaps understandable. The orgy of shooting that followed had no justification whatsoever. Soldiers fired upon terrified persons who were trying to escape into the courtyard—and they shot to kill.

The soldiers had been provided with ammunition but with strict instructions not to use it unless ordered to do so. The MVD officers in charge at the police station testified that no order to shoot was ever given. Maliutin was in radio communication with his superiors, but they had declined to give specific orders, instructing him only to act in accordance with circumstances. He claimed to have been on the second floor of the building when the shooting broke out, and immediately instructed the troops in the courtyard to cease firing.[26] If these testimonies are trustworthy—and there may never be certainty on this score—it was the excited soldiers rather than their commander who were responsible for the wanton shootings. One wonders what sort of training in crowd control they had been given, and whether their behavior accorded with their instructions.

What had occurred at the police station was undoubtedly communicated to Khrushchev, and resulted in a decisive shift to a belligerent policy. There is little direct evidence on this count, but a number of secondhand testimonies make it possible to surmise what happened. Staff Officer M. I. Vovchenko, sometime between 11:00 A.M. and 12:00 P.M., overheard part of a phone call from Khrushchev to Pliev. He quotes the leader as saying: "If the crowd tries to take the radio station or the state bank, open fire with live cartridges." This very specific directive is somewhat at odds with what another officer, V. I. Unitskii, reports having been told by Tank Division Commander Oleshko. This general, a subordinate of the NCMO commander, must have gotten the words he reportedly pronounced from Pliev: "Khrushchev ordered resort to arms if they begin to create an uproar [*debochirovat'*]." This vague instruction was open to interpretation, leaving it up to those on the ground to determine whether circumstances justified a resort to arms. In the same vein, at roughly the same time, General Shaposhnikov was told by General Parovatkin, who had just been with Pliev, that the latter had ordered resort to arms if necessary. Another officer, F. I. Podoprigora, deputy head of propaganda and agitation in the NCMO, proffered another bit of testimony. He had heard from staff officers that Khrushchev demanded the restoration of order by any means. No one attempted to seize the state bank or telegraph office, but the collision at the police station could readily be construed as an uproar. Given Kozlov's inclination from the first to resort to arms, Khrushchev's imperative to restore order at any cost would have fortified his resolve.

Recently published testimony by the late A. I. Mikoyan adds a significant perception to the last point. His earlier-noted, devastating opinion of Kozlov very likely derived, in some measure, from what he reports having witnessed at Novocherkassk on June 2. Upon learning what had triggered the strike, Mikoyan considered that the workers had legitimate grievances which ought to be addressed. In contrast, Kozlov's lurid representation of what was occurring "sowed panic" in Moscow, and resulted in the granting of permission to resort to arms. Khrushchev had panicked in response to "disinformation" which Kozlov had provided; so Kozlov was the "guilty" party.[27]

At noon the gorkom remained in the hands of the intruders and speakers continued to harangue the crowd from the balcony, although no one called for rioting or other illegal activity. In addition to large numbers of workers in the square and garden, there were very many onlookers, including no few teenagers. The bystanders included the wives of some officers, who had come to watch the proceedings. Also in the crowd were party activists who had been assigned to circulate among the people, doing "explanatory" work designed to encourage the demonstration to break up.[28]

Government agents, who until then had been remarkably passive, now went into action. Around 12:00, Battalion Commander Demin was ordered to have a group of his men break up the crowd in the square.[29] About the same time, Capt. V. V. Sakharov was directed to have his platoon clear the gorkom of its occupants. Finding thirty to thirty-five persons in the building, he ordered them to leave, and they complied without resisting. However, as Sakharov's men removed those on the balcony, a verbal objection was heard: "Comrade General, don't throw oil on the fire. Call off your soldiers, we're a peaceful demonstration."[30] When the building had been cleared, Demin noticed General Oleshko with some seventy or eighty armed MVD troops proceeding from Podtelkov Street through the garden to the gorkom. Pliev had chosen Oleshko to deal with the situation. Oleshko mounted to the second-floor balcony, while fifty soldiers were deployed in two semicircular ranks in front of the building. The soldiers, armed with semi-automatic machine guns, stood only a few yards from the crowd. Numerous witnesses—workers, onlookers, and military men, both officers and rank and file—recalled the mood and demeanor of the crowd. It was certainly noisy, but no one attacked the soldiers or attempted to seize their weapons.[31] No one sensed imminent danger. One observer recalled that some people were smiling and exchanging banter with the soldiers. Confronted though they were by armed troops, individuals in the crowd assured each other that the soldiers would never shoot.[32]

General Oleshko was accompanied to the gorkom balcony by other high-ranking officers. Through a microphone he called upon the massed people to quiet down and go home: "I order you to disperse immediately." He was greeted with whistles and shouts by a crowd determined to stand its ground. Someone in the throng called out: "And who are you to give orders?" One officer contended (in answer to this defiant question?) that Oleshko said he had a direct connection with the government; that is, he was authorized to make such a demand.[33] Another demonstrator called out that the people would not leave until Budenny came.[34] Others cried: "Let's hear Mikoyan." The general repeated his demand and, according to one who was present, promised that the people's concerns would be addressed.[35] Then Oleshko announced that he would count to three, and if the crowd did not begin to disperse, he would order his men to fire. At that the soldiers in the front rank of the two files facing the throng dropped to one knee, in position to fire. Perhaps in part because some in the crowd shouted: "They won't shoot at the people," Oleshko's counting fell on deaf ears. When he ordered "Fire!" the soldiers discharged a warn-

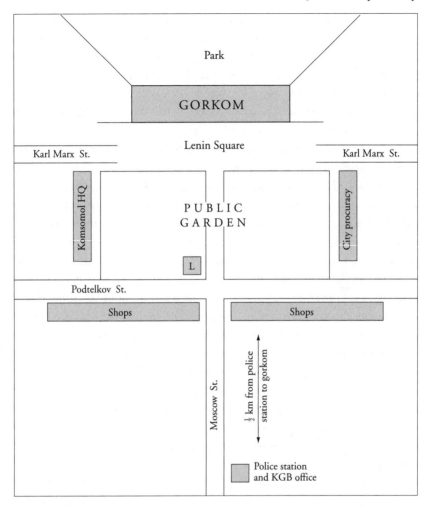

The vicinity of the gorkom (the city's party headquarters), the area where the massacre took place. (Original plan by Samuel H. Baron and G. R. Dobbs)

ing volley over the heads of the crowd, and puffs of gun smoke rose over the square. It was then around 12:30 P.M.[36]

Threatened with mortal danger for the first time, the crowd began to fall back. Then there were calls: "Don't be afraid, they're shooting blanks." At that the crowd again surged forward to within several yards of the soldiers. Whether or not Oleshko ordered a second volley is a matter of controversy, to which we shall return. There is today little argument, however, about what followed.

Bursts of gunfire went off and continued, according to witnesses, for anywhere from one to three or four minutes. A young woman near the square, hearing a salvo, cried: "They're shooting!" Her companion retorted: "Are you out of your mind? In our time they don't shoot." They drew closer to see what was going on, and both were injured by gunfire.[37] Once it became clear that men and women had been struck, with screams of horror rending the air and blood spattering all about, bedlam prevailed.

Now the terrified people scattered in all directions. Rather they attempted to, for the spaces before the gorkom were tightly packed with demonstrators and onlookers. To an extent, people were trapped while the fusillade continued, and this circumstance exacerbated the panic. No reports of people being trampled have come to light, but it would have been miraculous if something of the kind did not happen. Moments before, one woman remembered, when the crowd had surged forward, pushing and stomping, a sympathetic soldier beckoned her through a door, saying: "Come here, they'll crush you." Once the shooting began, another witness reported, "it was impossible to squeeze one's way through the crush of the fleeing crowd, and behind the automatic guns were working."[38] The people fled as they could, primarily from the square into the garden and beyond. The relentless firing was directed not only into the square but at the retreating crowd as well.[39]

Scores failed to escape the shots, which, rather than aimed at specific targets, were sprayed promiscuously. A missile struck a barrel of kvass at the right side of the square, causing its contents to gush forth. In the square and the garden both, men and women were hit and fell. The wounded who could do so kept running toward the far end of the garden, a few taking refuge at the base of the statue of Lenin at the corner of Moscow and Podtelkov streets. Bullets ricocheted off its pedestal, leaving marks that can be seen to the present day. A few individuals were struck beyond the garden, on Podtelkov Street, 170 meters from the gorkom. One of them, a woman whose life was snuffed out, was a hairdresser at work in a salon fronting that street. A man who was waiting for his wife outside a food shop on the same thoroughfare was so seriously injured that a few days later one of his legs had to be amputated above the knee. A youth who had run a little distance down Moscow Street, still farther from the gorkom, was struck in the back of his right leg. The bullet was removed at the hospital, but gangrene set in, and part of his right shank was amputated. Even more remarkable, a woman who was in the park *behind* the gorkom was hit in the hip and collarbone. She was pregnant, and to save her life the doctors had to abort the fetus.[40]

Many who were there described the horrendous scenes they witnessed. A demonstrator in the front rank, facing the gorkom, was hit in the right side of the head; the bullet carried a bloody mass with it as it spewed from the left side. A mother carrying a one- or two-year-old baby, the back of her dress blood-soaked, was seen frantically fleeing from the garden. A young onlooker saw running toward him an elderly man who suddenly keeled over, a fountain of blood spurting from his mouth. When an ambulance driver who had been told to be available heard shooting, he drove to the Podtelkov-Moscow Street intersection. There his vehicle was immediately loaded with six severely wounded citizens, whom he drove to the city hospital. He also discovered hiding in the bushes a ten-year-old boy with a bullet wound in his leg. Afterward he drove to the square, where he saw men in plain clothes throwing corpses into a truck. He counted no fewer than ten, he said. Ambulances were inadequate to the need, so compassionate men gathered up injured persons in the garden and put them on buses, which conveyed them to the hospital.[41]

As V. G. Bakholdin came up Moscow Street, he passed a bus, at whose open doors a man stood, shouting at the top of his lungs to passers-by: "People! See how many killed and wounded are in the bus." After that he saw a youth carrying in his arms a young woman with a broken leg, who moaned in pain; and then a woman in a bloody dress who was being taken away on a scooter by two men. When he approached the square, about one o'clock, he discerned six bodies on the grass near the Lenin monument. A female doctor who was examining them, while shedding bitter tears, said: "This one is dead too, and this one, and," pointing to the opposite side of the square, "there are dead over there too." He looked and saw several corpses laid out in a row. An elderly, grief-stricken woman bent over the body of a young man in worker's clothing until she was roughly pushed aside by two officious men in plain clothes. They carried the body away, leaving part of his skull and brains in a pool of blood.[42]

The stench of gun smoke pervaded the air, reminding one observer of the exhaust from motor vehicles. Soon after the shooting, many bodies, some motionless, some stirring, lay in the square, and heartrending cries and groans were audible. Their number was variously estimated, probably at different moments, as anywhere from fifteen to sixty; perhaps some estimates included felled people in the garden. When the square had been vacated, pools of blood remained on the ground; hats, shoes, and cartridge cases of both blank and live bullets were strewn about. Fire engines stationed nearby, evidently in anticipation that they would be needed, were rushed into the square, and the fire fighters did all they could to hose away the blood. Because the square had been paved with cobblestones, a good deal of it could not be removed, so a day or two later, a new coat of asphalt was applied to cover up evidence of the slaughter. The bloody water from the square flowed to the Podtelkov-Moscow Street intersection, where a witness came upon a crowd of wailing women. One of them put her hand into the stream of bloody water and bathed her face with it, crying that it contained the blood of her husband. It was a hot day, and the odor of blood hung in the air a long time.[43]

As if on cue, immediately after the shooting stopped, trucks entered the square from adjoining streets. KGB agents and policemen, all in plain clothes, loaded the corpses into trucks, which carried them to the morgue. The wounded, either in vehicles or on foot, came to the city hospital on Krasnoarmeiskaia Street. There were so many of them that medical supplies soon ran out and emergency stocks had to be opened. To make room for the unprecedented influx, patients already in the hospital were discharged the next day.[44] Tamara Stoianova, a surgeon, recounted the strained situation in the hospital:

> The wounded were brought into the first hospital in automobiles and ambulances. They were immediately sorted according to degree of seriousness of the injury. The first and third floors of the hospital were put at their disposal. Those who were lightly injured were sent to the polyclinic, after having been given first aid. The others required immediate help: treatment of wounds, operations. The entire personnel were occupied in the work. At times there were not enough physicians' hands. . . . During the first three days, the doctors and nurses didn't leave the hospital. Besides, on the second and third of June, a first-aid point was organized in the reception hall, and a mass of Novocherkassians with various light traumas passed through. A platoon of soldiers and police were posted in the hospital. Those who died were immediately removed.[45]

Infuriated people who had escaped injury returned to the square and vented their feelings upon the military men who remained on guard. "We thought the Red Army was our defender, but you are murderers!" some of them yelled at a platoon commander. From the garden, stones and turf were thrown at the soldiers, prompting some of them to shoot, but only into the air. Part of the crowd that fled down Moscow Street encountered trucks loaded with armed soldiers at side streets and, as a gesture of resistance, stubbornly prevented them from proceeding to the gorkom. A NEVZ metalworker who came to the square after the shooting had ended was so upset by what he saw that he could not contain himself. When a general drove up in a car, he blurted out: "Who are you shooting at, you sonofabitch?" Taken aback, the officer neither answered nor repaid the offender with punishment. I. F. Kolosov was reminded of 1905, and so terrifying was the butchery on the square that he could not bear to look. He then happened onto the keening woman who was washing her face in the bloody water, and so wrenching was the entire experience that in a few days his hair began to turn gray.[46] While many present were reminded of Bloody Sunday, a different thought occurred to others. Among them was a young girl who denounced the military men as "fascists"—a word that an officer later dolefully admitted "exactly defined our action."[47]

Not only the people assembled on the square were traumatized by what they had seen. A Caucasian soldier was observed weeping uncontrollably. In an effort to comfort him, his commander put his hand on the man's shoulder and bluffly said: "What are you slobbering about?" The soldier fired back: "Don't touch me, Commander. Get away." The platoon leader, who had been fiercely upbraided by people returning to the square after the shooting, later remembered that that night his men were so shaken by what had happened that they couldn't eat their rations. A woman with a flushed face hurled an accusation at a group of unarmed soldiers stationed by the state bank; one of them was crying too hard to answer.[48] It is difficult to believe that there was not more such revulsion among government servants, but the sources on their responses are skimpy.

A KGB report composed on June 7 mendaciously stated that the demonstrators at the gorkom had attempted to seize weapons from the soldiers, and this had led to the order to fire. There is overwhelming testimony that nothing of the kind occurred.[49] However, the report's count of the dead and wounded was not far off the mark. While army sources for a long time insisted that only five persons had been killed, according to this report twenty had perished, around forty had been wounded, and three of the wounded had subsequently died. In a report addressed to Khrushchev five days later, the number killed remained as before but the number of people treated at the hospital had risen to eighty-nine.[50] Ultimately it turned out that twenty-four had been slain or died of their wounds, a total of sixty-nine severely wounded had survived, and scores more had minor injuries. Sixteen lost their lives at the square, five were killed in the police station melee, and two boys who suffered wounds there later died. The twenty-fourth person, a man named A. E. Shul'man, had come from L'vov on assignment and had been out walking late on the night of June 2. A curfew had been established, and a sentinel ordered him to stop. Probably failing to comprehend what was afoot, he ran instead, and was forthwith shot dead.[51]

At least three wounded persons were obliged to have a limb amputated. Individuals were confined to a hospital, testimony indicates, from a week to as long as a year. Several of the wounded remained invalids the rest of their lives. At least three became eligible for state assistance.[52] Dr. Stoianova expressed the opinion that dumdum bullets had been used against the crowd. Rumors of the kind were widely believed—Solzhenitsyn was among those who credited the story—and constituted another reason for the popular (but quickly stifled) condemnation of the authorities. Official statements and the Military Procuracy report deny that such projectiles existed in the army's stock of ammunition.[53] The truth remains elusive. In a couple of recorded cases, innocent persons who were injured shunned hospital treatment for fear they would appear suspicious and be arrested. A student who suffered a gunshot wound in the leg was taken home by friends rather than to the hospital; and his concerned teacher insisted that his classmates bring him to class each day, as security agents tracking down demonstration participants would be searching for absentees.[54]

An analysis of the makeup of the slain is revealing. Of the twenty-four who died, three were women. Eighteen of the dead were between the ages of sixteen and twenty-six. The overwhelming majority of the injured, noted a KGB document, were between the ages of eighteen and twenty-five.[55] Twenty were workers, both male and female (the hairdresser included), four were students, and one the out-of-town visitor. Eleven of the workers were from NEVZ, the rest from other factories.

Someone who was allowed to inspect the police records has indicated that fifteen of the twenty-four killed were classified as bystanders, with Shul'man bringing the count to sixteen.[56] Two-thirds of the murdered, then, were innocent bystanders. Only one-third, notably those involved in the clash at the police station, were classified as active in varying degrees. Rather than killing the perpetrators of vandalism in the gorkom or individuals who had otherwise behaved aggressively, the promiscuous firing at the square had blotted out the lives of peaceful demonstrators, curious bystanders, and persons who just hap-

TABLE I

Names, Ages, and Occupations of Persons Killed or Mortally Wounded in Novocherkassk, June 2, 1962

Name	Age	Occupation
A. B. Artiushenko	16	Student, Novocherkassk Art School
A. N. D'iakonov	47	Department manager, Gormash factory
V. V. Drachev	21	NEVZ worker
V. F. Fedorkov	35	Quality inspector, consumer services
A. D. Gribova	40	Hairdresser
V. N. Gritsenko	21	NEVZ metalworker
V. K. Karpenko	18	NEVZ milling machine operator
K. K. Kelep	46	Temporarily unemployed
V. V. Konstantinov	22	Student, technical school
F. G. Limantsev	45	NEVZ assembly worker
V. P. Linnik	25	Worker, Novocherkassk Plant No. 7
V. I. Misetov	20	NEVZ foundry worker
V. P. Reviakin	24	Waterworks metalworker
V. A. Sitnikov	26	Stoneworker
M. G. Shakhailov	62	NEVZ worker
L. V. Shul'ga	19	NEVZ worker
A. E. Shul'man	25	Employee, L'vov construction trust
E. I. Slepkova	24	NEVZ metalworker
V. I. Solov'ev	24	Student, agricultural machinery school
G. N. Terletskii	16	Student, food technology school
I. F. Timofeev	22	NEVZ metalworker
V. V. Tinin	25	NEVZ worker
P. Ia. Vershinnik	18	NEVZ lathe operator
A. M. Zvereva	21	Worker

SOURCE: GVP, 142–43.

pened to be in the neighborhood. Among the latter was A. N. D'iakonov, a forty-seven-year-old party member, who caught a bullet just as he stepped out of a shop into which he had gone to buy some cigarettes.[57]

During the strike activity on June 1 and the demonstration the following day, soldiers of both the Soviet army and the internal security forces were harmed. None lost their lives; eighty-six were reported injured, but most of their injuries were minor, for only nine were hospitalized.[58] For all the official talk of the criminal behavior of the strikers, the offenses committed by crowds of 5,000 and more people against those charged with keeping them in line were remarkably paltry. The contrast with the mayhem perpetrated upon the demonstrators speaks for itself.

An Alternative Scenario

A widely credited version of what happened after Oleshko's warning salvo—that the people fell back in alarm, then surged forward again, and were immediately subjected to a murderous fusillade by the soldiers lined up in front of the gorkom—though plausible, has been sharply disputed. On the affirmative side, given the determination of Khrushchev and his agents in Novocherkassk to end the disorders, it is difficult to believe that Oleshko was bluffing, that he intended only to frighten the demonstrators, and was not prepared to follow his warning volley with a deadly burst of fire. In fact, a number of eyewitnesses have asserted that they distinctly heard a second volley on the heels of the first. One of them added a detail: the soldiers first fired into the air and then gradually lowered their weapons and fired into the crowd. Col. P. P. Falynskov agreed that a second volley followed the first, but without a command having been given.[59] The preponderant testimony, however, contradicts that version of the story. Many witnesses recalled that people began falling to the ground as soon as the soldiers fired into the air. No one consistently claimed to have heard Oleshko order the troops to fire a second time, and he adamantly denied having done so.[60]

An integral element of the widely credited view is that the troops lined up before the gorkom fired directly into the crowd, but this proposition may also be called into question. The compiler of the Military Procuracy materials, among others, flatly characterized N. A. Taiushkina's testimony that the soldiers fired into the crowd as "mistaken."[61] If the troops had fired their semiautomatic weapons point-blank into the throng, the number of casualties would surely have been far greater. Persons on the scene estimated that the firing continued anywhere from one to three or four minutes, and the magazines of the soldiers' weapons contained thirty bullets, half of which would be discharged in one burst. Significant, too, is the area-wide distribution of persons who were shot. It would obviously have been impossible for the soldiers before the gorkom to wound the woman in the park behind it. And it would have been most unlikely that shots fired directly into the crowd could have cut down people at ground level as far away as Podtelkov Street.

We are left with a conundrum, which Oleshko put into words when he is said to have exclaimed: "I didn't give an order, but a volley occurred." [62] In the face of these perplexing circumstances, the conclusion is inescapable that the firing came from elsewhere; although we should perhaps not exclude the possibility that one or a few individuals among the troops before the gorkom discharged their weapons as well, either because their nerves had been stretched to the breaking point or because they had heard shots from elsewhere. Numerous witnesses testified that they noticed men with weapons on the roof of the gorkom and in the upper windows or on the roofs of buildings adjoining the public garden—Komsomol headquarters on the left, the city procuracy on the right. This might explain how it happened that two men who stood facing the gorkom were struck from the side. The presence of men on the roof of the gorkom would also make intelligible the raining down of empty cartridge shells on the soldiers in front of the building, which one of them recalled. [63]

Especially arresting is the recollection of O. N. Ianovskii, commander of a platoon of the 505th MVD Regiment, who around noon was posted with his troops not far from the central entrance to the gorkom. He observed the expulsion of the demonstrators from the building, the appearance of Oleshko on the balcony, and the general's attempt to get the crowd to disperse. While this appeal was in progress, several Red Army men with semi-automatic machine guns, led by an officer holding a pistol, emerged from the building onto a porch at the second-story level. The officer raised the pistol and gave the command to fire, whereupon the soldiers unleashed a fusillade upon the people in the square, causing some thirteen to fifteen to fall to the ground. [64]

Lending credence to this observation is the independently offered testimony of V. A. Demin, commander of the 406th Tank Division. He heard a second volley follow the first, and while it was under way he saw an officer on the porch fire his weapon upward. [65] The two testimonies diverge, one depicting the shooting from the porch as coinciding with the warning volley, the other with a second volley. But the likenesses outweigh the incidental difference in recall as to the timing. The firing of the officer's raised pistol appears to have been a signal to soldiers positioned in places other than the square to shoot into the crowd. If Demin said nothing about the armed troops accompanying the officer, he contributed a nugget of information in identifying the officer as

Capt. V. P. Chetverikin, a member of the intelligence battalion of the 18th Tank Division.

Chetverikin was also interrogated in the course of the Chief Military Procuracy's investigation. He told of having been assigned to secure two of the entrances to the building, and of standing with five to seven soldiers on the porch of the central entryway. No doubt unaware of what the two other officers had testified and (we infer) anxious to conceal a dubious action in which he had engaged, he concocted an original tale of how the shooting began: On the left flank of the file before the gorkom, a soldier suddenly discharged a short burst, and immediately all the troops posted along the facade fired into the air, his men joining in as well.[66] Chetverikin's account of what happened then is chaotic and confusing, but it does record his firing his pistol into the air.

The evidence thus far adduced suggests a sequence of events contrary to the widely credited understanding of what occurred on Bloody Saturday. If it smacks of conspiracy, there is additional information to bolster that perception. The compiler of the Military Procuracy's investigative material makes much of the testimony given by D. I. Mel'nichenko, who in 1962 was a third-year student in the Novocherkassk party school: The morning of June 2, around 10:00 A.M., he and his classmates were ordered by KGB agents to go to the gorkom to do explanatory work among the people assembled there and to take measures to quiet them down. They were in the garden "after twelve" when several KGB agents in plain clothes told him, as the lead person in the group, to accompany them to the basement of the nearby procuracy building. They remained there forty to fifty minutes — it should be kept in mind that the shooting occurred around 12:30 — and then were permitted to return to their school. In the early 1990s, Mel'nichenko surmised that the authorities had planned to use weapons against the crowd and, wishing to keep the party school cohort out of harm's way, had had the group conducted to the basement.[67] Such protective measures evidently did not encompass all government-connected people mingling with the crowd. A police lieutenant complained to a friend that he and some colleagues dressed in plain clothes were in the throng observing activists for subsequent detention when the shooting began, and he was wounded. Indignant at this negligent treatment, he quit the service that very day.[68]

The testimony in the Military Procuracy compendium includes two exceedingly brief items whose relevance the compiler overlooked. Demin, as noted earlier, was ordered around noon to have a group of his men break up the crowd in the square. But a few minutes later, no clashes having occurred, he was ordered to withdraw them. In his testimony, he drew no conclusions about this odd sequence, but there is an obvious correspondence between Demin's and Mel'nichenko's evidence, strongly indicating that Mel'nichenko's surmise is correct. As it happens, a fifteen-year-old onlooker, M. N. Abrosimov, told of something he personally heard that dovetails neatly with what has already been remarked. Just before the firing began, he heard an officer on the balcony cry: "Soldiers, leave the crowd." [69]

That something of the kind took place is confirmed—and extended—by the testimony of several soldiers of the platoon that was deployed in front of the gorkom. When the reminiscences of five of them are combined, the following picture emerges: Shortly after Oleshko confronted the crowd, an officer called out from the balcony: "Soldiers! Move closer to the wall of the building!" When they did so, they immediately heard an order to fire, and blasted into the air. Almost simultaneously, they heard shooting break out above them, from either the second story or the roof of the gorkom. It sounded like the bark of a machine gun, and empty cartridges rained down on them. Continuing for a few moments, the fire was directed at the fleeing panic-stricken crowd. One of the soldiers recalled how puzzled he had been to see people falling to the ground when he and his fellows had only shot into the air. He realized what had happened when he saw two sergeants with machine guns emerge from the building onto a porch. When some of the crowd came back into the square, the same soldiers triggered short bursts, which drove them away.[70]

With these suspicious circumstances before us, a number of questions present themselves. Who were the men that fired upon the people? At whose bidding? With what purpose? Because the evidence is sparse, the answers must be speculative in part. Mel'nichenko's testimony that KGB men ushered his cohort from exposed places to the basement of the procuracy building obviously implicates the organization to which the agents belonged. The involvement of Captain Chetverikin points in another direction. It was apparently he who gave the signal for men positioned outside the square to fire; the small detachment with him on the porch also fired into the crowd, and he elaborated a cover story to becloud what had happened. Inasmuch as Chetverikin was a Soviet army officer, it is plain that at least some elements of the army were involved. It should not be forgotten that Chetverikin belonged to an intelligence battalion, and it may not be farfetched to posit cooperation between the KGB and military intelligence forces. The military intelligence *forces* are indicated, because a captain could have implemented such collaboration but certainly could not have initiated it. Looking further, one notes with a start that the intelligence battalion to which Chetverikin belonged was a subdivision of the 18th Tank Division, whose commander was none other than Oleshko. It is inconceivable that an intelligence unit within his division could have taken on an assignment without his knowledge. So, as he claimed, Oleshko could have refrained from giving a second order and yet have connived in the plan to have the crowd fired upon: "I didn't give an order, but a volley occurred." Demin doesn't indicate who gave the order to have his men withdraw from the crowd, but according to Abrosimov, such a call came from the balcony, and it was there that Oleshko and his subordinates were standing. Lt. Col. A. A. Tiurin, commander of the 98th Detached Battalion of MVD troops, contributed another likely piece of the puzzle. On June 5, 1962, in a report on the events of June 2, he wrote: "With the aim of suppressing the outrages, soldiers of the Soviet army fired a warning volley, which failed to produce a sufficient effect on the hooligans. Therefore at 13:10, upon signal, a certain unit [*opredelennaia chast'*] of the military was obliged to resort to arms."[71]

The cryptic phrase "a certain unit" brings to mind the Special Forces, a branch of military intelligence that was given especially sensitive assignments. Men of that branch, it will be recalled, liberated Basov from his confinement in the NEVZ administration building the previous night. Another possibility, given Tiurin's official position, is that the "certain unit" was made up of troops drawn from an MVD counterpart to the army's Special Forces, possibly his own "detached" battalion. Consistent in a way with the guarded information Tiurin proffered in June 1962 is his already noted testimony in the early 1990s—so contrary to what many others testified that it has the ring of disinformation—that after the gorkom had been cleared, disorders in the square increased, with demonstrators pushing and kicking soldiers in the stomach.

Oleshko would certainly not have conceived such a plan without Pliev's knowledge and approval, nor would Pliev without an order from the Presidium members ensconced in the military staff headquarters. What they, and particularly Kozlov, had in mind may only be conjectured. If they were determined, as Khrushchev had reportedly dictated and Kozlov repeated after the fact, to put an end to the disorders by any means, that still left open just how to go about it. Of course, an effort would be made to persuade the crowd to break up and, in effect, call off the demonstration. In the light of all that had occurred since the outbreak of the strike, however, it would have been ingenuous to suppose that the insurgents would comply, and ingenuous the Presidium members were not. So what was to be done in case of noncompliance had to be considered. To men steeped in the history of the Russian revolutionary movement, the massacre in Palace Square on January 9, 1905, was a soul-searing event. Knowing, too, how large this abominable episode figured in popular lore, they were loath to sponsor a frontal attack on the demonstration. In this hypothetical reconstruction, at some point an operation was put into play involving cooperation between the KGB and selected military units, probably both army and MVD. Marksmen (and perhaps machine gunners) were to be positioned on the roofs or in upper stories of the gorkom and the adjacent buildings. The gunmen would be instructed to fire into the crowd at a signal, to coincide with Oleshko's call for a warning salvo. The demonstration would thus be broken, the disorders ended, and bewilderment sown among the people as to what had happened.[72]

If this construction seems fanciful, it must be noted that the activists in Novocherkassk, those who have been most concerned about the massacre, firmly believe that it was not the troops arrayed along the facade of the gorkom but gunmen deployed elsewhere that carried out the shooting on June 2, 1962. Their conviction on this score surely stems in the first instance from Siuda, who had adduced reasons for that belief in notes on the subject published in 1990. Mardar' adopted the idea in her influential pamphlet, which appeared two years later.[73] Siuda had learned that just before the firing began, over a microphone an officer had ordered: "All soldiers are to leave the crowd." The conclusions of the man in charge of the Military Procuracy's investigation, Col. (now Gen.) Iu. Bagraev, were based on the testimony of Mel'nichenko, Tiurin, and others cited above. He may have been ignorant of Siuda's article, whose view of the matter predated his own. Of course, the testimonies Bagraev collected gave a solid foundation to what was for Siuda only a speculation.

Bagraev deserves accolades for having amassed so much important material, and his effort to arrive at independent judgments. However, the very abundance of material, the many inconsistencies in it, and perhaps other circumstances kept him from noticing data in his compilation that would have strengthened parts of his portrayal. We are indebted to him also for the intelligence that a thorough search of the CPSU archive revealed that the Presidium discussed the Novocherkassk events on June 10, 1962, but disclosed nothing substantive, gave no hint as to the mechanics of the decision-making process or who precisely carried out the policy chosen. In explanation of this lacuna, Semichastnyi coyly observed: "In such circumstances, no one wants to assume responsibility."[74] Bagraev concedes that no definite identification is possible, but supposes that KGB or MVD units were the likely executors.

Contrary to widely held opinion, Bagraev's key conclusion is that the army was not culpable. The subhead of a major article he and a journalist published in the army newspaper, *Krasnaia zvezda*, in 1995 reads: "The investigation has established: The army did not shoot at the people."[75] This proposition is questionable. The testimony referred to above, notably the appearance of Red Army Captain Chetverikin on the porch and his behavior, plus the certainty that he must have been implementing what higher-level officers had planned, points to army participation. Too, the observed emergence from the building of two sergeants with machine guns is suggestive, although it is not clear whether they were army or MVD troops. Without calling into question Bagraev's intention to be objective, we should perhaps not be surprised that this investigator exonerated the service to which he belonged. How could he not have identified with the institution in which he had spent his professional life, not have avoided the intrusion (albeit unconscious) of subjectivity? Indeed, it seems incongruous that a branch of the army, the Chief Military Procuracy, rather than an independent entity was given the task of investigating the army's role in the disorders and the circumstances leading to the taking of arms.

Curiously, Bagraev evidently didn't notice that what he affirmed in the article contradicted the very first sentence of the 170-page summary of the Chief Military Procuracy's investigation: "On June 1–2, 1962, in Novocherkassk, Rostov oblast, with the help of a part of the Soviet army and the MVD's internal troops, the disturbances [caused by] the workers of the electric locomotive factory were suppressed." The summary appears over the signature of none other than Iu. Bagraev.[76]

Chapter 4   After the Massacre

Ironically, it was only after the bullets had taken their toll that worker representatives finally gained an opportunity to meet the Moscow leaders—but there is disagreement on how and where the meeting came about. On the matter of timing, Mardar' supposed that the meeting took place shortly before the shooting, but, as will become clear in a moment, it actually was held afterward.[1] The preliminary investigation record identified B. N. Mokrousov, a worker in the machine-building plant, as the one who initiated an appeal for the selection of a delegation. He did so when, after his work shift ended at 1:00 P.M., he heard about the firing and hurried to the square. Profoundly shaken by what he saw and heard, he circulated from one cluster of people to another, furiously denouncing those he considered responsible and calling for a group to confront them. In the prevailing chaos there was no way of holding an election, but nine volunteers, at least three of them Komsomol members and one a woman, joined him.[2] (They were not delegates, strictly speaking, but will be so designated in what follows.) One of the persons involved later recalled that the group wanted to draw up a list of demands but couldn't find a piece of paper.

In another version—the two are not necessarily entirely contradictory— A. S. Antonov, a tank officer at the time, related that it was Mikoyan who sought a meeting. He had insistently wished to speak to the demonstrators from the gorkom balcony, perhaps in part because individuals in the throng had called for him to do so. But Pliev, who deemed such an action hazardous, dissuaded him. After he retreated with the other leaders to the military cantonment, Mikoyan expressed a desire to meet with worker representatives. Antonov escorted the delegation to Mikoyan, who offered them seats. Hoping to find common ground, Mikoyan remarked that those on both sides were Soviet people, and the demands of the strikers should be heard and discussed.[3] In a radio speech later that day, he said that the workers had been attentively listened to, but he touched on only one of the items treated: in answer to the complaint that they should have been apprised of the impending price increases well ahead of time, he explained that advance notice would have given rise to speculation and precipitated disorders in the shops.[4]

In the Antonov account, after hearing the complaints of the strikers, Mikoyan proposed a compromise. He and his fellows had learned of the change in work norms, a matter that could be reviewed and—it was intimated—perhaps altered; but there was no chance whatever that the increase in food prices could be undone. Antonov had to step out at that point, and didn't hear the delegates' response before he was instructed to escort them back to the square. When one of them tried to recount the conversation to the assembled people, he was accused of being a traitor and not permitted to speak. Although there is no independent verification of Antonov's account, it is credible for the most part. If any one of the Moscow group had wished to engage worker representatives, it would have been Mikoyan—which is not to say that he alone dealt with the delegates. It would have been sensible for him, a supple negotiator, to try to find a middle ground, and the one he posited was likely to be acceptable to his colleagues. Indeed, in the radio address Kozlov gave the following day, he made much the same proposal, adding a promise to secure better provisioning of the food shops.[5] More doubtful is the alleged unwillingness of the crowd to listen to the delegates when they returned. According to the preliminary trial record, Mokrousov did not in fact return to the square but instead— perhaps disheartened by the results of his initiative—went home.[6]

In the radio broadcast he made soon afterward, Mikoyan made no reference to the shootings, only remarking obliquely that he and Kozlov were in Novocherkassk on a very unpleasant occasion.[7] One would never guess from his words that there had been a bitterly contentious session with the delegation, that Mokrousov would shortly be indicted not only for having incited the crowd but for his behavior vis-à-vis the party leaders. He was charged with having been "insolent," gesticulating with his fists, and hurling threats and insults.[8] He was probably the one who complained of the poverty the people endured, and exclaimed (according to a hearsay report) that only Khrushchev, Brezhnev, and their like lived well in the USSR.[9] Mikoyan and his associates were bound to take umbrage at the charge that they lived well at the expense of those who were supposedly the beneficiaries of the Soviet state. But probably more objectionable was Mokrousov's demand, highlighted in the record of the preliminary investigation, that the military forces be withdrawn from

Novocherkassk. His vehemence on this score surely bespeaks his outrage at the killings, and the corpses and pools of blood he either witnessed or heard about. The withdrawal of the troops would at least prevent a repetition of the slaughter.

One can readily imagine the party leaders' indignation at a rank-and-file worker who dared to make such a demand, and their scornful rejection of it. They (especially Kozlov?) wished instead to burden the delegates with the task of persuading the crowd to "end the disorders" and go home. Their indignation must have been mixed with guilt about the shootings, aggravated by Mokrousov's reported recitation of passages of a poem by a Soviet icon, the nineteenth-century writer N. A. Nekrasov. Composed in 1873–77 but published only in 1879, the poem is titled "Who Can Be Happy and Free in Russia?" Referring to tsarist times, it includes lines remarkably apposite to the circumstances in Soviet Novocherkassk:

> You've heard how the peasants
>
> . . .
>
> Revolted for causes entirely unknown
> As they say in the papers
>
> . . .
>
> The Tsar packed a messenger
> Off in a hurry
>   he coaxed them
> And cursed them together
> But when he was tired
> Of these peaceable measures
> Of calming the riots
> At length he decided
> On giving the order
> Of "Fire" to the soldiers.[10]

A well-informed individual and a warm sympathizer with Russia's common folk, Nekrasov probably based this episode on a real incident that had occurred in April 1861, some months after the tsar issued the proclamation emancipating the serfs. The incident, described in absorbing detail by Daniel Field, is worth examining because of its remarkable resonance with the Novocherkassk clash a century later.[11] Peasants in and around the village of Bezdna, in Kazan Province, were convinced by one of their number, Anton Petrov, that the emancipation proclamation provided true freedom to the peasants. They understood this to mean the acquisition of land they tilled at no cost, the end of labor and other obligations to the landowners, and release from taxes and military service. Certain that this was the tsar's intention, the peasants were convinced that the landowners and officials who explained the decree in far less favorable terms were trying to deceive them. Some thousands of peasants who refused to work on the landlords' estates, as they were still required to do under the emancipation terms, gathered at Bezdna, intent on preventing the authorities from arresting their idolized Petrov. Many efforts were made to disabuse the peasants, but as the governor of the province, P. F. Kozlianinov, advised the minister of internal affairs: "All persuasion is fruitless." A day later he wrote of "their terrible stubbornness . . . the degree to which they were aroused, and . . . their confidence in the rightness of their cause." [12] The contending parties were deadlocked.

Perhaps to circumvent the censorship, in his poem Nekrasov represented that the seemingly imminent shooting was averted at the last moment. In fact, it was not averted at Bezdna. The marshal of the nobility, Count A. S. Apraksin, "counting on the moral influence of the presence of troops," brought in companies of soldiers. The peasants were no more overawed than the Novocherkassk workers. According to a reliable witness, they said: "How could they shoot the *narod* [people]? We aren't rebels, are we?" [13] Like Kozlov and his colleagues later, Apraksin feared to face the crowd, and ordered his agents to do so in his stead. In response to the people's demand to hear the tsar's emissary, he finally emerged, but was no more successful than others in turning the assembled peasants around. Apraksin reported to Tsar Alexander II that the peasants were repeatedly warned of the grave consequences of disobeying the authorities. But instead of giving way, he untruthfully claimed, the peasants prepared to assault the soldiers with pikes, "threatening to surround and crush my undermanned unit." To head off a "general rebellion," therefore, he ordered the soldiers to fire. They discharged a series of volleys, resulting in scores of deaths and injuries. [14] (The governor estimated the number killed at 70, Apraksin at 51; privately, an estate steward with no ax to grind counted 109 plus around 200 wounded who fled and later died. As late as 1990, high-ranking army officers who had been present in Novocherkassk on June 2 insisted that only six persons had been slain.) [15] After the fusillade, the surviving peasants returned to work, and Petrov was court-martialed and executed. Only a few others were tried, and they received light sentences. Like the Novocherkassk arrestees, all of those who were detained confessed their guilt. Approximately anticipating Khrushchev's sentiment a century later, the tsar remarked: "Sad though it is, there was nothing else to do."[16] Many particulars of the two events are almost as identical as two drops of water, as a Russian saying goes, with the Soviet authorities acting in 1962 the parts played by the tsarist authorities in 1861.

The lengthy Apraksin report, like the KGB reports after the Novocherkassk events, became the official version of what had happened at Bezdna. Unlike the later official version, however, the one concerning Bezdna was widely published, but it could not be called into question. Apraksin himself later amended his version, laying the blame for the killing squarely on Petrov, whose stubbornness, he insisted, was the cause of the great loss of life. Similarly, as late as 1991, an authoritative military spokesman quoted approvingly a former secretary of the Rostov party's executive committee as follows: "Those fundamentally responsible for the loss of lives were the hooligans, among whom there were former convicts. They were the ones who provoked the collision between the demonstrators and the police and soldiers, obliging the latter to take up arms."[17] Like Semichastnyi later, Apraksin claimed that the measures implemented had a great prophylactic effect. Individuals who took issue with the report—for example, F. A. Polovtsov, the governor's military adjutant—were dismissed from their posts.[18]

Mikoyan's radio speech, couched in conciliatory terms, was broadcast repeatedly through the late afternoon and evening. It was one of a series of diverse measures taken after the massacre to pacify the people. Reinforcements were brought in and posted throughout the city, and when a curfew scheduled to last from 9:00 at night until 6:00 in the morning was announced and enforced, the crowds dissipated. In the evening a great fireworks display exploded over the city as military units unleashed a multitude of tracer bullets to facilitate observation.

A Polytechnical student who had been visiting a friend's room before 9:00 didn't leave for his own dormitory until around 11:00 P.M. and had a difficult time avoiding the network of guards put in place to enforce the curfew. The occupied town was eerily silent, except for an occasional burst of gunfire somewhere or other, and the sound of hobnail-studded boots of patrolling soldiers. When the student, Mikhail Los', approached the Polytechnical Institute, he saw an armored troop carrier standing guard. He hid until it moved on, but as he went farther along he was spotted by a group of three soldiers. When they ordered him to halt, he took to his heels. Unlike the unfortunate Shul'man, who in similar circumstances was cut down, the student escaped, as the soldiers fired over his head instead of at him. In an unsuccessful effort to reach his dormitory, Los' wandered through many a side street; he had to avoid the main thoroughfares, brightly illuminated by powerful searchlights on the military vehicles parked at the intersections.[19]

That same night, at the command post, the authorities discussed what should be done with the corpses filling the morgue.[20] The KGB report to the Central Committee of the CPSU and the Council of Ministers, dated June 6, laconically indicated that "the corpses had been buried in various places in the province." In the early 1990s, Lt. Gen. D. A. Ivashchenko recollected matter-of-factly the ghoulish conversations that had led to the decision:

> The whole question was where and how [to bury the dead]. For five hours straight, we attempted to come to a unanimous decision. Mikoyan, Kozlov, Pliev, the head of the MVD regional office, Strel'chenko, and I were present. At first, it was proposed that we should bury them in a humane way—people would understand. But what if they did not understand? If the burials would cause a new wave of unrest? No, we couldn't take on such a responsibility. Then it was suggested that the corpses be given to the families for burial. But this had to be rejected as well. . . . Funerals, funeral feasts. . . . We decided to take a refrigerated car, load it with the coffins, send it by railroad to Central Asia, and bury them somewhere in the sand. But we shrank from this, too. Then Strel'chenko proposed burying them in the sea: [put them] in sacks, together with rocks, load them onto flat-bottomed boats, and dump them in Taganrog Bay. But we could not agree on that, either. There remained only the alternative to which everyone agreed: to bury the corpses two by two in different cemeteries. Mikoyan proposed this. . . . Strel'chenko was entrusted with organizing the burial.[21]

In the dead of night, around 2:00 A.M. on June 3, twenty corpses were loaded into two military trucks and carried away. They were driven to a forested area, where each was photographed, examined by a court medical expert, and tagged with a number; a record was made of the number and descriptions of the individual's clothing. Once the disposition of the corpses had been decided, they were transported to cemeteries away from well-populated places—the villages of Tarasovskii, Martsevo, and Novoshakhtinsk. Their graves were marked with other people's names. Men considered trustworthy dug down in an old grave until they struck a coffin, threw in a corpse, and restored the grave to its former appearance. Almost eighty persons, mostly policemen from towns in Rostov Province, participated in these grisly operations, and all were obliged to sign statements solemnly binding them to remain silent about what they had done and seen.[22] The relatives were unable to find out where their loved ones were buried until 1992.

A concerted effort was made to mobilize the faithful for a propaganda offensive. Before June 2 had ended, and the next day as well, Kozlov and Mikoyan met with party activists, first at NEVZ and then at the synthetic products factory.[23] No doubt they urged their comrades to unmask the fellow workers who had participated conspicuously in the strike and demonstration, to engage in intensive "educational" activity, and to stage counterdemonstrations. A mass of tanks and armored vehicles had preceded the Presidium members to NEVZ and were deployed throughout the factory to ensure their safety. After the meeting there, the force had bellicosely passed through the streets of the hushed workers' village to demonstrate, as a participating officer ruefully recalled, the might of the national army, which had dealt savagely with its own people.[24]

Early on the morning of June 3, groups of workers at NEVZ began gathering once again, although in much reduced numbers. Apparently Saturday's terror had effectively persuaded many of the strikers to back off. The actions of the bold remnant reveal what was on their minds. On foot and by car, they went to the headquarters of the police and local KGB, where many of their fellows had been incarcerated. Crowds began to show up near the gorkom as well. One can readily imagine the rage vented over the previous day's orgy of violence and its likeness to Bloody Sunday. At the police station a woman cried hysterically that her son had been killed. Her lamentations attracted the attention of many people, and soon some 500 had collected. The aroused crowd continued to grow, and it advanced toward the barrier of soldiers guarding the building. The throng demanded the release of the detainees but made no attempt to force their way in. To distract and influence the crowd, a loudspeaker was set up at the movie theater just across the street, and the speech Mikoyan had broadcast the day before was repeated, as well as Khrushchev's speech to the Cubans (or, more likely, part of it). At noon, party members, other loyalists, and druzhinniki were brought to do "agitational work." In a heated exchange with someone in the crowd, one of the druzhinniki argued that those who had been shot the day before had gotten what they deserved. Back came the words: "You should be wearing a black [i.e., fascist] armband rather than a red one."[25]

The pacifiers apparently failed to accomplish their mission, for at 3:00 Kozlov made a broadcast.

Reviewing the reasons advanced in the May 31 announcement of increases in food prices, he said that the leadership had made the decision "with a heavy heart." In explanation of what had occurred the day before—there was no mention of shootings—he fulminated against "hooligans," "drunks," and "provocateurs," under whose malign influence "nonconscious" workers had fallen. Papering over the abyss between the people and the party highlighted the day before, he assured his listeners that in the USSR's "social democracy," the workers possessed "their own social organizations, their own state, [and] there own party, whose entire activity is directed to the happiness and well-being of the people." As we have seen, he held out the prospect of concessions, but there could be no tolerance for "mass disorders" that subverted the workers' state, party, and well-being, and were condemned by the overwhelming majority. The KGB report on which this account of the June 3 events is based— it is the only source currently available on the matter—asserts that Kozlov's speech marked a turning point. It caused the popular mood to change, and the crowd began to disperse.[26] It is unlikely that Kozlov's arguments changed many minds. Rather the crowd was reacting to the closing words of his address: "Normal order will be reestablished in the town, by whatever means may be necessary"—a thinly veiled threat of a renewed resort to force.[27] Even so, not everyone fell into line. On the nights of June 3 and 4, 240 persons were detained for violation of the curfew.

Kozlov contended in his radio speech that the workers (and the city's residents, with whom, he claimed, he and Mikoyan had spoken on the streets) overwhelmingly approved the government's policies and condemned those who "had disorganized the normal life of the city." To restore things to normal in the town and its institutions and enterprises, it was imperative "to isolate and restrain" the provocateurs.[28] Accordingly, the KGB and police forces sought to apprehend persons suspected of active involvement in the strike and the demonstration. They made a good beginning with the arrest of the thirty persons who were trapped at the police station during the clash there. Their subsequent efforts were assisted by Komsomol and party members, who, once they had lost control of the situation, functioned as spies, staying close to the action and fixing in mind the faces of "malign" elements, so that they could later point them out to the authorities. The hunt was carried on intensively over a period of at least three weeks, fragmentary data indicating that two of the key individuals were arrested on June 6, another on June 8, three more on June 9, and one not until June 22. By June 12, the authorities had identified 150 of the "most active participants" and had already arrested 53. The total number of those arrested at one time or another was probably over 300, but the majority were released after questioning. Among them were curious onlookers who had been caught in a camera's eye and others on whom nothing could be pinned.

Rumors about the arrests and their disposition flew through the town. One of them had it that truly mass arrests were carried out, the numbers attaining such proportions — as many as 5,000 — that the detainees had to be penned in the stadium. According to another story, the party leaders entertained the idea of deporting the town's mutinous residents en masse. Reports were abroad that numerous trucks, their beds covered by gratings, were brought into the city for the purpose, but at some point the idea was vetoed.[29] Skepticism about this tale has been countered by the testimony of a former KGB man who, in the early 1990s, told of having heard the plan discussed within the agency after the massacre.[30] This point has been verified in Mikoyan's recently published memoir. He asserts that Kozlov wished to carry out a mass deportation, which he, Mikoyan, vigorously opposed, and the idea was abandoned.[31]

The press was brought into play to help calm the city. The Novocherkassk newspaper, a publication of the city's party organization, always came out Tuesday through Sunday. But the extraordinary times called forth an extraordinary response: a Monday edition was brought out on June 4. Needless to say, no coverage was given to the bloody events of June 2; nor was an effort made to blanket the town with the party's tendentious version of what had happened. Instead, the centerpiece was the text of Khrushchev's speech to the Cubans.[32]

As already indicated, Khrushchev is said to have advised Kozlov on June 2 to proceed in the spirit of that address. Although the speech was equivocal, the message to be communicated in the aftermath of the slaughter was that Khrushchev gave his blessing to Saturday's forceful actions against those who "may be dressed in the same worker shirt as you." A bit of secondhand evidence confirms the point. Commander Maliutin was told by one of his officers who went to staff headquarters immediately after the shooting on the square that Kozlov had just spoken to Khrushchev about what had happened. Khrushchev responded grimly but approvingly that "millions had perished on behalf of Soviet power, and it was right to use arms against people who challenged that power."[33] The threat of more of the same was the point of Kozlov's radio broadcast. It should be pointed out in this connection that after the shootings, worrisome rumors spread that the soldiers who had witnessed the shootings were to be liquidated. To assuage fears in the ranks, on June 5 Kozlov met with the staffs of the Novocherkassk garrison and subdivisions of the MVD armed forces in the military compound. He assured them in the name of the Central Committee that those who had suppressed the disorders had performed well, and he passed along Khrushchev's personal thanks for their steadfastness.[34]

Propaganda and intimidation took various forms. Local party and Komsomol leaders as well as some of the Moscow dignitaries fanned out to the factories and institutes to impose the official view.[35] Witnesses later detailed the high-handed conduct of party officials and other authority figures with respect to "comrades," especially students, who dared to ask questions. The secretary of the USSR's Komsomol organization, Pavlov by name, held forth at a student dormitory "on all manner of things, even his desire to be in Cuba with Fidel Castro. But when he was asked, 'Who gave the command to fire?' he feigned surprise, and accused the questioner of being incorrectly informed. In general [he insisted], nothing had happened here." The same question was posed to Polianskii at a meeting with Institute activists. "Who said that?" the Presidium member shot back. And when an individual stood up, Polianskii ordered, "Leave the room. You're no longer a student." A friend of the narrator of this episode was taken aback by the deathly silence in the hall as the young man left. He accused himself of cowardice, and asserted—the narrator seriously doubted this proposition—that had he said one word in self-defense, the whole room would have erupted in outrage.[36]

Another witness described a meeting at the Polytechnical Institute where both Ilychev, one of the Central Committee secretaries, and Pavlov spoke. Ilychev drew laughter and indignation when he told the students that a soldier's weapon had fallen to the ground and gone off accidentally. Pavlov drew a parallel between the 1956 events in Hungary and what had happened in Novocherkassk, characterizing the strike as something like a counterrevolutionary mutiny. Manipulating the students with invented tales of worker outrages, he asked: "Was it necessary to shoot at them?" and received a rousing affirmative reply. At that Pavlov remarked: "I was certain that here we have our true youth," and the assembly passed a resolution condemning the strikers.

In the course of the meeting several courageous students had tried to express their actual thoughts on the events, but were assailed with hysterical invective. One person contended that everything that had been said about the strike and demonstration was false. From the dais he was asked to identify himself. He gave his name and identified himself as a miner from Shakhty. He was at the meeting, he explained, because he was an extension student who had come to town for an examination and had witnessed the events. Someone in the hall cried: "It's a provocation!" The charge was taken up at the speakers' table, followed by a demand that the "provocateur" be thrown out, and he was.[37]

G. Marchevskii, a student who happened to be at Lenin Square at the time of the fusillade, spoke out forcefully to neighbors and other acquaintances about the "Bloody Saturday" he had witnessed. Someone informed on him, and days later he was escorted to the police station. Four officers eyed him while they leafed through an album of photographs taken during the demonstration. They did not find his image, but berated him for his loose tongue and intimated that he would pay for it. Days later, Marchevskii—whose father had perished in the 1937 purges—was summoned to a meeting with the Polytechnical Institute's party committee. Obliged to explain his behavior to the head of the local KGB, he was afterward hailed before a meeting of the Institute's Komsomol. His friends, equipped with cameras and tape recorders, were misinformed by the authorities about the time and place of the trial and were unable to attend. Present were members of the party committee; representatives of the rector and the faculties of the history of the CPSU, political economy, and Marxist-Leninist philosophy; members of the KGB; and fifteen students. Marchevskii was expelled from the Komsomol for "amoral conduct and demonstrated irresponsibility." But that wasn't the end of his ordeal.

After he defended his thesis in the Faculty of Military Studies, a meeting was arranged in the Institute's concert hall. All the students completing the Military Studies program had assembled before the rector and the heads of the Institute's Professional Committee and the KGB appeared. The Professional Committee chief, N. S. Durov, announced that the assemblage was to make a binding judgment on the behavior of certain comrades during the recent events. Marchevskii was named, along with one other student. It was his final chance to recant, to condemn his behavior and repent. He declined, but the proceedings appeared so unjust that the students, unexpectedly, were loath to follow their leaders. When the three managers proposed to terminate the hearing, the students demanded that the issues be thoroughly discussed. The demand was ignored, and Marchevskii was arbitrarily deprived of his diploma and his commission as a reserve officer. Although Marchevskii undoubtedly felt severely dealt with, in the context of that time and place the punishment seems surprisingly lenient. A year later he was granted the degree, but he continued to be defined as "unreliable," and this characterization dogged his professional career indefinitely.[38]

The people were effectively cowed into silence. The head of the local branch of the KGB observed weeks later that the town's population was so afraid of saying anything, of speaking about the trials then going on, that they even warned one another, "Don't open your mouth or you'll be put in prison."[39] The hidden sentiments of a considerable part of the population may have been expressed in what one of the demonstrators reported having seen at the NEVZ administration building where a portrait of Khrushchev had formerly been displayed: a dead cat suspended on the wall, together with a placard reading: "Under Lenin, she lived; under Stalin, she wasted away; under Khrushchev, she croaked."[40] One Novocherkassian told long after the event—and there may have been many more like him—that because of what he knew, he later declined an invitation to join the party.[41]

KGB Deputy President Ivashutin concisely summarized the activities of June 4, 5, and 6

> to bring about the definitive normalization of the life of the city and work at the enterprises. The curfew was lifted, and the army forces that had been in the city were withdrawn. [Mokrousov's demand was heeded, after all.] Vehicular transportation was restored. In accord with a decision of the city's party active component, meetings were held at the factories, enterprises, and educational institutions that condemned the criminal actions of hooligan elements who had provoked the disorders. A number of shortcomings in the commercial sector were eliminated, [and] the provision of food supplies to the population was improved.[42]

Along with repressive measures—146 persons had been arrested and an "open" trial of the most active participants in the disorders was envisaged— the authorities apparently sought to appease the Novocherkassk population with concessions: the lifting of the curfew, withdrawal of (part of?) the army, and increased food supplies. Another important measure of the kind was the removal of several lightning rods. On June 4 B. N. Kurochkin, the despised NEVZ director, whose insensitivity certainly contributed to the troubles, was discharged, and two months later he was expelled from the party.[43] His replacement was P. A. Abroskin, who had occupied that position in the 1950s and reportedly was well liked by the workers. He recognized the many shortcomings in working and living conditions, and was able to report detailed plans for improvements to the provincial party committee as early as July 6. By then Abroskin had already suited action to words, noting, for example, the addition of 500 seats in the dining halls and places for the workers to rest and wash up; and that construction of worker housing, establishment of new kindergartens, and paving of roads and sidewalks in the workers' village were under way. An energetic and sympathetic administrator, Abroskin was following in the footsteps of the factory owner and utopian socialist Robert Owen, who had learned a century and a half earlier that over time workers were more productive when given evidence of concern for their well-being.[44]

In the popular mind, Generals Pliev and Oleshko were the executioners; they were responsible for the shooting. On that score, a month or two after the events they (and other figures in the NCMO command) were transferred to new assignments. Oleshko was ordered to the Far East, where he became deputy commander of an army corps before assuming a post as an instructor in the General Staff Academy in Moscow. Pliev was put in charge of Soviet forces in Cuba, where he presided over the installation and then the dismantling of missiles aimed at the United States.[45] A fourth figure who had earned the enmity of the workers was Basov, the secretary of the Rostov Province party committee. Of course, he had participated in neither the decision to raise the prices of meat and butter nor the change in work norms at NEVZ. But inasmuch as the disorders had occurred on his watch, in his region, and his efforts to curb them had fallen flat, he too was pulled from his post, and given an assignment in the diplomatic field. At a lower level, one of the party leaders at NEVZ and several officials of the Novocherkassk party organization were reprimanded for their failings.

Throughout the first half of 1962, *Znamia kommuny* printed many triumphant articles on the fulfillment and overfulfillment of production targets at NEVZ and other Novocherkassk plants. Ludicrously, along with a piece on the party leadership's wise decision to increase the prices of meat and butter, the issue of June 3 included an article hailing the fulfillment of the first half-year plan for 1962 ahead of schedule. These public assertions were belied by information aired behind closed doors at meetings of the party leaders. One of the reports to a province-level conference on August 13—it was delivered by two of Novocherkassk's top party officials—was headed: "On serious deficiencies in the organizational and mass-political work of the party organization at

NEVZ." The upshot of the meeting was Kurochkin's expulsion from the party and the reprimanding of others, but the criticism and self-criticism that preceded those actions are revealing. Although no production figures were presented, the remarks about "slack performance," the want of a "conscientious attitude toward work," and numerous violations of work discipline inspire skepticism about the claims of plan fulfillment and overfulfillment. The underlying difficulties indicated may be grouped under two interrelated rubrics: the inadequacies of party work and inattention to the needs of the workers.

Under the first head were references to the disjunction between the factory's trade union and party organizations and the mass of workers; the failure to carry on educational work and to serve as good examples; a formal, unimaginative mode of performing essential functions; the abysmal record of exercising influence on young people and women; and insufficient vigilance in dealing with antisocial behavior (hooliganism, drunkenness, theft of state property, and religious activity). Because of the failure to inculcate comradeliness, initiative, and the capacity to overcome difficulties, such vices as apoliticism, indifference, and nihilistic attitudes flourished.

The party organization was faulted, under the second head, for its failure to understand conditions in the various departments and the moods and needs of the workers. The way wage rates were determined was not satisfactory; the collectives had an opportunity to discuss such matters all too infrequently. And meetings that were supposed to deal with production problems were not working as they should. Far too little effort was devoted to improving the workers' cultural and living conditions. Sanitary conditions were poor and eating places were inadequate. Perhaps as a way of supporting Abroskin's good intentions, the head of the province's economic office was to be compelled to expend funds allotted by the Council of Ministers for the provision of amenities in the factory and for housing and other everyday needs in the NEVZ worker village. In fact, over time housing was so much improved that it became distinctly better than that provided industrial workers in neighboring towns.[46]

The report also leveled sharp criticisms at the tempo and the quality of production. It is well known that very many Soviet enterprises worked at a slow pace in the early part of the month and speeded up ("stormed") toward the end in order to fulfill the plan for that period.[47] *Znamia kommuny* often accompanied reports on plan fulfillment with assertions that the enterprises were working "rhythmically," meaning at a steady pace. But the data on NEVZ for the second quarter of 1962 reveal no sense of rhythm at all. In the first ten days of one month, production attained a paltry 3.4 percent of the target—about one-tenth of the 33.3 percent it should have scored if the plant had been operating rhythmically. By contrast, the output in the last ten days came to 78.6 percent of the target for the month. These statistics are of more than academic interest. They suggest demoralized workers who, rather than conforming to the dicta of political leaders and economic managers, applied themselves to the work in accordance with their own inclinations and convenience. Moreover, this mode of work was bound to affect the quality of production, and it did. In the first six months of 1962, the workmanship on one of the locomotive models produced at NEVZ was so poor that railroad divisions to which they had been furnished demanded replacements for forty-two of them, whereas there had been only nine defective ones in the entire preceding year.[48] This unsatisfactory situation could only have been aggravated by the early June troubles.

Of course, the violent suppression of the strike and the subsequent "prophylactic" activity of the security organs alienated a great many workers, not to mention students and other town residents. It could not help having an adverse effect on the workers' morale and on their attitudes toward the authorities and toward their work. When on June 12 a meeting was held at NEVZ to condemn the recent disorders, only 700 of the 13,000 workers turned out. This showing is the more striking because, according to a former KGB agent, there were 1,400 party members in the enterprise.[49]

It goes without saying that the price increases on meat and butter were not rescinded, and despite intimations that the work norms at NEVZ would be reviewed, there is no evidence that they were altered either.[50] But the concessions made—the dismissal of Kurochkin, the increase in the town's food supplies, improvements in working conditions at the factory and living conditions in the workers' quarter, and in general greater sensitivity to the workers' needs—were significant. These changes had been brought about as a result of the strike, so from this angle, the stoppage was not fruitless.

Moreover, the outbreak at Novocherkassk had repercussions throughout the Soviet Union. For one thing, it rudely awakened the country's leadership to the inadequacy of provisions for a wide range of needs of the entire population. On August 10 a lengthy document "on the further improvement of everyday services for the population" was drawn up by the Central Committee and the Council of Ministers.[51] It set forth a litany of shortcomings, ranging from the want of facilities for repair of apartments, refrigerators, sewing machines, radios, and television sets to shoes and clothing; the insufficiency of spare parts, baths, dry cleaners, and hairdressing parlors for women; the scheduling of daily work shifts, days off, and hours for breaks without regard for the convenience of customers. And much more. The document, as a matter of course, prescribed corrective action and periodic checkups. Such self-criticism and resolutions to improve matters were not unusual, but it is generally agreed that in the next ten or fifteen years the leadership made good to some extent on its promises. Subsequently, for complex reasons to be touched on in the concluding chapter, it proved impossible to continue delivering the goods, with ultimately catastrophic results.

The Novocherkassk events also produced a considerable impact in the realm of state security. Deeply disturbed by the unexpected upheaval, the leadership sought to understand what had happened and prevent a recurrence. It was all well and good to prescribe better living conditions for the population, but the regime's resources were inadequate to achieve all its desiderata, domestic and foreign. It was essential, therefore, to be able to deal efficiently and effectively with inevitable manifestations of discontent. This consideration impelled the head of the KGB to review the work of the organization critically and to publish in July 1962 a comprehensive thirteen-point directive on ways and means of "strengthening the struggle of the security organs against hostile manifestations by anti-Soviet elements." Among other things, surveillance of released convicts and nationalist and religious elements was to be stepped up, more agents were to be recruited, greater attention was to be given to their training, and collaboration with the MVD was to be intensified. Conspicuous were mandates clearly deriving from the Novocherkassk troubles: greater emphasis was to be placed on operations in large industrial enterprises and educational institutions, so that potential problems would be identified and dealt with expeditiously; and at all levels plans were to be drawn up for dealing with "mass disorders." In addition, because a significant number of ex-convicts lived in the southern region, and people of that sort were believed to have been prominent in the Novocherkassk events, a special passport regime was to be established in the south.[52]

In July and August the security organs assured the party leadership that everything had returned to normal. As a matter of fact, in August and September well over a hundred arrested persons were brought to trial in a series of court proceedings. Novocherkassk's Calvary was far from over.

(Above) *The gorkom, formerly the ataman's palace, now the town hall. In 1962 the facade was not yet partially obscured by trees.*

(Below, left) *This statue of Lenin was erected in place of a statue of Ataman Matvei Ivanovich Platov, founder of Novocherkassk, after the Bolshevik Revolution.*

(Below, right) *Another statue of Platov was set in place after the collapse of the Soviet Union.*

(Above) *NEVZ, the factory where the strike began. Officials who spoke to the massed strikers from the balcony-like platform at the second-story level left of the entry were showered with missiles. (Photo by Samuel H. Baron)*

(Below) *The Polytechnical Institute, many of whose students participated in the demonstration. (Photo by Samuel H. Baron)*

(Above) *Placard inscribed with the signature slogan of the strike:*
"Meat, Butter, a Pay Raise!" (KGB photo)

(Below) *Preparing to block a train on the Saratov–Rostov line.*
(KGB photo)

(Above) Strikers gathered before the top of the entrance to the railroad underpass, which served as a rostrum for speakers. The placard is attached atop a power line. (KGB photo)

(Below) Massed demonstrators, marching with a portrait of Lenin and red banners, before the Tuzlov River bridge on their way to the gorkom. (KGB photo)

Andrei Korchak, one of the most remarkable of the strikers singled out with X marks for arrest as an agitator. (KGB photo)

Another striker singled out for arrest is believed to be E. P. Levchenko, who instigated the attack on the police station. (KGB photo)

(Above) *The military headquarters building in Novocherkassk, in which the principal trial was held. (Photo by Samuel H. Baron)*

(Below) *From left to right, Mikoyan, Kozlov, and Khrushchev enjoying a concert in May 1962. (Copyright Bettmann/CORBIS)*

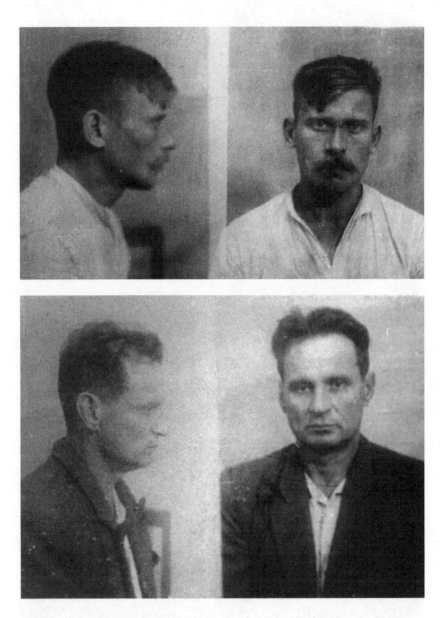

Rogue's gallery pictures of the seven who were condemned to death and executed: V. D. Cherepanov (above), A. A. Korchak (below). (KGB photos)

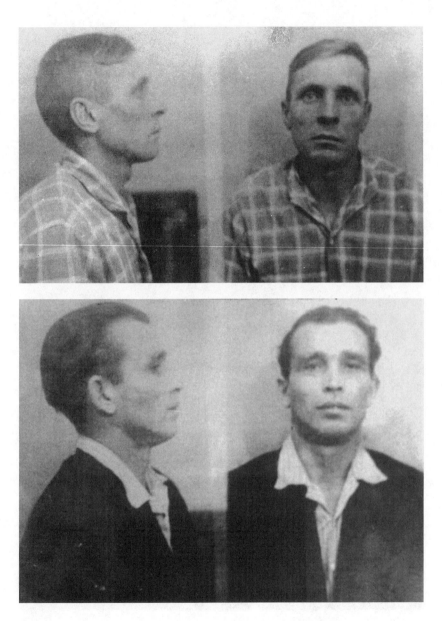

M. A. Kuznetsov (above), B. N. Mokrousov (below). (KGB photos)

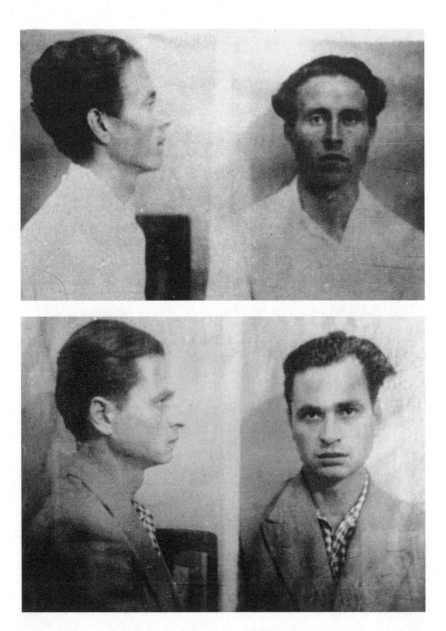

V. G. Shubaev (above), *S. S. Sotnikov* (below). *(KGB photos)*

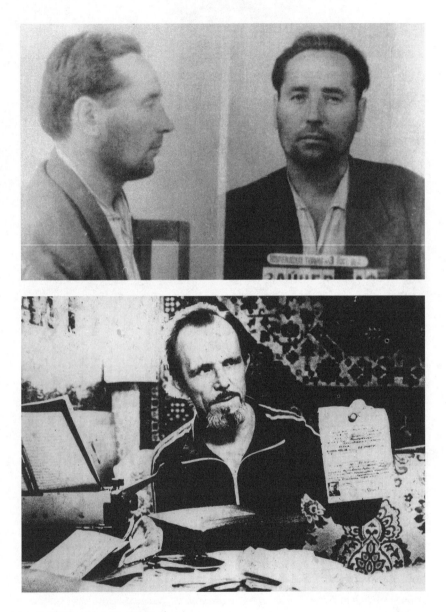

A. F. Zaitsev (above). (KGB photo)

(Below) The NEVZ striker P. P. Siuda became the chronicler of "the Novocherkassk tragedy." (Photo courtesy of Emma Siuda)

(Above) *Gen. M. K. Shaposhnikov was discharged from the army and expelled from the party because of his efforts to publicize the events in Novocherkassk. (Photo courtesy of Nina Shaposhnikova)*

(Below, left) *Ol'ga Nikitina wrote the first article on the Novocherkassk affair to be published in an official newspaper, and several more thereafter in unofficial publications. (Photo courtesy of Ol'ga Nikitina)*

(Below, right) *Iurii Bespalov wrote the first article on Novocherkassk to appear in one of the All-Union party-sponsored newspapers (Komsomol'skaia pravda) and continued to discover and publish ever more relevant information. (Photo courtesy of Iurii Bespalov)*

(Above) *Irina Mardar', journalist, first president of the Novocherkassk Tragedy Founda-tion, and author of the most considerable work on the events published until 1999. (Photo by Samuel H. Baron)*

(Below) *Valentina Vodianitskaia, one of the most vocal of the former strikers. (Photo by Samuel H. Baron)*

Tat'iana Bocharova, television news reporter and second president of the Novocherkassk Tragedy Foundation, addressing a memorial ceremony on the thirty-fifth anniversary of the massacre. (Photo by Samuel H. Baron)

(Above) *M. I. Kraisvetnyi, an archaeologist instrumental in finding and exhuming the secretly buried bodies of the victims. (Photo by Samuel H. Baron)*

(Below) *Members of the Novocherkassk Tragedy Foundation excavating bodies of the victims in 1991. (Photo courtesy of M. I. Kraisvetnyi)*

(Above) The cemetery in Novocherkassk, where the remains of the victims were buried in 1992. Inscribed on the cross are the words: "Victims of the 1962 shootings." (Photo by Samuel H. Baron)

(Below) Memorial obelisk erected in 1992 at the square where the strikers were shot. It is marked: "June 2, 1962." (Photo by Samuel H. Baron)

N. E. Stepanov, one of the strikers, standing outside NEVZ in 1998, under a plaque placed on the wall to commemorate the events. It reads: "Here began the spontaneous initiative of workers driven to despair, which ended June 2, 1962, with a fusillade in the city's central square and further repressions." (Photo by Samuel H. Baron)

Chapter 5   The Trial

One hundred and fourteen persons were brought to trial in a series of eight to ten proceedings, each involving anywhere from three to fourteen defendants. The trials, held mainly in the Novocherkassk city court or the Rostov oblast court, took place in August and September. The most important of them, the one on which we shall concentrate, was held in August in the military head-quarters building in Novocherkassk. It involved fourteen defendants: V. D. Cherepanov, V. I. Chernykh, Iu. P. Dement'ev, G. A. Goncharov, G. G. Katkov, A. A. Korchak, M. A. Kuznetsov, E. P. Levchenko, B. N. Mokrousov, G. M. Shcherban, V. G. Shubaev, I. P. Sluzhenko, S. S. Sotnikov, and A. F. Zaitsev.[1]

A brief examination of the legal order then in place may serve as a useful framework for what follows. In the wake of Khrushchev's denunciation of Stalin at the 20th Congress of the CPSU in 1956, many areas of Soviet life were reformed in some measure, among them the legal system. Because legality had been one of the most serious casualties of the Stalin era, in 1960 both a new Criminal Code of the RSFSR and a new Code of Criminal Procedure were promulgated.[2] George Feiffer has conveniently summarized many of the principal points:

> Conviction by "analogy" had been repudiated; "social danger" had been narrowed to mean only crimes specifically described in the criminal code; and the class origins of the parties before the court was no longer a matter for the consideration of the judges. Civilians were no longer tried in military courts, except in cases of espionage. Unpublished criminal statutes had ceased to [serve as the basis for prosecutions]. The MVD's boards, which formerly convened secretly on the basis of secret procedure and issued secret, nonappealable decisions, had been abolished; all crimes were now tried in the regular court system. The procurator's obligations to the accused had been clarified and increased throughout the criminal process.

93

In court, the burden of proof was more clearly on the prosecution, and the standards of proof had been raised; confession alone could no longer convict the accused.[3]

The new Code of Criminal Procedure was peppered with such impressive juridical phraseology as prosecution only "in accordance with the procedure established by law"; "inviolability of person"; "inviolability of dwelling space"; "equality before the law"; "independence of judges and their subordination only to law"; "thorough, complete, and objective analysis of the circumstances of the case"; "rights of the accused"; and "duties and rights of the defense counsel."[4] Such concepts, insofar as they were honored in practice, certainly merit praise. Yet they were deceptive because, like *Hamlet* without the Prince of Denmark, the code never once mentions the CPSU. Meanwhile, Article 126 of the Soviet Constitution describes the CPSU as "the leading core of all organizations . . . both social and state"—and the criminal justice system was no exception.

The system consisted of three core elements: the judiciary, the procuracy, and the advocacy. "The RSFSR Supreme Court," reads Article 38 of the Code of Criminal Procedure, "shall have jurisdiction over cases of special complexity or of special social significance." In the eyes of the authorities, the Novocherkassk case clearly possessed "special social significance," so it was tried before a panel of the RSFSR Supreme Court. It goes without saying that a large majority of judges generally, and certainly any who had risen to such eminence, were members of the party and subject to its discipline. Their subordination to the party was obviously at odds with the Criminal Code's assertion of "the independence of judges and their subordination only to law."

The procuracy was of "crucial importance in the Soviet system of law." It was solely responsible for the prosecution of criminal cases in court, and in performing this function it was obliged "to ensure strict execution of the laws." Still, the procuracy was not free of outside constraints. In the principal Novocherkassk proceeding, the case against the accused was to be made by the procurator general of the RSFSR, A. A. Kruglov. Inevitably, political considerations were to be taken into account along with the laws.[5]

The third element of the tripod that constituted the criminal justice system was the defense counsel, or, as it was known in Soviet Russia, the advocacy. No lawyer could participate in court proceedings without first being admitted to one of the so-called colleges of advocates. These colleges were voluntary organizations in the sense that they were not an integral part of the state structure. It will come as no surprise, though, that these organizations were not completely autonomous. The Judicial Commission of the Council of Ministers was charged with supervision of the colleges, and the head of a college, who was invariably a party member, was admonished to "increase the ideological-political level of its members." (In 1961, 53 percent of the advocates were either members or candidate members of the party.)[6] The accused in a criminal case had the right to select defense counsel or, alternatively, the advocate would be appointed by the judge or procurator. It is not clear how the nine lawyers who served as advocates in the principal Novocherkassk case were chosen, but it would almost certainly have made no difference one way or the other.[7] When the KGB was involved in a case, and it was deeply involved in this one, no advocate could undertake to serve without its approval.

It would be interesting to know whether the advocates played an active role in the Novocherkassk case, but it is safe to suppose that they did no more than go through the required motions. Although in theory Soviet defense attorneys enjoyed parity with prosecutors, in practice they were routinely treated condescendingly or worse by judges and procuracy staff alike. Even if the advocates perceived serious flaws in the prosecution's case, they were hardly likely to conduct an aggressive defense of people charged with "especially dangerous crimes against the state." They surely were aware, in the words of a woman who worked as an advocate for some thirty-seven years, that "any lawyer who . . . came into head-on conflict with the prosecution" was likely to be disbarred as a consequence.[8] A well-informed author has observed that "the advocates not only made no effort to defend their clients but [some of them] even failed to appear at the trials."[9]

V. E. Semichastnyi, the KGB chief, and R. A. Rudenko, procurator general of the USSR (who was also a member of the Central Committee), jointly outlined the procedure to be followed in the principal trial. The two considered it expedient that the proceedings take place in open court, with the accusation brought by the procurator of the RSFSR and a number of NEVZ workers.[10] It was customary to involve a "social accuser," in this case selected workers from the factory, to advertise that not just the state but society in general had an interest in prosecuting violations of established norms. The inclusion of (handpicked) NEVZ workers was calculated to give the impression that the overwhelming majority of the workforce condemned the strikers.

The trial was to be open, but not to the general public. Indeed, not a word about the trial appeared in the press.[11] Attendance was by way of invitations sent to "workers of Novocherkassk factories, party activists, and representatives of social organizations."[12] It can be stated confidently that not just any workers from the Novocherkassk factories or members of social organizations were invited, but solely party and trusted Komsomol members, and perhaps some fellow travelers. Even so, security arrangements were rigorous. A senior instructor at the Polytechnical Institute who served as a member of his faculty's party bureau was among those sent a ticket of admission. Around 1990, he recalled that at the entrance to the site of the trial he was required to show his ticket and other documents as well. As he advanced into the building, he was asked to show his admission ticket again, and then a third time.[13]

The trial ran from August 14 to 21, both mornings and afternoons, but apparently with several recesses. Each of the ten sessions was attended by 450 to 500 people for a total of 4,500 to 5,000, among them 45 NEVZ workers.[14] With the NEVZ workers constituting no more than 1 percent of the total, is it not reasonable to suspect that many others, traumatized by what had occurred, declined invitations to participate? This kind of thing evidently caused the authorities to worry that new disorders might be in the offing, for "during the trial vigilance was heightened, and all objects and vulnerable places were put under guard and control."[15]

One wonders why the authorities opted for an open trial. If the intention was to give a lesson to the country at large, there could have been a more genuinely open trial, one tendentiously reported in the press. But the authorities certainly wanted to conceal what had occurred from foreign eyes, and were probably no more willing to expose the events to their own subjects. To do so would surely have provided grist for the mills of dissidents, and it could well have raised questions much more widely about the allegedly reformed nature of the post-Stalin order. To publicize a strike so massive as to require six of the party's top leaders to fly to the scene and large military forces to be called up could serve no positive end. Confining the trial to the area whose residents already knew about the strike, holding the proceedings before a select audience, depicting the defendants in the most repulsive way, and meting out frightful punishments might make the best of a bad situation. In fact, Ivashutin (wishfully) claimed several times that the trial had produced a "great educative and prophylactic effect" on the people of Novocherkassk.

The KGB inquiry into the disorders had already begun on June 3, with twenty-six agency officers participating in the investigation. The indictment was drawn up July 11 in Rostov by Lieutenant Colonel Shchebetenko, a KGB investigator, and approved and countersigned by the agency's vice president.[16] The fourteen were all charged with violation of Article 79 of the Criminal Code, which is headed "Mass Disorders." It reads in full: "The organization of mass disorders, accompanied by pogroms, acts of destruction, arson and other similar actions, or the direct commission of the aforementioned crimes by participants in them, or the offering by such persons of armed resistance to the authority." Persons convicted of such violations were to be imprisoned for two to fifteen years. Eight of the fourteen (Cherepanov, Korchak, Kuznetsov, Levchenko, Mokrousov, Shubaev, Sotnikov, and Zaitsev) were charged as well with violation of Article 77, "Banditry." It is defined as "the organization of armed bands for the purpose of attacking state or social institutions or enterprises or individual persons, or participation in such bands and attacks committed by them." The punishment mandated was "deprivation of freedom for three to fifteen years with confiscation of property and with or without additional exile for two to five years or death with confiscation of property."

The presiding judge was L. G. Smirnov, the chairman of the RSFSR Supreme Court.[17] As was customary, two "people's assessors" were named judges as well. One of them, A. T. Gruzhin, recounted in 1990 that he had been summoned to party headquarters before the trial and asked how he felt about the case—a procedure undoubtedly designed to ensure a "correct" stance on his part and surely in conflict with the independence of judge and assessors required by the Code of Criminal Procedure. After he had examined the record compiled in the preliminary investigation, he was convinced that the accused were guilty of participation in mass disorders as defined in Article 79 of the Criminal Code. He considered, however, that the accused were not guilty of banditry as defined in Article 77, and expressed his doubts to Smirnov. The latter, who had already brushed aside the assessor's objections on other counts, responded condescendingly: "You are still young," as if to say, "You don't yet understand how things are done." When Gruzhin warned that he would write his own opinion, Smirnov retorted: "Write it, but you will accomplish nothing."[18]

Of the fourteen defendants in the principal trial, thirteen were men; E. P. Levchenko was the lone woman. They ranged in age from twenty-two to forty-five; most were between twenty-two and thirty-two, again an indication of the disproportionately large part played by young people in the events. Of the fourteen, twelve were Russians and two Ukrainians. They stemmed from all parts of the USSR: two from Siberia, another from the Moldavian Republic, still others from Vologda, Nikolaev, Tambov, and Kiev and Rostov oblasts.

Most of them had three to five or six years of schooling, but two had completed nine years. Almost all were factory laborers, both skilled (metalworkers,
lathe operators, and an electrician) and unskilled (a tractor driver and a loader).
The other accused were a diverse lot: a Polytechnical Institute student, a brigade leader on a state farm, a cook in a boarding school, and a guard in the
construction administration. One of the fourteen, Sergei Sotnikov, was a party
member, whose official evaluation had described him as "disciplined in the fulfillment of work, [having] overfulfilled tasks, [being] actively involved in the
social life of his department and [serving as] the commander of his department's druzhinniki."[19] That such a paragon had cast his lot with the strikers
and demonstrators indicates the depth of feeling the reduction in wage rates
and increases in food prices had evoked. Two others among the accused,
Chernykh and Dement'ev, were Komsomol members, and Chernykh was a
member of the leadership of his factory department's Komsomol.

Five of the fourteen had been convicted before, and perhaps it was partly
on this score that they were charged with the most serious offenses. The heads
of the security forces contended that the troubles in Novocherkassk were caused
largely by criminals who inflamed the situation, and exaggerated the number
of the arrestees who had been convicted of earlier crimes. Some perspective on
this matter is in order. Three of the five, it turns out, had been convicted of
embezzlement of state property (though not that alone in one or two cases), a
common practice in a society where compensation was meager.[20] Aleksandr
Bovin, a high-level consultant in the Khrushchev and Brezhnev eras who once
related to Brezhnev how difficult it was for people on low incomes to get by,
was told by his boss: "You don't know what life is like. Nobody lives on their
wages. When I was studying at the technical college we earned extra money by
unloading freight trains. How did we manage? Three bags or a container would
go to them and one to us."[21] Statistics published by the Correctional Labor
Institution (Ispravitel'noe Trudovoe Uchrezhdenie) at the end of the 1970s indicated that one in every four males up to age thirty had been tried for some
offense.[22] S. S. Oganesev, an advocate for Goncharov, one of the accused, remarked in 1990 that the accused were chosen less for their specific acts than
because they were most conspicuous (i.e., turned up in photographs) or had
been convicted in the past.[23]

Rather than detail the specific charges against each of the accused, those leveled against the fourteen are here presented in composite, summary form. Individuals were indicted for initiating and promoting the continuation of the

strike at NEVZ and elsewhere, setting the factory whistle going, producing the agitational placard attached atop the power-line pole, bursting into the gas depot with the intention of cutting off the flow of fuel, calling for the seizure of the state bank and the post and telegraph offices (a charge the strikers denied), denouncing Khrushchev and heaping opprobrium and occasional blows on the local Communists and the intrusive soldiers, calling for the liberation of detainees thought to be in the police station and then invading that building, forcing their way into the gorkom, engaging in vandalism, and making inflammatory speeches from its balcony.[24] In sum, they were charged with engaging in a strike, participating in a demonstration, and a few of them with having perpetrated some collateral violence. They were charged, in short, with the sort of labor actions the Soviet authorities enthusiastically applauded when they were committed in a capitalist country.

Words pronounced by the strikers were cited against them by witnesses during the preliminary investigation, and undoubtedly were repeated during the trial. Their exclamations offer glimpses into how they viewed their world. In the struggle for support of the strike, one announced: "Anyone who goes to work is a fascist." Korchak called workers who would not come out "traitors," in contradistinction to those who, he said, risked their lives. On June 1, near the Lokomotivstroi railroad station, Kuznetsov, who appears to have been inebriated, shouted: "Forward! We must . . . destroy everything so they'll know our strength." When vehicles carrying soldiers came to the factory area, Katkov declared: "Here is your soviet democracy, they're going to smother [*dushit'*] the working class." Zaitsev rebuked the soldiers: "What are you doing here? The workers have come with their demands, and you have no business here." To encourage his fellows, Sluzhenko (falsely) claimed that the workers at Rostselmash, the great agricultural machinery plant in Rostov, were striking. Kuznetsov urged: "Make sausage out of Khrushchev," and after the shooting warned some soldiers: "We'll deal with you tomorrow." Korchak, the most articulate of the lot, railed against the sending of aid to less developed countries while Soviet workers lacked necessities. In answer to someone who contended that the price increases were only temporary, he cried: "We've been deceived for forty-five years, not allowed to speak out . . . let them imprison me but I will not remain silent." Mokrousov, having determined that an officer accompanying his delegation to Mikoyan and Kozlov was a party member, said derisively: "No use talking to him, he's a Communist." After the shooting at the square, one called the soldiers "murderers, fascists, and traitors." Shubaev shouted:

"Hang the Communists!" and allegedly pleaded with the soldiers to turn their guns on "those who compel you to fire on the people."[25]

A telling feature of the investigation was the makeup of the witness cohort, which numbered seventy persons. The overwhelming majority of those who testified against the strikers were party or Komsomol members, joined by numbers of police and military officers, and a very light sprinkling of nonparty people. At this level, most conspicuously, the trial was an unambiguous case of the Communist Party versus the workers. Typically, testifying against Shubaev were three party members and one candidate, two Komsomols, one sergeant, one captain, and one nonparty worker; against Kuznetsov, four party members, two Komsomols, and one nonparty individual; against Mokrousov, two party and six Komsomol members. The sole exception involved Korchak, against whom eight party members, one Komsomol, and six nonparty people testified.[26]

This exception to the rule stems from the fact that, in the eyes of the authorities, Korchak was the most formidable opponent and therefore the one it was most important to discredit. He was respected by his fellow workers, who considered him an authoritative person and addressed him by his name and patronymic. When he declared in his department that the men should strike, a large number laid down their tools. He also succeeded in bringing out the workers of other departments. In short, he was a genuine leader. Moreover, he was not one to cringe before the powerful. When they spoke of "hooligans" who came to his department to seek support, he insisted that he had seen no hooligans, only a delegation of workers. He refused to name his fellow strikers. In the preliminary investigation he denied guilt under Articles 77 and 79 of the Criminal Code, and admitted only that he had joined the strike out of solidarity with the NEVZ workers. Korchak testified that he had threatened no one and had not resorted to force; he denied any involvement in hooligan activity. Fifteen witnesses were called against him, twice as many as against most other defendants; and, to bolster the government's effort to defame him, it was no doubt considered essential to find more than a token number of nonparty people to testify against him.[27]

In the preliminary investigation, all those indicted initially denied the charges. Each was then confronted with many witnesses, who confirmed the activities the accused had allegedly committed. After that, all but two, Korchak and the student Dement'ev, reportedly confessed to all or most of the particulars raised against them, and repented what they had done.[28] Three of the defendants (Zaitsev, Kuznetsov, and Sotnikov) attributed their behavior to heavy drinking.

The accused in criminal cases had an opportunity toward the end of a trial to pronounce his or her "final words." Brief statements found here and there were in all likelihood drawn from the final words of several of the defendants. A KGB report quoted the self-abasing pronouncements of two confessions: Shcherban declared: "I consider my actions a crime against the fatherland, and I repent." Said Shubaev: "I condemn my criminal acts and profoundly repent before the Supreme Court. I understand now that [the soldiers] shot not at innocent people but at pogromists and hooligans, and they were right to shoot." Sotnikov, the former party member, explained that the workers had been brought to despair by their cheerless existence, and begged the judges to save his life. "I have always been proud that my father died in the war as a hero. . . . It is bitter for me to realize that my children will think of me as an executed bandit." Four others (Korchak, Zaitsev, Levchenko, and Mokrousov) who attempted to mitigate their guilt were exposed by witnesses as "out-and-out criminals, self-seekers, and morally degraded people."

Quite surprisingly, a KGB report to the highest authorities claims that Korchak ultimately admitted his guilt. Besides, it was said at a meeting of the Novocherkassk party activists, Korchak stated that none of the honest workers followed him, and that he was part of an insignificant group of rioters and hooligans. Because this assertion is so out of keeping with the character of the man, one is impelled to think that if physical pressure was applied to anyone, he was its most likely target. The experience of a person involved in one of the lesser trials suggests an alternative explanation, that assertions of admission of guilt could be fictitious. Some time after he had been convicted, A. I. Prankin protested in a letter to the authorities that he had been reported at the trial as having confessed his guilt, but he denied that this was so.[29] The same turns out to have been true in Korchak's case. An official document composed three years later remarked that Korchak "did not acknowledge that he was guilty."[30]

One can only speculate as to reasons for the confessions. Beginning in 1960, a confession alone was considered insufficient for conviction. But the principle established by Andrei Vyshinsky, that "a confession was the best result attainable," evidently remained in effect, despite the fact that the prosecutor of the great purge trial of 1938 had been discredited.[31] Unquestionably, the prosecution sought to obtain confessions, but why did the accused provide what was wanted? Whether it was because the evidence seemed irrefutable, whether physical pressure was applied to secure the confessions, or for some other reason, we cannot say with assurance. A former advocate adduced a number of reasons why innocent people might confess in the course of a preliminary investigation: the investigator would not believe an accused person, particularly if he or she had been convicted of some offense before; every attempt to prove one's innocence was rejected out of hand; the defendant lost hope of convincing the investigator, and gave in to promises that the sentence would be mitigated if a confession was forthcoming.[32] It should be noted, moreover, that the Code of Criminal Procedure gave defense counsel access to defendants only after the preliminary investigation was completed—a circumstance certainly disadvantageous to an accused individual subject to relentless interrogation.

A baffling problem still remains: how were confessions obtained with respect to the charge of banditry, when the activities attributed to the defendants were flagrantly at odds with the Criminal Code's definition of this crime? Let us recall what Article 77 of the Criminal Code stipulates: "the organization of armed bands for the purpose of attacking state or social institutions . . . or participation in such bands." But there were no armed bands, and no witnesses in the preliminary investigation testified to their presence. It is certainly worth noting, too, that this article prescribed alternative punishments, one for a prison term of three to fifteen years, the other for execution. Despite the fact that no armed bands had been organized, the court chose to bypass the lesser punishment and inflict the extreme penalty. Only one explanation is possible: the party leaders had resolved that political considerations should take precedence over the law. More than alarmed by what had occurred at Novocherkassk, the Presidium must have demanded the extreme penalty. For that reason, Rudenko had charged eight of the strikers under Article 77, and then demanded the death penalty rather than the lesser punishment. The judges had no choice but to comply with his demand. If the penalties inflicted on the other defendants might conceivably be justified by reference to Article 79—punishments prescribed under Soviet law were notoriously harsh—for those condemned to death this was a kangaroo court.

The accused were all convicted of inciting mass disorders, and the eight accused of banditry as well were judged guilty of that offense. Seven of the eight were condemned to death, and the lone woman among them—surprisingly, because it was her incitement that had brought forth the first shootings—to twelve years of imprisonment. All the others were sentenced to ten to fifteen years in severe-regime correctional labor camps.[33] (Their terms were later com-

TABLE 2

Names, Ages, Occupations, and Sentences of Defendants
in Principal Trial, RSFSR Supreme Court

Defendant	Age	Occupation	Sentence
V. D. Cherepanov	26	Metalworker, mining machinery factory	Death
V. I. Chernykh	24	Metalworker, NEVZ	12 years
Iu. P. Dement'ev	27	Student, Polytechnical Institute	15 years
G. A. Goncharov	22	Metalworker, NEVZ	10 years
G. G. Katkov	36	Tractor driver, electrode plant	11 years
A. A. Korchak	45	Electrician, electrode factory	Death
M. A. Kuznetsov	28	Metalworker, electrode factory	Death
E. P. Levchenko	27	Guard	12 years
B. N. Mokrousov	39	Machine-building factory	Death
G. M. Shcherban	27	Assembly worker, Neftemash	10 years
V. G. Shubaev	25	School cook	Death
I. P. Sluzhenko	32	Loader	12 years
S. S. Sotnikov	25	Lathe operator, NEVZ	Death
A. F. Zaitsev	35	Brigade leader, state farm	Death

SOURCE: *KD*, 29–30.

muted to shorter periods.) The information at our disposal suggests that the prosecutor pressed the case against the strikers relentlessly and with a generous seasoning of vituperation. Those in the dock were painted in the darkest colors—as morally degraded, among other things—to leave no trace of a doubt that they should be destroyed or banished. To that end, a number of points were emphasized: that the accused were all criminals—actually, only five of the fourteen had criminal records—and the dastardly acts they had recently perpetrated were but the latest, though the most reprehensible, of their criminal activities; second, that two of the accused (Korchak and Katkov) were detestable parasites—they ranted about the poor living conditions of the workers while they themselves were well off. They were said to possess their own homes and dachas, and one owned an automobile, the other a motorcycle. (There was some exaggeration here, but the two *were* relatively well off because they were better educated and more skilled than their fellows.) The prosecutor apparently sought to exploit envy in the mass of spectators in the courtroom.

Third, the prosecution aimed to elicit outrage against the group for the effort one or two of its members had made to cut off the fuel at the gas depot. Had this maneuver succeeded, it was argued, it would have inflicted a severe financial loss on the state, put many of the workforce out of work for a time, and possibly have caused a devastating explosion.[34] Forcefully advancing such themes, the prosecutor whipped up a lynch-law atmosphere in the courtroom. The KGB reported that many workers in attendance expressed the opinion that the "criminals" did not deserve an investigation and trial but should be shot forthwith. One who attended a session of the trial noted that the proceeding was "often interrupted by applause in honor of witnesses who are unmasking the criminals." Rather than discourage outbursts of the kind for the sake of decorum, such interventions from the audience were welcomed. The announcement of the court's decision at the conclusion of the trial "was met with lengthy applause in the crowded hall."[35]

During and after the trial, communications sent to the uppermost party and state organizations included numerous quotations indicating the highly favorable sentiments of the audiences. Said one: "We are struggling in our division to earn the title 'brigade of communist labor,' and these parasites think about creating riots." Another hyperbolically spoke of these "bandits" as having been condemned three or four times and married six or seven times. Two characterized the accused as "skunks," one declaring that they should "be isolated from society and punished in the most severe manner"; the second, after the verdict was announced, that they got what they deserved, "to teach others a lesson." "They went against their brothers and fathers," one worker mystifyingly contended. "It's right that they should be shot." Not wasting words, another declaimed: "A dog's death to the dogs!"[36]

One might suppose that the quotations were concocted by the KGB to assuage the anxieties of the leaders whom they were addressing. This is definitely not the case, as reports of party meetings held in the course of the trial make clear. Whether at the direction of the top party leadership or not, the local leaders of the CPSU organized meetings on a daily basis concurrently with the trial. Each gathering brought together party members who had attended a session of the trial, giving them an opportunity to vent their sentiments. The meetings sometimes began with assurances by the local leadership that the great majority endorsed the price increases, that those who opposed them had no social support whatsoever. Then individuals, mostly workers from different enterprises who had attended some portion of the hearings, offered their opinions. Their remarks emphasized how shocked they were by the disorders, and by the disrespect of the "criminals" and "hooligans" for all that had been achieved in the Soviet Union. (At a meeting on June 4, immediately after the shootings, one Communist worker had indignantly blurted out: "A strike is a disgraceful thing.") Now, rising one after another, all the speakers violently denounced the accused and demanded that they be shot. One condemned the strikers as "the dregs of society, people without conscience or honor," for giving themselves out as "real workers." Those "villains" and "enemies of the people" should be put up against the wall. The head of a factory committee at the electrode plant exclaimed scornfully: "Instigating disorder, rioting in the city, repelling local authorities, the vile scoundrels conducted themselves insolently and 'heroically'; but before the court they behaved like pitiful lambs, tried to soften their guilt and escape punishment." "How disturbing it was," a woman fumed, "that among these evil and dangerous criminals were young people born in 1938 and 1940. How they became so abominable is beyond understanding; so let them be subject to the most severe punishment of Soviet law." [37]

These were statements of the faithful, of course, and they were mouthed formulaically. Those pronouncing the words knew what they were expected to say, but whether the words corresponded to their inner feelings we shall never know. In all probability, these vindictive outbursts echoed what the speakers had heard from the mouth of the prosecutor. The worker who demanded "a dog's death for the dogs" may have been paraphrasing the prosecutor; unwittingly, almost echoing Vyshinsky's demand in the 1938 trial of Nikolai Bukharin and others that "the enemy must be shot like dirty dogs." [38] It is doubtful that the people who called for blood knew anything about the content of Article 77, and that to inflict the death penalty meant grossly to violate the law.

A large number of the more than a hundred others who were convicted were sent to severe-regime camps in Siberia. Upon their arrival, prisoners who were already there quickly dubbed the newcomers "the Decembrists from Novocherkassk." [39]

Chapter 6   Anatomy of a Cover-Up

Phase 1: 1962–1988

The Soviet government, determined to keep news of this extremely damaging occurrence from getting out, put in place an effective multifaceted cover-up. The local KGB went into action almost as soon as the strike erupted. Moscow learned of the strike quickly, and 140 agents from Kiev, Leningrad, and elsewhere were dispatched to Novocherkassk.[1] They penetrated wherever militant strikers were in action, observing, recording, and photographing. The most immediate task envisaged was to keep the strike localized by preventing information about it from spreading. While it was in progress, to block possible transmissions both internally and abroad by local amateur radio operators, five counterespionage cars equipped with radio-locating capability were rushed to the scene.[2] All roads leading out of the city were closed, and telephone communication with the outside world was cut off. A Soviet engineer who was in Novocherkassk on business when the strike erupted confided to an American resident in Moscow that he had been unable to leave the city for three weeks.[3] A Novocherkassk taxi driver told me of the difficulty his family had—he was then a youngster—in regaining admission to their home town upon returning from a vacation in the Baltic region.

Immediately after the shooting, men in plain clothes loaded the bodies into trucks and drove them away. Fire engines that had been stationed nearby entered the square and hosed away the blood. According to some reports, a fresh coat of asphalt was laid down to cover up traces of the blood that could not be removed.[4] To avoid what would have been a massive and probably explosive public funeral, the bodies of the dead were secretly buried at night at places well removed from Novocherkassk.

The physicians who examined the victims and those who buried the corpses

106

were compelled to pledge that they would never reveal what they knew.[5] Terrorized by the slaughter and the draconian punishments inflicted on those brought to trial, the local people sought to distance themselves from what had happened. A woman who was injured at the square reported that friends asked her not to come to their homes, for fear of difficulties they might suffer if they were associated with her. A worker who had seen a man wounded during the June days began to speak about it when they met some years later, but the man interrupted and asked him not to tell anyone about it.[6] After those who had been imprisoned for a number of years were released, they were warned periodically to refrain from talking about the events.

Readers of the Soviet press could have learned nothing whatever about the strike and its suppression. The media assured their readers that the country had received the news of the price increases with understanding and approval. Shortly after Bloody Saturday, the Novocherkassk daily, *Znamia kommuny*, ran a full front page headed: "Workers of Novocherkassk approve measures adopted by party and government for rapid growth of animal-husbandry products." The letters and articles arrayed below the headline, written by two factory workers, an institute teacher, and the director of a dining-hall trust, bore the labels: "Now It Is Necessary," "Unanimity," "Our Labor Contribution," and "The Measures Taken Are Correct." The newspaper's readers were bombarded with similar messages for many days. The June 4 and 5 issues of *Pravda* "demonstrated" that these sentiments were shared throughout the country by printing applauding letters from Novocherkassk, Tashkent, Kazakhstan, Leningrad, the Kharkov region, Stavropol, Frunze, Baku, the Lithuanian Soviet Republic, and Ukraine. The June 4 issue also signaled international support for the new policy with items from (Communist) newspapers in London, Prague, and Budapest, affirming the soundness of the Soviet price rises.[7]

On June 4 the head of the KGB reported directly to Khrushchev on measures his organization was taking: "The spread of rumors about the Novocherkassk events is being restricted, and various provocative conjectures connected with them are being suppressed. We are giving special attention to correspondence, trains coming from Rostov, markets, and places where the public gathers."[8] Top-level officials believed, not without reason, that the cover-up was effective. Long after the fact, Vladimir Solodin, the chief of the Soviet literary censorship organization (Glavlit), revealed that his organization was "required not to allow into print matter that disinforms the public"—a euphemism for things people should not know. The principle "functioned marvelously," in his opinion, until the Chernobyl incident in 1986. "Even major events such as the firing on demonstrators in Novocherkassk were known to very few people. They knew something, heard that some sort of trouble had occurred. But no one knew anything for sure, not how many were dead, not how many participated in this affair, and so forth." [9]

With the Cold War in full cry, their adversaries were as eager to discover news hurtful to the USSR as the Soviet authorities were to conceal it. And, as Mme de Staël reportedly observed long ago, "In Russia everything is secret, but there are no secrets." Tens of thousands of people in the Novocherkassk region, including Rostov and other nearby towns, knew something of the events. After a while, residents of the region were free to travel elsewhere; and relatives, friends, and others from other parts of the country could come in and out of the southern Russian towns. Given so porous an interface, no matter how reluctant many people were to talk, a good deal was bound to seep out. With so many Soviet citizens aware that something dreadful had occurred at Novocherkassk, foreigners in the USSR were bound to hear about it too.

Aleksandr Solzhenitsyn erred when he wrote: "No one abroad got to know about Novocherkassk, there were no Western broadcasts to inform us of it." [10] Almost two months did go by, however, before the foreign press had an inkling of what had happened, and four before a skeletal and moderately accurate account appeared. The first item to come out, in *Paris-Presse* on July 27, was on the mark in some ways but wildly off in regard to the outcome. It told of a strike at a locomotive factory in Novocherkassk, set off by the announcement of steep price increases on meat and butter and reductions in wage rates. Faced with unbending resistance by the workers, the government was compelled to retreat: it suspended the price increases, restored the old wage rates, and fired the objectionable factory director. Consistent with this rendition, the story was headlined "A Strike Succeeds in a Soviet Factory," and the episode was represented as "an example of the liberalism of the Soviet government." With unintended irony, the article concludes: "In the USSR, this story is viewed as a fairy tale."

A week or so later, a flurry of very brief notices about more serious trouble at Novocherkassk came out. *Posev*, a Russian-language anticommunist newspaper published in Frankfurt, claimed on August 5 that strikes had spread from Novocherkassk throughout the Donbass. The *London Telegraph* (Aug. 7) came closer to the truth with a story (picked up by *Le Monde* the following day) headlined "Russians Killed in Food Riots." [11] A *New York Herald Tribune* story, datelined Moscow, August 8, inaugurated the numbers game—it would long endure—with a suggestion that Western sources considered reports of 800 casualties near Rostov "irresponsible." A much more circumstantial report from Washington by Max Frankel appeared in the *New York Times* on October 8. His report, as well as a shorter piece in the *Herald Tribune* the next day, was based on remarks made at a press conference by Lincoln White, spokesman for the U.S. State Department. White's comments clearly derived from dispatches sent to Washington by the U.S. embassy in Moscow.

The two organizations most interested in ferreting out information about Soviet difficulties were the U.S. embassy in Moscow and Radio Liberty. On July 27, the same day the *Paris-Presse* article appeared, the first of a series of memoranda relating to Novocherkassk was composed for the ambassador by R. T. Davies, the embassy's first secretary. The importance attached to the matter is indicated both by the repeated attention given—there were follow-up reports by Davies dated August 10 and 17 and October 19, and memoranda by others dated August 3 and 14—and the forwarding of copies not only to the Department of State but also to the U.S. embassies in London, Paris, Rome, Bonn, and Vienna, and also to Munich (the site of Radio Liberty), Frankfurt, and Berlin. The first report, the details of which Davies characterized as "scarce and vague," was based on information provided by "a reliable Western correspondent in Moscow with good contacts among Soviet citizens." From what he learned from several persons, he had pieced together a brief account of a serious disturbance in Novocherkassk, but was uncertain whether fatalities had occurred. The report signaled that something important, warranting further investigation, had happened there.

However, it quickly became known that the area had been sealed off: a scheduled visit to Rostov by a U.S. farm delegation was canceled, as were visits by some U.S. tourists, U.S. students at Kiev, and a Princeton professor. One reason given for barring travel to Rostov was that the roof of a major hotel there had collapsed and was under repair. The students were kept away, they were told, because a large international meeting was to be held in Rostov in late July–early August, so rooms would not be available. Most consistently, Soviet officials emphasized the necessity of quarantining the area because it had been stricken by a cholera epidemic. The embassy staff suspected that the quarantine was a pretext to bar outsiders; and the suspicion was confirmed when *Pravda* (Aug. 7) reported an influx of more than 2,000 boys and girls to Rostov for a five-day all-union athletic event (a *spartakiada*). Nor did the "quarantine" prevent the Rostov soccer team from playing a match in Moscow on August 10, also reported in *Pravda* (Aug. 11).[12]

Although there was no possibility of obtaining firsthand information, embassy personnel managed to learn more by closely examining newspapers, both central and local (Novocherkassk and Rostov). They saw evidence of trouble in a *Pravda* report (June 9) on a meeting of party activists in Rostov, featuring a good deal of vigorous self-criticism apropos of the weakening of links between some party organizations and the masses and a "disdainful attitude toward the needs and questions of the toilers." They were intrigued by published information that Kozlov, Khrushchev's second in command, had somehow been involved in the Novocherkassk events. And when *Pravda* announced the ousting of Basov, first secretary of the Rostov region party committee and a full member of the Central Committee, they viewed his dismissal as "the strongest evidence" that something of major consequence had happened in the area over which he had presided.[13]

It seems odd that the *Times* story published on October 8 should have come from Washington. Frankel, who had spent many years as the *Times* correspondent in Moscow, filed a story that one might have expected to be posted by his successor in Moscow, Seymour Topping. According to Whitman Bassow, then the *Newsweek* correspondent in Moscow, the embassy shared such information as it possessed on the matter with U.S. journalists, but they were reluctant to use it for fear of the consequences.[14] This consideration could have seemed especially significant to Bassow, who was expelled from the USSR in mid-August 1962 for having written "crudely slanderous dispatches about the Soviet Union, which have evoked the righteous indignation of Soviet public opinion." Probably more important, as late as August 10, Davies was writing to Washington: "What may have happened in Novocherkassk on June 1 [*sic*] cannot, at present, be established in detail and beyond a doubt." Responsible journalists could hardly be blamed for failing to send dispatches based on rather shaky evidence, especially after Bassow was expelled.[15] On the other hand, information released at a press conference in Washington, even though it could not "be established in detail and beyond a doubt," might serve a national purpose without jeopardizing the correspondents in Moscow. Frankel's report reflected the uncertainties of the embassy: it contained errors of omission and commission; it gave no hint of the mass arrests, the trials, and their harsh outcomes.

The sort of restraints that may have worked on U.S. and other Western correspondents in Moscow did not operate on Radio Liberty, based outside the

Soviet Union, in Munich. An instrument of U.S. policy in the Cold War, it possessed an ample research staff; and it followed troublesome developments in the USSR more closely and was better informed than the U.S. embassy in Moscow. If the Soviet censorship's mission was to keep a lid on "matter that disinforms the public," Radio Liberty's task was to inform that same public of matter the Soviet government wished to keep secret. Not surprisingly, then, the organization became intensely interested in the Novocherkassk events. As its files show, its personnel did an impressive job of picking up every possible scrap of information: scourings from Soviet media and from the Western press as well; dispatches from the U.S. embassy in Moscow; and conversations with tourists who had visited Russia and Soviet citizens who traveled abroad.[16] It had the resources to collate the materials collected into coherent, if rather carefully hedged, reports.

Through the month of August the station had broadcast fragmentary accounts based on the reports in the European press. Meanwhile, its researchers had gathered a good deal of background and contextual data by a sensitive reading of the April through July issues of the Novocherkassk newspaper. As these materials were combined with evidence from other sources, the picture of what had occurred began to come into focus. The excitement generated was palpable as the text to be broadcast was read and commented on by various staff members.[17] At last, on September 10, 1962, a fairly lengthy newscast—the script fills two single-spaced pages—was beamed to the USSR. With a view to reaching as many people as possible, the report was broadcast in Russian and sixteen other Soviet languages, and not just once but around the clock. The report was evidently based on a more considerable paper produced by Albert Boiter, then Radio Liberty's director of research. How many people actually heard the broadcast will never be known, but it must have reached some of those for whom it was intended.

Over the next dozen years or so, little information about the Novocherkassk events appeared either in the USSR or abroad. What did appear was mostly a rehash of what would already have been known to anyone seriously interested in the subject. For example, a brief notice from Paris by Philip Ben, headlined "Pressure on Khrushchev," came out in the *New Republic* edition of March 9, 1963. An issue of *Problems of Communism* published at the beginning of 1964 included an article by Boiter on labor unrest in the Soviet Union, whose centerpiece was an account of the Novocherkassk upheaval much like the one he had composed in September 1962.[18] Although its data were not new, this piece was important for making available outside the Soviet Union what had been gleaned on the subject by the then most knowledgeable individual in the West. However, it is remarkable how little attention was given this piece, or the Novocherkassk story in general, in serious works published in the next several years. When in 1967 the distinguished French journalist Michel Tatu published a massive tome titled *Power in the Kremlin: From Khrushchev to Kosygin*—it concentrates on the years 1960–66—he devoted only a couple of footnotes to Novocherkassk. Incredibly, given its focus, one looks in vain for anything on the subject in Mary McAuley's 1969 monograph, *Labor Disputes in Soviet Russia, 1957–1965.*[19] Robert Conquest offers nothing on the matter in the body of his *Industrial Workers in the USSR* (1967), although he has a few words about it in the Preface.

Only in the years 1973–76, with the appearance of *The Gulag Archipelago*, was the affair again given a notable airing—indeed, the most significant thus far, and for the next dozen years or so as well.[20] A couple of brief treatments had been published in rather obscure places in the preceding years. In a memoir by John Kolasky, a former Communist leader in Canada who heard about the affair during a period he spent in Ukraine, it figures as one of the causes of his disillusionment with the Soviet regime.[21] His account was drawn upon in an interesting article analyzing the situation of labor in the Soviet Union.[22] Solzhenitsyn reportedly had gone to Novocherkassk at some point to investigate an event that seemingly fired his imagination when he heard about it.[23] His account indicates that he found well-informed eyewitnesses who were willing to tell what they knew. Understandably, then, his account is far superior to Boiter's, and not only in the amplitude of detail it offers. Solzhenitsyn was the first writer to describe accurately the terrain on which the events occurred, and the first to get the chronology right. He traces various stages of the strike action, including the train stoppage, efforts to spread the strike, and the June 2 march to the city. He reports the arrest of thirty people during the night of June 1–2, and the subsequent efforts of their fellows to liberate them. He notes (not quite correctly) that six members of the Central Committee rushed to Novocherkassk, that a delegation of workers conferred with them after the shooting, and that both Kozlov and Mikoyan made radio speeches. He appears to have been the first writer to realize that a series of trials were held and death penalties imposed. His literary skill enabled him to shape the abundant data at his disposal into the most vivid account of the June days yet to appear.

Like all its predecessors, however, Solzhenitsyn's account contains a good many errors. Reference has already been made to his assertion that no one abroad knew about Novocherkassk, and that no Western broadcast dealt with it. The six who went from Moscow to Novocherkassk were not simply Central Committee members: four—Kozlov, Mikoyan, Kirilenko, and Polianskii— sat in the Presidium; and two—Shelepin and Ilychev—were major party secretaries. The authenticity of his portrayal of the events obviously depended on the reliability of the testimony he obtained. But the knowledgeable informants with whom Solzhenitsyn spoke were not fully informed. Unwittingly they relayed to him as facts—and he in turn relayed to his readers—what were actually only widespread rumors, which we now know to be false: that an officer had committed suicide in front of his men rather than order them to fire on the demonstrators; that a volley fired over the heads of the crowd massed in the square killed a number of boys perched in nearby trees to get a better view; that seventy or eighty persons in all were killed, forty-seven of them by dumdum bullets; that the families of the victims were exiled to Siberia.

The Gulag Archipelago was first published in Paris by the YMCA Press, in the original language (1973). A German translation appeared the same year, and an English one in 1974–78. It had a wide readership. One need not agree with Solzhenitsyn's hyperbolic estimate of the significance of the Novocherkassk eruption—"We can say without exaggeration that this was a turning point in the history of modern Russia"—to appreciate how signally his account increased its visibility. For some years it would serve as the authoritative reference for anyone concerned with the subject.

Still, so far as I have been able to determine, writing on Novocherkassk between Solzhenitsyn's treatment and the advent of glasnost was meager. In 1979 the editors of a pamphlet on labor disturbances in the USSR pointedly noted that *Pravda* had recently played up the execrable behavior of agents of the U.S. ruling class against workers in the Haymarket affair of 1886—Chicago police had fired wildly at people attending a demonstration, wounding scores, and seven workers were subsequently sentenced to be hanged—while never uttering a word about an incident much closer to home. These editors issued an underground leaflet in May 1977 to mark the fifteenth anniversary of the Novocherkassk massacre, which some eighty-five dissidents had signed. After a short (and faulty) recounting of the events, it concluded: "These deaths must never be forgotten or forgiven! We call for June 2 to be a day of remembrance of the victims of despotism, a day of struggle against the bloody official terror!" Earlier the pamphlet declared: "If it had not been for the persistent, courageous work of Aleksandr Solzhenitsyn . . . the world would not have known anything about [the events] to this day." Fittingly, the editors also reprinted a substantial portion of *The Gulag Archipelago*'s treatment of Novocherkassk.[24]

Obviously Solzhenitsyn's revelations clandestinely reached the Soviet Union and were appropriated by and lent momentum to the dissident movement. Among the signers of the leaflet were Maj. Gen. Petr Grigorenko and his wife, Zinaida, and Andrei Sakharov and his wife, Elena Bonner.[25] The leaflet was composed by Grigorenko, who in 1963 had formed the Union of Struggle for the Revival of Leninism. Not long after, he was stripped of his rank, expelled from the party, and confined for fifteen months in a psychiatric hospital. After his release, he devoted his life to the defense of human rights so relentlessly and selflessly that he was said to have done more than any other individual to inspire the groups that made up the democratic movement.[26] Grigorenko had written the leaflet ("The Dispersal by Shooting of the Workers' Demonstration in Novocherkassk") on the basis of information related to him by an acquaintance who had been there. His intention, of course, was to publicize what he viewed as the dastardly action of a repressive regime, made worse by the cover-up. KGB agents arrested him after raiding his apartment in Moscow and finding copies of the offensive document.[27] It is impossible to know how wide a distribution the leaflet enjoyed, but it is safe to say that awareness of the Novocherkassk events was henceforth a matter of vital concern to the dissident movement and a major item in its bill of particulars against the Soviet order.[28]

Phase 2: 1988–1993

In his first speech after assuming the post of general secretary of the CPSU in March 1985, M. S. Gorbachev pronounced the word *glasnost'*. Openness would perform an instrumental function, he explained, for "the more informed people are, the more consciously they will act, the more actively they will support the Party, its plans, and its fundamental goals."[29] Gorbachev's statement appears to be a startling reversal of the well-known predilection of the party-state for tight control of information as an essential condition of its existence. Unaware of the contradiction or, more likely, intending to expand but still limit the release of information to the public, he supposed that this course would be helpful in fighting debilitating corruption, inefficient management, and an unresponsive bureaucracy. Gorbachev set the tone with increasingly sharp attacks on the Brezhnev era, now castigated as an era of stagnation and corruption. However, strict limits on openness remained in place yet a while, giving way only after the Chernobyl nuclear catastrophe in April 1986. Information about the disaster was released haltingly and piecemeal, failing to reach the front page of *Pravda* until two weeks after the explosion. This event severely undermined the people's confidence in their rulers and shattered the complacency of the governing structures. Critics were now emboldened to press their views. Gorbachev's government was all but forced to loosen controls, and what began as a modest flow developed into a torrent of criticism. Far from helping the party to carry out its plans and meet its fundamental goals, glasnost would play a central role in discrediting and bringing down the Soviet regime.

In the two years after Chernobyl, a series of sensational developments took place. Toward the end of 1986, Sakharov was released from administrative exile, and the Georgian-made film *Repentance*, about a vicious dictator reminiscent of Stalin, was also released. Khrushchev's famous denunciation of Stalin at the 20th Party Congress in 1956 was at last published in the Soviet Union in 1987. The jamming of BBC and Voice of America broadcasts was discontinued. Around the same time, Gorbachev declared there ought to be no "blank spots" in Soviet history or literature. Key members of the intelligentsia eagerly responded to the challenge, with remarkable results. Nikolai Bukharin, Grigorii Zinoviev, Lev Kamenev, and Karl Radek, Old Bolsheviks who had been branded as enemies of the people and been condemned to death in Stalin's notorious purge trials, were declared innocent and rehabilitated posthumously, while Andrei Vyshinsky, Stalin's prosecutor, was denounced. Works of Boris Pasternak (*Doctor Zhivago*) and Anna Akhmatova (*Requiem*), writers who had been subjected to ferocious abuse, were brought out to acclaim in 1988. Even more surprising, two of the most pungent anti-Soviet novels produced in the West, Arthur Koestler's *Darkness at Noon* and George Orwell's *Animal Farm*, appeared in Soviet editions.[30] In 1988 the officially atheist Soviet Union celebrated the thousandth anniversary of Christianity's advent in Russia. Mirabile dictu, in 1989–90 Solzhenitsyn's monumental exposure of the atrocities committed in his homeland, *The Gulag Archipelago*, appeared in Moscow.

With the repudiation of so many measures of the Soviet regime proceeding apace, sooner or later the Novocherkassk story was bound to come out. Two circumstances may have stood in the way for a time. It was the central press that showed initiative in digging up revelations, while the provincial press lagged well behind. Yet, as it turned out, the lead in bringing the Novocher-kassk events to light was to be taken at the local level. Also, during the first few years of the Gorbachev era, reform-minded people inside the government and out were bent on destroying the image of Stalin; meanwhile, the reformers were celebrating Khrushchev, who had initiated the assault on the dictator, as the precursor of the perestroika program then under way. For that reason, per-haps, they were inclined to avert their eyes from one of the most discreditable events of his years in power. The breakthrough finally came toward the middle of 1988.

The exposure of the cover-up owed far more to Petr Petrovich Siuda, the son of an Old Bolshevik who in 1937 had died in the purges, than any other individual. He had been involved in the strike, was arrested early on the sec-ond day, was put on trial along with the others, and was sentenced to twelve years of imprisonment.[31] Despite his absence from the Saturday massacre, Siuda would become the chronicler of "the Novocherkassk tragedy." After his arrest but before his dispatch to a labor camp in Siberia, and in the camp as well, he spent a good deal of time with activists who had lived through what he had missed. From them he zealously gleaned all possible evidence, check-ing and rechecking the details for the sake of an accurate reconstruction of the story. Beginning in 1989, when it had become possible to publish articles for-merly prohibited, he managed to get several pieces printed, though in rather inconspicuous places.[32] They were brief, and each one told much the same story, more or less elaborated. More important, with efforts under way to fill in the "blank spots" decried by Gorbachev, Siuda was frequently interviewed by investigative reporters and was widely quoted in the progressive press. In a dramatic case of "the return of the repressed," for the first time a participant in a massive yet long-concealed strike described what had happened—and from the perspective of the strikers. As an editorial introduction to one of his pieces put it, "Because the official press had suppressed the story for almost three decades, the few testimonies by participants in the events are all the more valuable."[33] Later many other participants were located and what they recalled was recorded, but none came close to matching Siuda's depiction in extent, coherence, and clarity. Moreover, because Siuda had attained a degree of his-torical and political understanding, he was able to make the Novocherkassk upheaval more meaningful.

Siuda's agitation did not commence with the publication of his articles. Be-ginning in December 1987, with letters addressed to the Central Committee of the CPSU, the Presidium of the Supreme Soviet, and the Supreme Court, he launched an intensive campaign for the reconsideration of what had occurred and the rehabilitation of the victims. In March 1988 he quit his job to devote himself full-time to this cause. Predictably, he ran into official obstruction everywhere. Perhaps more disappointing, although perestroika was under way, even those families whose members had been slain or incarcerated would not assist him for fear of reprisals.[34]

Unbowed by these rebuffs, he went to Moscow, where the atmosphere was less constrained, to press his case in every possible venue. In April, at a discussion meeting of the Soviet Committee for the Defense of Peace, for the first time he publicly laid out his story. He arranged to have an abbreviated version of his memoirs circulated as samizdat. Just before President Ronald Reagan and Secretary of State George Shultz visited Russia to confer with Gorbachev, he passed copies of his writing to officials at the U.S. embassy, along with a request that the rehabilitation of the victims of the Novocherkassk tragedy be taken up in scheduled negotiations with the Soviet government on behalf of human rights. He also endeavored—with some success, as will shortly become clear—to promote international publicity about Novocherkassk.[35] Finally, he contrived to have articles brought out in such obscure unofficial publications as *Nabat, Levyi povorot*, and *Obshchina*. In May he presented his story to the staffs of a number of central periodicals and to a group of progressive writers.[36]

After returning home, Siuda set out to arouse the citizens of Novocherkassk to protest against what had been inflicted on them or their relatives, forebears, or friends twenty-six years before. In late May and early June, Siuda distributed around town a leaflet bearing the title "On the Novocherkassk Tragedy of '62." It was subsequently made available also in Rostov, Taganrog, Krasnodar, and other towns. The leaflet reviewed the causes of the strike, the unwillingness of the authorities to negotiate with the workers, and the "bloody suppression" of the disturbances. Siuda pointed to all those—the druzhinniki, administration and party officials, police, and detachments of the Novocherkassk garrison— who proved incapable of putting down the strike movement. Consequently, tanks and soldiers of Caucasian nationalities were brought in to force the unarmed, fundamentally nonviolent people into submission. Thus the party-state officialdom was guilty of criminal behavior, which extended to the trials of at least 105 persons (*sic*), with seven sentenced to death and many more to imprisonment, on the basis of fabricated accusations. Even now the number of the slain and their place of burial remained unknown. Likening the Novocherkassk tragedy to Bloody Sunday in 1905 and the Lena gold field massacre of 1912—he would do so repeatedly—Siuda called for the public condemnation of what had been perpetrated and of the persons responsible and for the rehabilitation of the victims.[37]

Siuda's agitation was directed as well at local authorities. He submitted an article to Novocherkassk's newspaper, *Znamia kommuny*, and rebuked its editors for remaining silent about this deplorable happening in the town's history, despite the central government's proclamation of glasnost. To strengthen his bid, he pointed out that he had proposed to write for Moscow publications, distributed many copies of his memoirs in Moscow, and circulated his writings in samizdat. He had spoken at least ten times to meetings of the Soviet Committee for the Defense of Peace. He had distributed leaflets in Novocherkassk and elsewhere, and intended to go on distributing them. And he anticipated that material on the Novocherkassk events would shortly be published abroad. Realizing that for once he had the upper hand, that there was no longer any way to stop the flow of information, he was not prepared to bargain. So, while requesting publication of his article, he served notice that he would under no circumstances alter it, should the editors ask him to do so.[38] The editors, no doubt chagrined by his audacity and unaccustomed to being placed on the defensive, brusquely declined to publish the article. Nevertheless, Siuda's activities were destined to produce a historic breakthrough. More immediately, a meeting of party members was convened at NEVZ to discuss Siuda's leaflet critically and shore up the justification of the party's position.[39]

Before the breakthrough, he unleashed another attack in the form of an open letter to N. K. Artemov, the NEVZ worker who was secretary of the factory's party organization and a delegate to the 19th Conference of the CPSU, to be held in Moscow in June. The letter indicates that Artemov had tried to defame and discredit Siuda for his efforts. Siuda rebuked him on that score, but his principal concern was political, not personal. At a time when Stalin and his works were being repudiated by party leaders, Siuda characterized what had occurred in 1962 as a disgraceful Stalin-style assault on the people, a mode of behavior that had unfortunately survived the dictator. He identified June 2, 1962, with January 9, 1905, and April 4, 1912, as one of a series of reactionary assaults on the working class, and charged Artemov with the responsibility, *as a worker*, to rise from his knees and secure consideration of the Novocherkassk events at the party conference.[40]

Amazingly, the pressure of one ordinary but uncommonly determined individual compelled the provincial party organization to retreat. Convinced, however reluctantly, by Siuda's observation that the flow of information was unstoppable, L. A. Ivanchenko, secretary of the Rostov Province party organization's executive committee, decided on a countermove. If the Novocherkassk events would inevitably become public, he evidently reasoned, at least the damage might be minimized. The local party organization should seize the initiative and publish the first report on the events. An authorized version could save face, and it might take the steam out of Siuda and his kind, who he feared were bent on sensationalizing the story and blackening those in power.

Thus it happened that the first article ever published on Novocherkassk in an officially sanctioned outlet—the piece filled five-sixths of a large-format page—appeared in the June 22, 1988, edition of *Komsomolets*, the Rostov organ of the Young Communist League. Its author, Ol'ga Nikitina, gave it a weighty title: "Days of Darkening, Days of Illumination," and the subtitle "History with No Pages Torn Out."[41] The editors underlined the dramatic character of its revelations by setting the first words in white against a black background and the last in black against a white background. In a subsequent article, Nikitina mentioned in passing that Ivanchenko had pressured the provincial office of the censorship to "unseal" the subject, and had assumed responsibility for publication of her piece.[42] In an interview she filled out the intriguing story of how she came to write the article.[43]

Although she was the head of the propaganda department of the province's Komsomol and a correspondent for *Komsomolets*, she had not been particularly interested in the Novocherkassk events and knew next to nothing about them. Then one day in May, out of the blue, she was called in to meet Ivanchenko. He told her indignantly that "extremists" in Novocherkassk were spreading leaflets about an alleged massacre of workers in 1962. Were she to look into the matter, he assured her, she would find that nothing of the kind had occurred: "The Soviet power does not shoot workers." These canards had to be stopped, and he would ask the KGB to help her do so.

She went to Novocherkassk, together with Iurii Bespalov, the Rostov correspondent of *Komsomol'skaia pravda*. Bespalov had already been investigating the case, and he seized what looked like an opportunity to obtain new information. Nikitina and Bespalov first talked to Iu. Sukhomlinov, the secretary of the city's party committee, and then the three of them proceeded to the local KGB office. Taking no chances, its head, V. A. Bukhanov, indicated that he had been instructed to deal with Nikitina alone, so the others were obliged to leave.[44] Nikitina asked to see the relevant KGB archival materials, but was told there were none.[45] Bukhanov did grant her permission to speak with NEVZ workers.

At NEVZ she found a group of people assembled to talk with her. It was evidently a handpicked group, led by Artemov, who presented the party line on what had occurred. Others in the group followed suit. Ivanchenko may have misjudged Nikitina, assuming she would be satisfied with what she would hear at NEVZ. In fact, she sensed that she was not getting the whole truth, and as a conscientious journalist she resolved to press on. She looked up participants in the events, spoke with Siuda for two hours, and devoted about two-fifths of her article to him. She now understood that there were two contradictory versions of the events and was not about to accept either of them unconditionally. Siuda's writing struck her as somewhat "hysterical"; she sharply criticized him as an agitator, comparing him unfavorably with his father, "a true son of the party," who, she was confident, would have behaved quite differently. But she now could not doubt that workers had been shot, and this truth shocked her. To be sure, her report reflected the official view in emphasizing hooliganism and drunkenness on the part of some of the strikers, and the presence of criminal elements among them. But all the same, she could not refrain from making an adverse personal judgment: "It is extremely painful and bitter for me to write of this. Under such circumstances [as then obtained], I consider that fire should not have been opened"—especially in view of the fact that most of the people in the square before the gorkom were simply curious onlookers. The party should have foreseen trouble, listened to the people's grievances, isolated the provocateurs, and worked things out peaceably instead of calling in the army.

Once the article had been written, the problem of getting it published loomed. Ivanchenko read the piece, and although he could not have been entirely happy with it, at least she had not introduced lurid details. According to Nikitina, he asked her to make only a few minor changes, to soften some sharp edges; when she had done so, he approved its publication. However, his certification alone was insufficient. Agreement of the provincial censorship organization (Oblit) was indispensable as well, and those in charge would not rubber-stamp the article merely on Ivanchenko's say-so. The approval of the local KGB would first have to be obtained—and its chief refused his consent. Upset by this turn of events, the editor of *Komsomolets* communicated the bad news by phone to Ivanchenko. To resolve the standoff between party officials and the

KGB, a meeting of the principals, including Nikitina, was convened in Rostov. Along with Novocherkassk's KGB chief, Bukhanov, both the head of the provincial KGB, Kuznetsov by name, and his deputy were on hand. Ivanchenko made the case for publication, arguing that withholding the piece would leave the field to "our ideological enemies." It was an article of the KGB faith that, whatever the circumstances, secrecy was the best guarantee of security. At any rate, Kuznetsov was unconvinced by Ivanchenko's argument and adamantly refused to sign. Losing patience with his stiff-necked opponent, at one point Ivashchenko ordered Kuznetsov to sign — to no avail.

The standoff had not been resolved and the meeting was breaking up when Nikitina cried out in protest. Her article had already been set in type — indeed, the entire edition of the newspaper was ready to be printed. It was then 4:00 P.M., and the press run had to be completed by 6:00. Determined to meet the deadline, she insisted that the news staff would not be able to proceed without the KGB's assent. After holding out yet a while, Kuznetsov finally yielded to the continuing pressure. In a cowardly maneuver to escape any possible censure from above, however, rather than commit himself in writing, he directed his deputy to sign. The article appeared on June 22, the anniversary of the German invasion of Russia in 1941, and Nikitina felt as though she had won a war.[46]

Siuda was grateful for the airing of "the Novocherkassk tragedy" in an official organ but, predictably, his gratitude was offset by dissatisfaction with many aspects of the article. Four days after it appeared, he penned a letter to the newspaper's editor, listing twenty-two points of disagreement.[47] A verbose, repetitive harangue (with a hint of hysteria), it sought to correct errors, refute misconceptions, fill out omissions, and justify his contact with U.S. embassy officials. Siuda berated Nikitina for rebuking him instead of condemning the "anti-Bolshevik apologists for Stalinism" who had covered up and still strove to conceal the criminal action against the workers in June 1962. In the final analysis, though, he recognized that the article had performed a great service had "awakened a civic spirit" among the people, manifested in an outpouring of telephone calls, letters, and visits he had received from people of both Novocherkassk and Rostov. For the most part, they shared his dissatisfaction with the article, and wanted to correct and supplement it. Moreover, later in the month he observed a welcome ripple effect: other journalists were encouraged to investigate the case and prepare articles, although they had not yet succeeded in publishing their work.[48]

Nikitina, too, was swamped with critical communications, and they made her realize that her piece had been rather one-sided. Accordingly, she searched further, found new witnesses, and produced a second, more critical article under the same title as the first. She then learned that the deliberate suppression of information was not just a thing of the past. Ivanchenko forbade her to publish anything more, and two years passed before the further progress of glasnost enabled her to bring out a second installment of "Days of Darkening, Days of Illumination," on the anniversary of Bloody Saturday.[49]

Nikitina's first article enjoyed wider exposure than she realized. The NEVZ worker Artemov, it will be recalled, had been selected as a delegate to the 19th Party Conference in Moscow in June. Ivanchenko, or perhaps the Rostov party leadership as a whole, may have feared that a damning report on the Novocherkassk events—Siuda claimed to have leaked information to outside sources—would soon appear in the West. As Nikitina's article had been commissioned to forestall something of the kind locally, it might serve the same purpose with respect to the outside world. This consideration in all likelihood explains how it happened that while Artemov was in Moscow, he passed a copy of Nikitina's piece to Jonathan Steele, the *Manchester Guardian* correspondent there.

The report Steele wrote, headlined "A Sausage Roll That Sparked a Massacre" (a reference to Kurochkin's flippant remark), was featured in the July 15 edition of the *Guardian*. The story relies on Nikitina's article, but only in part. Internal evidence plainly indicates that Steele possessed the material Siuda had spread around during his stay in Moscow. Steele was evidently unfamiliar with earlier revelations by Boiter, Solzhenitsyn, and others, and so had been reluctant to use Siuda's material before it was somehow confirmed in the Soviet press. The Ivanchenko-Artemov tactic misfired, for with the Siuda material in hand, Steele was able to deconstruct Nikitina's article and make his own an unequivocal exposé. The subhead provided by the editor—"Jonathan Steele reports from Moscow on a survivor's account of the killing and secret burial of unarmed civilians"—indicates the article's emphasis. Steele's piece did not resonate through the Western press, but the BBC picked it up immediately and broadcast it almost in toto to the USSR the same day.[50]

A full year passed between the publication of Nikitina's first article and the appearance of the first story on Novocherkassk—a more critical piece, composed around the same time as Nikitina's—in a central Soviet organ, *Komsomol'skaia pravda*. Far from being vanquished, the opponents of glasnost continued to resist the disclosure of injurious information long kept secret.

Bespalov has detailed the story of how he and Valerii Konovalov eventually managed, in the face of long-enduring obstruction, to bring out their article.[51]

He emphasized the obliteration of memory of the events by reference to an episode in Gabriel García Márquez's novel *One Hundred Years of Solitude*, wherein a person climbs out from under a mountain of corpses, citizens gunned down in the course of a strike, and a few days later is unable to convince anyone that the episode was not just a dream. Growing up in Rostov, Bespalov himself was skeptical of hushed talk he had heard in kitchens about pools of blood in the square and trucks hauling away bodies, supposing the stories to be the inventions of persons hostile to the Soviet order. As a journalist in the perestroika era, however, he decided that this matter deserved investigation, so he invited an older colleague, Valerii Konovalov, to come from Moscow, and they worked together on the project for a month. Not dissidents, they were initially oblivious of the need for circumspection in their undertaking, never imagining that they would be subjected to police surveillance.

Their incautious telephone conversations were overheard, and they became aware that they were being followed everywhere. Not deterred, they went to the Polytechnical Institute in Novocherkassk, where they found several witnesses who gave invaluable and terrifying accounts of the events. They interviewed General Shaposhnikov, now retired (he had been deputy commander of the North Caucasus Military District at the time of the shooting), one of the defense lawyers, and others as well. They managed to identify and phone a court medical expert who had participated in the burials and agreed to tell about them. When they arrived at his apartment fifteen minutes later, however, the man stammered that his memory had failed him, and he had no knowledge of any bodies. Their call had been intercepted, and the KGB had warned the man to say nothing. The KGB did not interfere completely with their collection of reminiscences, but did strive to bar access to documents.

Many people in Novocherkassk pleaded with the journalists not to reopen old wounds, but they persisted; they wished not only to fill in a blank spot but also to dispel the "syndrome of fear" hovering over the city. Individuals who had signed pledges not to speak of what they knew still felt bound by them twenty-six years later. Many people who had lost relatives in the square or to prisons had purged their memories of the victims, destroyed their photographs, and concealed what had happened from their children and grandchildren. When their article finally appeared, it unleashed a flood of repressed memory and feelings.

The two men submitted their completed article to the chief editor of their newspaper, who agreed to try to publish it. The censor would not let it through. A telephone appeal to someone in the Politbiuro yielded advice to wait two or three months, because conditions just then were strained. Three further attempts to publish the piece failed. On one of these occasions, Konovalov phoned Bespalov from Moscow to say that the article had been set in type for the next issue. Bespalov bought some food and drink, gathered a group of friends, and together they waited. With the paper scheduled to come out at nine o'clock, he phoned Konovalov at five, to learn that the piece had thus far survived. When another call at seven brought the same reply, Bespalov's heart began to pound. At eight-thirty, however, Konovalov phoned to say that the article had once again miscarried. Episodes of the kind continued for a year, but the article was finally published "by chance" on June 2, 1989, the twenty-seventh anniversary of the massacre. Lithuania had just declared independence, and when its delegation to the newly created Congress of People's Deputies ostentatiously left the chamber, creating a crisis atmosphere, Konovalov surmised that the attention of top-level figures who had repeatedly blocked the article would be occupied elsewhere, and it might be possible to slip the article past the censor. He proved correct. A call from the Politbiuro reached the editorial offices too late: the presses were already printing a run of more than 18 million copies.[52]

The article produced a twofold impact. First, it caught the attention of several members of the Congress of People's Deputies, among them the dean of Leningrad University's Law Faculty, A. A. Sobchak. Actually, Sobchak had heard about Novocherkassk earlier from another member of the Congress, V. M. Kalinchenko.[53] This deputy from Novocherkassk, once elected, was visited by numerous residents who wanted him to request an inquiry into the June 1962 events. The most articulate and importunate visitor was Siuda, who showed him various materials and discussed the matter with him at length. Impelled to do something, Kalinchenko requested but was not granted a meeting with Gorbachev. He did speak to A. I. Luk'ianov, a Gorbachev ally and Speaker of the Supreme Soviet, who discouraged him from doing anything. What use would it be, he asked rhetorically, to go into an event that had occurred so long ago? In other words, he—and he probably spoke for Gorbachev as well—wished to perpetuate the cover-up.

Kalinchenko then spoke to Sobchak, who told him of his intention to make a speech about the killings in Tbilisi in April, and suggested that his fellow deputy speak out about Novocherkassk. When, early the next day, Kalinchenko told the scheduling official he intended to speak, he was asked what he proposed to speak about. The proceedings got under way, and hour after hour slipped by, but Kalinchenko was not recognized. At last he complained to the official, who lamely replied that a great many people wished to speak. The deputy's insistence that he had been among the first to sign up got him nowhere. The leadership, he inferred, had resolved to bar him from speaking on a matter it found embarrassing and unpleasant. Under these circumstances, the publication of the Bespalov-Konovalov article on June 2 was indeed opportune, providing an opening for an interpellation. At a session on June 11, Sobchak cited the piece in support of a request to the presiding officer (Gorbachev) that a protest to the procurator general and the rehabilitation of the victims be placed on the agenda.[54]

As for the article's more immediate impact, once the story was out in the open, Bespalov continued his investigations, and *Komsomol'skaia pravda* published several more pieces on the subject. The first article's revelations, incomplete as they were, stimulated other journalists to search for additional witnesses and more documentation. Attention remained focused on Novocherkassk, of course, once the issue was brought up in the Supreme Soviet and that body called for a reconsideration of the case. In the three years after the publication of the June 2, 1989, article, at least forty pieces were printed in various organs. They were especially prominent in such reformist publications as *Literaturnaia gazeta, Izvestiia*, and *Trud*, but also came out in similarly oriented organs both central and local. Exposés overwhelmed the few counterattacks in conservative publications such as *Pravda, Sovetskaia Rossiia*, and *Voenno-istoricheskii zhurnal*, and unquestionably won the public relations war.

It should not be imagined, glasnost notwithstanding, that the guardians of the old order abandoned efforts to cover up as much as they could. Reporters who in June 1989 went to the office of the MVD in Rostov in search of information were told that it possessed nothing on the affair, and the KGB provincial office followed suit. Information about where the corpses had been buried was especially tightly withheld because military officers who had been involved continued to deny that soldiers had fired on unarmed people. An *Izvestiia* correspondent had no luck in his efforts to secure access to the KGB archive in Moscow, but was given access to some Supreme Court material after she complained to the procurator general. The filmmaker Mikhail Mar'ianov, who was producing a documentary on Novocherkassk, was subjected to all kinds of harassment. Photographs taken at the time of the strike, locked away for twenty-nine years and only recently brought out, mysteriously disappeared, and so did various documents. Measures were taken against individuals who were prepared to show where the corpses had been buried.[55] Writing in the spring of 1992, Nikitina lamented: "Almost all the documents that shed light on the Novocherkassk tragedy are still hidden away in secure archives and remain behind the steel doors of official safes."[56]

As a matter of fact, materials for historical research had already begun to emerge from their hiding places in 1990. At Gorbachev's order, masses of material were being declassified and transferred to open collections. Oddly enough, in 1992 the post-Soviet government bureaucratized the procedure inordinately, thereby greatly slowing the process. It also hampered research by classifying the materials into three collections. The first, containing party documents for the period up until 1952, was open to researchers; the second, consisting of party documents below the Politbiuro level from 1952 to 1991, was comparatively difficult to access; the third, the presidential (formerly Politbiuro) archive, is off limits.[57] This situation makes all the more remarkable the publication in 1993 of a stunning collection of documents on the Novocherkassk affair drawn from the presidential archive.[58] The publication offers fourteen communications, marked "Absolutely Secret," from the KGB chief, V. E. Semichastnyi, or his deputy to the Central Committee and the Council of Ministers. Six of them are based on virtually round-the-clock observations by the swarm of agents who operated in Novocherkassk at the time of the strike. Others identify and give information about the most active of the persons arrested, plans for the trials to be held, the indictments and the verdicts, the disposition of the corpses, and measures taken to correct conditions regarded as the causes of the disorders. These documents, written from the perspective of the establishment, have to be used critically. Nevertheless, they are so revealing that their publication marked a "tectonic shift" for every student of the Novocherkassk events.

This does not mean, however, that access to all the relevant archival material is now at hand. I have attempted in vain to obtain permission to study the eight-volume record of the most important of the trials. The same holds for the thirty-one volumes of material collected by the Chief Military Procuracy in response to the Congress of People's Deputies' request in 1989 for a thorough reexamination of the whole affair. Unfortunately, many Russian officials continued to be influenced by the Soviet ethos of secrecy, and set the bounds of confidentiality far wider than in many advanced countries. As things now stand, the outlines of what happened at Novocherkassk have been disclosed and can be freely discussed in the Russian press. Nevertheless, a partial cover-up remains in place.

Chapter 7   Shaposhnikov and Siuda

Two individuals involved in the Novocherkassk events deserve special attention. Although their social origins were not dissimilar, the paths they traveled
could not have been more different: one became an army general, the other a
NEVZ worker who was arrested and imprisoned in 1962. In a sense, they stood
on opposite sides of the barricades. But both were traumatized by the bloody
suppression of the Novocherkassk strike. Each in his own way strove to bring to
light a horrendous action that had been relegated to oblivion and to secure justice for those who had been killed, wounded, or imprisoned, and their names
dishonored. Both were persecuted for their beliefs and both became trenchant
critics of the Soviet regime.

Matvei Kuzmich Shaposhnikov was born to a middling peasant family in
Voronezh Province in 1906.[1] As a boy, Matvei heard a good deal about the military exploits of his great-grandfather and grandfather, and these tales may have
influenced his choice of a military career. He completed seven years of schooling in 1923 and then enrolled for a while in the campaign to wipe out illiteracy
among the peasantry. He next worked four years as a miner in Krivoi Rog, and
this experience may have left him with lasting empathy and identification with
working people. Matvei was then admitted to a military training school in
Odessa. He had joined the Komsomol in 1926, and at the age of twenty-two,
while still in school, Matvei became a party member. He was active, moreover,
serving as secretary of his party cell. After graduating near the top of his class,
he was assigned to command a rifle platoon in Kiev. He evidently served with
distinction in this and subsequent posts, for in 1936 he was inducted into the
military order of the Red Star. Thereafter he successfully completed a course
of study at the prestigious Frunze Military Academy in Moscow.

Shaposhnikov had his first experience of combat during the war against the

Finns in 1940, and performed well enough to be decorated. He fought as a tank officer from the beginning to the end of World War II, on the Kursk, Dnieper, and Baltic fronts. By 1943 he had attained the rank of colonel. In that year the troops he commanded forced their way against German resistance across the Dnieper River. For this signal achievement he was named a Hero of the Soviet Union. By the end of the war he had become a major general. After the war he attended the General Staff Academy, and then served four years as commander of the Second Guard Tank Army in East Germany. In 1960 he assumed his next (and last) post as first deputy commander (second in command) of the North Caucasus Military District, one of the sixteen into which the country was divided. It would turn out to be a fateful assignment, for Novocherkassk lay within its borders.

Late in life, Shaposhnikov recorded an event that occurred during his service in Germany, instructive for what it reveals about his character. Khrushchev and he held divergent views on strategic matters, and their differences surfaced in a notable episode. Khrushchev had become enamored of nuclear armaments and correspondingly less supportive of the traditional forces. He not only spoke vigorously in favor of nuclear rockets and the like, but in the 1950s he had twice drastically reduced expenditures on the other forces. These moves entailed the discharge of many skilled and experienced personnel. Shaposhnikov was among the army leaders who considered this policy wrongheaded and dangerous.[2] At a banquet in Germany in honor of Khrushchev, the latter spoke enthusiastically and at length about Soviet production of nuclear weapons, which he dubbed his "favorite child." He contended that they would have the decisive role in a third world war, and was inclined to write off planes, artillery, tanks, and motorized infantry. Upset by this stance, and especially by the belittling of tanks, Shaposhnikov raised his glass and boldly expressed a discordant view. He diplomatically recognized the importance of atomic weapons, but also the devastating consequences their use would visit on the earth. Human reason might therefore prevail, and these devices might never be employed. In that event, the other forces, above all tanks, would be critical to success. He proposed a toast to the development of the country's tank forces, which, he said, had been and always would be the motherland's dependable shield. Miffed by this jab at his policy, Khrushchev declined to raise his glass.[3]

Shaposhnikov left the army in 1967, at the age of sixty-one, and lived quietly in Rostov-on-Don for the next twenty-two years. In the late 1980s, with glasnost in the ascendant, newspaper articles about the Novocherkassk events began to appear. Now Shaposhnikov suddenly emerged from obscurity to celebrity. If the army deserved to be condemned as the perpetrator of Bloody Saturday, reformist writers argued, one of its members deserved the highest praise for his principled behavior. Shaposhnikov was now lionized as the hero of the Novocherkassk episode, for his refusal to order his troops to shoot at the striking workers.

The details were presented in the general's own words several times, with significant variations.[4] Here is a version he wrote in mid-1992:

> Sometime between May 21 and 29, 1962, my chief general, I. A. Pliev, received an order: place the district army on military alert. . . . From his explanation, it followed that the order had come from N. S. Khrushchev personally. The district army was put on military alert [and] was given not only weapons but ammunition as well. In Novocherkassk, in keeping with the military alert, tanks fully equipped with ammunition were called up. On the first of June, by order of General Pliev, a large part of the army was concentrated in the NEVZ area, and the lesser part in military cantonments in a state of military preparedness. I was put in command of the forces at NEVZ. Pliev assumed direct responsibility for all the forces in the cantonment, and deployed one of the tank regiments at a medical dispensary.
>
> From the start I was against deploying our district army, especially with weapons and ammunition, against the factory workers and the crowd. My position was based on the Program of the CPSU, which says: "With respect to the internal conditions of the Soviet Union, there is no need of an army." And it was from this position, in the first meeting with Comrades Kozlov and Mikoyan, that I spoke of my fear of "the possibility that great trouble might ensue." They reacted very condescendingly to my warning, and Kozlov declared: "The commander of the army, General Pliev, has received all the necessary instructions."
>
> Before my arrival, the forces located in the NEVZ area were headed by Lt. Gen. D. N. Parovatkin. When I arrived, both General Parovatkin and the commanders of the sections informed [me] that elements of the forces situated around the factory territory were equipped with loaded submachine guns and carbines, and that this had been done in accordance with General Pliev's direct order.
>
> Since from that moment on, responsibility for the army's action in the NEVZ area rested squarely with me, I decided and ordered: "Submachine

guns and carbines will be unloaded and the ammunition put under the control of the company commanders." And I emphasized that ammunition was not to be distributed unless I so ordered.

It was a strange scene: in the morning [June 2] people came to the factory, gathered in the departments, but no one began to work. They demanded to see the [factory] director.

To our surprise, the representatives from Moscow did not appear at the factory. I think they were simply afraid of the people. At the time passions were inflamed. It turned out that only we, the military, were in contact with the workers and listened to their grievances.

Although the situation was extremely unpleasant, it was no more than the usual sort of trouble. But [then serious] trouble came to pass. A great crowd carrying red banners marched toward the [city] center. I declare that there were no hostile actions on the part of the workers. I tried to ascertain the workers' intentions. To my question, one wiseacre replied: "If the mountain won't come to Mohammed, Mohammed will go to the mountain" [i.e., if the leaders would not come to the factory, the people would go to them].

By radio I informed General Pliev that a column of many thousands of people with unfurled red banners was moving into Novocherkassk. "Hold them back! Don't allow them to go on!" he cried over the phone. "The head of the column has already crossed the bridge over the Tuzlov River," I replied. "And besides, the forces at my disposal are insufficient to restrain so many people." "I will send you tanks. Attack," the commander went on. "I don't see before me a foe we should attack with our tanks," I replied firmly. With that the "dialogue" ended. It later turned out that Pliev had thrown down the phone.

Foreseeing trouble, I got into my car and drove forward. Shortly I met General Parovatkin, whom I had sent to consult with Pliev. He advised: "The commander has ordered the use of weapons." "That can't be!" I exclaimed. Then Parovatkin took out a notebook and opened it. One of the points [written there] indicated "use weapons."

Meanwhile, the column with many thousands of workers, surrounded by an enormous crowd of citizens, arrived at the square before the building that housed the city's party committee and executive committee. In my vehicle, together with Parovatkin, we hastened forward: a bloody action must not be allowed. But we were too late. We had got to some 400 meters from the square when we heard massive submachine gun fire.

The next morning, D. A. Ivashchenko, a member of the Military Council, told me [in confidence] that the generals of the law enforcement organs [Tupchenko and Strel'chenko] together with the MVD agents who had come from Moscow [Shchelokov and others] had secretly buried the bodies. . . .

Unfortunately, at the time there was not a single organization or a single person I could turn to without serious risk to express my judgment of the events and my relation to them. Nevertheless, I wrote a letter to the writer Konstantin Simonov. But unfortunately, Simonov, like everyone else, remained silent. Then I wrote four more letters [elsewhere he said five], and addressed them simply to "Soviet writers." I counted on their elevated morality, their special sensitivity, their honesty, their intolerance of any kind of injustice, and their implacable opposition to unjustified cruelty.

But all in vain. And it was not long before there were reprisals against me: I was compelled to retire [from the army]; and after a long, tiresome investigation by the military procurator and the KGB, I was expelled from the CPSU.[5]

Shaposhnikov told his story for the first time, albeit very briefly, to Iurii Bespalov and Valerii Konovalov, who included it in the important article they published in *Komsomol'skaia pravda* on June 2, 1989. A fuller account followed in *Literaturnaia gazeta* on June 21, 1989. Sometime between the beginning of 1990 and mid-1991, he went over the same ground again as a witness in the Chief Military Procuracy's fresh investigation of the Novocherkassk events. The 1992 account quoted above is his fourth rendition. The fifth and last time, he reviewed what had happened in his conversations with Mikhail Arkhipov, which the latter published in 1995, after Shaposhnikov's death (he died in 1994).[6] To evaluate the general's account is no easy task. I have found no corroboration in other sources of much that he relates, and in fact several of his main contentions have been contested. A comparison of his several accounts reveals many significant inconsistencies. And there are glaring errors as well, most conspicuously in his first rendering of the story in 1989.

A good deal of what he said in the account quoted above appears also in the 1989 interview, but a close reading reveals disturbing errors and inconsistencies, not least in chronology. First, in both accounts Shaposhnikov speaks of a communication from Moscow to Pliev sometime between May 21 and 29, ordering him to place the district forces on military alert. Second, in the 1989 article Shaposhnikov asserts unequivocally—this would be consistent with the first point—that NCMO forces were deployed in Novocherkassk before the price increases were announced. He also places Kozlov and Mikoyan in No-vocherkassk and himself at NEVZ before the announcement. These proposi-tions presuppose that the announcement of the price increases was expected to cause serious trouble. But if that were the case, why were the party organiza-tions throughout the country not alerted to what was coming until one day be-fore the announcement?[7] More to the point, in their testimony to the military procurator's inquiry, other NCMO officers unanimously agreed that the forces were not put on alert until *after* the strike had begun. The district army staff's top men had been engaged in an exercise in Krasnodar and flew to Rostov only after an order came from Moscow on June 1. They proceeded to Novocher-kassk, where they arrived the afternoon of the same day. As for Kozlov and Mikoyan, it is certain that they arrived in the troubled city only on June 1–2.[8] Plainly, Shaposhnikov was wrong on all these points, and he also confuses events of June 1 and 2.

In subsequent accounts he corrected some but not all of these errors. He was able—or compelled—to do so as more information about the events ap-peared in glasnost-era publications. In his Military Procuracy testimony (1990–91), Shaposhnikov shifts the order to Pliev to bring the forces to military readi-ness from the week of May 21 to the end of the month—closer to but still short of the actual date. He was almost surely impelled to do so by the evidence adduced in an article contradicting his statement in the 1989 interview.[9] But he showed little consistency in keeping the details properly aligned: in the ar-ticle quoted above, published the following year, he dates this event once again before the end of May, while this time correctly reporting his arrival in Novo-cherkassk on June 1. He still maintains, erroneously, that Kozlov and Mikoyan were already there when he arrived. For many years Shaposhnikov had kept a diary, but at some indeterminate point he had destroyed all the material in his possession relating to the Novocherkassk events.[10] Accordingly, he had no rec-ords to rely on when he told his story, and was obliged to summon up from memory the details and the sequence in which they had occurred. Obviously his memory was unreliable, but it is hardly surprising that he could not recall accurately events that had occurred twenty-seven years before. It must be kept in mind, too, that Shaposhnikov was eighty-three years old when he was inter-viewed by *Literaturnaia gazeta*. In one of his accounts he frankly acknowl-edged that he did not remember all the circumstances of that far-off time.[11] It follows that his testimony must be treated cautiously.

Rather than examine in full Shaposhnikov's errors and inconsistencies, let us turn to the core issue in his story, the claim that he refused an order to have his men fire on unarmed people. There can be no doubt that he was deeply troubled about the intervention of the army in a labor dispute. He expressed his doubts and fears on this score to Pliev, who, he remarked in one of his accounts, also had misgivings.[12] We have no independent corroboration that Shaposhnikov raised objections with Kozlov and Mikoyan, but it would have been consistent with his outlook and character to do so.[13] A. S. Davydov, the head of the political sector of the 18th Tank Division, encountered Shaposhnikov at NEVZ the evening of June 1. The general agitatedly complained to him, he testified, about the sending of army forces to solve a problem that should be dealt with by the local organs and the police.[14]

Shaposhnikov took command of the Novocherkassk garrison troops deployed near NEVZ, charged to prevent disorders by the workers but without specific instructions on how to do so. When he arrived at NEVZ, he relates in one of his testimonies, a meeting of the workers was in progress. He spoke to some of them, learned why they had quit work, and advised them to send a delegation to state their grievances and wants to Khrushchev. They told him they would not be allowed to go to Moscow, and instead of meeting Khrushchev would wind up in prison. Only a strike could secure attention to their demands.[15] Shaposhnikov deployed his troops around the factory but made no effort to suppress the strike. When a company of tanks manned by cadets from the Rostov military school appeared, according to Davydov, he ordered them to leave.[16]

Although he apparently sympathized with the strikers, he was not unmindful of the need to do his duty. In one of his accounts he speaks of having taken steps (evidently late at night) to clear the top of the railroad underpass of the workers who were using it as a rostrum to address the crowd. His men also removed the barriers that had been set up on the tracks, thereby enabling rail traffic to resume, and he posted guards over that section of the track.[17]

Although he does not mention it, two other officers credit him with having liberated Basov from his place of confinement in the administration building. He called in *Spetsnaz* troops, who entered the building disguised in workers' clothing and contrived to bring Basov out.[18] Another relevant matter is noted by P. P. Falynskov (but not by Shaposhnikov). Falynskov, deputy commander of the 406th Heavy Tank Regiment, was at NEVZ the evening of June 1. Sent by Pliev to size up the situation at the factory, he of course spoke with Shaposhnikov. The latter asked him to send two boxes of smoke grenades, which he thought to use against the strikers if things got out of control.[19] When Falynskov reported this request to Lieutenant General Ivashchenko, a member of the District Military Council, Ivashchenko reportedly exclaimed: "Has Shaposhnikov gone out of his mind, thinking to use smoke against the workers?" He forbade Falynskov to report this matter to Pliev. This request seems to reflect accurately Shaposhnikov's state of mind at the time: his sense of duty dictated that he take resolute measures if necessary; his sympathy for the strikers required him to opt for the least painful measure possible. Whether the troops' weapons were loaded or not, unruly crowds might thus be dispersed without resort to violence.

One of the most remarkable claims Shaposhnikov makes in four of his five accounts is this: dismayed to learn that the troops at NEVZ were equipped with both weapons and ammunition, he ordered the weapons to be unloaded and the ammunition put in the custody of company commanders. Curiously, this claim is absent from his testimony to the Military Procuracy; yet in this same account, for the first and only time, Shaposhnikov reports having ordered the disarming of tanks on the bridge over the Tuzlov. We possess no independent confirmation of either claim. In an essay designed to refute the *Literaturnaia gazeta* article (1989), Falynskov flatly denied that the troops under Shaposhnikov's command had been supplied with ammunition, so that he could not have ordered their weapons unloaded.[20] In an all too brief rejoinder to the essay, Shaposhnikov did not address Falynskov's rebuttal.[21] One might be inclined to consider this matter insoluble, or perhaps to discount Falynskov's claim as a defensive maneuver on the army's behalf. A major buttress of Falynskov's assertion, however, is Siuda's observation that the Novocherkassk garrison soldiers sent to NEVZ had no weapons, and that the workers and soldiers fraternized.[22]

On the morning of June 2 the general observed the workers appearing at the factory, refusing to work, forming a column, and heading for the city. He did nothing to stop what was apparently a peaceful demonstration, having received no orders to do so. Shaposhnikov informed Pliev by radio that a mass of workers was on the way to the city center, intending to speak with Kozlov and Mikoyan. As we have seen, he was ordered to stop the column, but reported that it had already moved out, and besides, his forces were inadequate to do any such thing. Pliev responded that he would send tanks to enable his deputy to attack and halt the march. At that point Shaposhnikov purportedly pronounced the words that have often been quoted, and for which he has been celebrated: "I don't see before me a foe we should attack with our tanks." According to the general, the exchange ended there; but soon after, his emissary to Pliev showed him a notebook with a written message from his superior ordering him to resort to arms.[23] Of course, he and his men never did, but whether this amounted to refusal to obey an order is less than clear.

If and when Pliev *first* ordered Shaposhnikov to stop the demonstration, he would not necessarily have meant that arms should be used. This inference appears justified when we note that military forces deployed before the bridge to block the way were unarmed and did nothing to stop the procession when it approached and moved through them.[24] Is it not reasonable to assume that they behaved as they did because they had no orders to fire? More critical was the confrontation on the bridge. When Shaposhnikov advanced toward the city in an attempt, as he said, to intercept the tanks being sent before they came face to face with the procession, he presently arrived at the bridge. The crowd had already passed through the array of tanks that had been sent to block the way.[25] Would it have made sense for Pliev to send tanks to Shaposhnikov when tanks were already stationed on the bridge? At this choke point, armor would obviously have been most effective. How could another group of tanks have crossed the river if the bridge was already chockablock with tanks? Most important, if Pliev wished to employ arms to stop the procession, why didn't the tanks he had deployed on the bridge fire their weapons? Colonel Mikheev, the commander of the fifteen tanks at the bridge, asserts that ammunition had been distributed Saturday morning, but no orders given to use it.[26] The conclusion indicated, that they had not been ordered to fire, appears to undercut Shaposhnikov's depiction definitively.

At this point, one cannot help being reminded of the confrontation on June 1 between General Pliev and the Presidium member Kirilenko, described earlier. To repeat: Kirilenko thrice asked Pliev how he intended to keep the workers from coming into the city. Pliev indicated he would set a barrier of tanks on the bridge, but did not plan to take other measures against the workers. Against this background, what happened at the bridge is perfectly intelligible. It is a matter of more than passing interest that Shaposhnikov first became aware of the Kirilenko-Pliev exchange only in 1992, by exposure to portions of the testimony the Military Procuracy had collected. According to his biographer, the general implicitly believed the story, and it altered his attitude toward his former chief, whom he now viewed more favorably.[27] In his response to the polemical article directed against himself earlier, Shaposhnikov had accused Pliev of demonstrating a lack of "civic courage" in Novocherkassk.[28] However, in 1992 Shaposhnikov evidently did not perceive—he was now eighty-six years old—that to credit the Kirilenko-Pliev episode was to discredit his own story.

The analysis here presented may appear excessively speculative, but it is supported by considerations of another kind. If Shaposhnikov had disobeyed a direct order from his commander, it is inconceivable that he would not have been severely punished—and not merely by expulsion from the army. In Pliev's eyes, nothing the general had done or failed to do appeared unforgivable, it may be confidently inferred, for he brought no charges against his deputy. Far from rebuking Shaposhnikov publicly or privately, when Pliev was transferred to a post in Cuba shortly after Bloody Saturday, he raised no objection to Shaposhnikov's appointment as his replacement.

Given that Shaposhnikov's honesty is not in question, how can his affirmation of a manifestly untrue story be accounted for? Reflection suggests the following hypothetical explanation. In his rendering of the confrontation on the square between demonstrators and soldiers, Solzhenitsyn asserts in *The Gulag Archipelago* that an order to open fire "was not carried out because the captain who received it killed himself in front of his men rather than pass it on. That an officer committed suicide," Solzhenitsyn continues, "is beyond doubt"— although "the circumstances are vague and no one knows the name of this hero of conscience." As a matter of fact, although this incident was widely credited, it was a rumor that has never been confirmed rather than an event "beyond doubt." Shaposhnikov could well have heard and believed the story, even before Solzhenitsyn learned of it and passed it on as fact.[29]

It requires no stretch of the imagination to suppose that the general strongly identified with the protagonist of the tale. Like the captain, he had in principle adamantly opposed the use of weapons against the striking workers. The captain had been thrust into an existential situation, which required him to choose between performing his professional duty and acting in accord with his conscience. Because he had chosen to immolate himself rather than betray his sense of right, he was properly considered, in Solzhenitsyn's words, a "hero of conscience." Shaposhnikov had good reason to consider himself a hero of conscience, too. His efforts to expose the murderous fusillade on June 2 had resulted, as he said later in life, in his "moral execution." His plight, which lasted over twenty years, could be construed as a kind of equivalent of the captain's self-sacrifice. The powerful resonance between the story of the captain and Shaposhnikov's lived experience may have brought about, in the general's mind, an unconscious erasure of the boundaries between the two, and the psychological incorporation of the younger man into himself. As a consequence, Shaposhnikov unwittingly made the story about the captain his own.

On the conscious level, Shaposhnikov was of course aware that the captain's situation on that fateful day did not correspond exactly to his own. The problem worked out on the unconscious level involved the imaginative creation of an equivalent of the captain's behavior in the rather different circumstances that had figured in the general's case. For one thing, as a much higher ranking officer, Shaposhnikov could have taken a step not available to the captain—ordering the disarming of his troops—and thus avoided the kind of confrontation that had produced such a lamentable result in the junior officer's case. He repeatedly asserted that he had done just that. More important was the matter of the response to an order that required an individual to make an excruciatingly difficult choice. For Shaposhnikov to perform a heroic act equivalent to the captain's, he had to be commanded to do something that flagrantly violated his moral sensibility. The supposition that he had been ordered to attack the column of demonstrators and had firmly refused to do so was the false memory concocted to fill the bill. Solzhenitsyn's remark that no one knew the name of the hero of conscience offered to Shaposhnikov, another hero of conscience, the opportunity to stand in for the unknown captain and receive the plaudits he deserved.

Matvei Kuzmich was expelled from the army not immediately after the Novocherkassk crisis but five years later. Nevertheless, his ultimate disgrace was certainly related to Novocherkassk. As already demonstrated, Shaposhnikov was profoundly disturbed—as were the workers—by the introduction of army units into the NEVZ dispute. He raised objections to Pliev, purportedly to Kozlov and Mikoyan, and he urged that an appeal be made to Khrushchev—all in vain. Traumatized by the massacre, he was immediately impelled to do something about it. He suggested to a top-level colleague that they press Kozlov and Mikoyan to hold responsible those who had fired at the people, but was assured they would not be heeded. He let it be known that he wished to address his concerns to a meeting of the Rostov Province party organization, but was not invited to attend. He drafted a letter to the top leadership, but after concluding that Khrushchev had authorized the shooting, he decided not to send it.[30] A convinced Leninist and a historically minded individual, Shaposhnikov assigned a subordinate to find Lenin's pronouncements on Bloody Sunday and the Lena gold field massacre.[31] He repeatedly cited a provision of the Rules of the CPSU, to the effect that under Soviet conditions there was no need of an army in the country's internal affairs. Actually, there is no such provision in the rules, nor in the Soviet Constitution, but this conception was an element of the dogma that sought unequivocally to demarcate the Soviet regime from its reactionary predecessor and the "imperialist" states.[32] Shaposhnikov was horrified to recognize that his government had replicated the despicable acts committed by the tsarist regime. He was incapable of assenting to the idea that crimes and betrayals were essential for the good of the state.

Obsessed by such thoughts, he could not let the matter rest. As indicated in his account quoted at length above, he wrote to the prominent writer Konstantin Simonov. The letter, dispatched in December 1962, is not extant; but it is not difficult to guess that its intent was to enlighten Simonov and enlist his help in bringing the gruesome story to public attention. Receiving no reply, he penned a series of letters to the Union of Russian Writers. Instead of affixing his own name, he signed the letters "Furious Vissarion," a token of his identification with the famous nineteenth-century literary critic Vissarion Belinskii, the implacable enemy of injustice, dishonesty, and hypocrisy. Here is a fragment of one of them, a cry from the heart of a man whose bedrock beliefs had been shattered:

> The party has been transformed into a machine, driven by a poor chauffeur who often drunkenly violates the traffic laws. The time is long past when the chauffeur's right to drive must be taken away to avoid a catastrophe. . . .
>
> It is now extremely important that the working and productive intelligentsia gain an understanding of the nature of the political regime, the conditions in which we live. They must understand that we are under the power of the worst form of autocracy, operated by an enormous bureaucratic and military force.
>
> People must begin to think, instead of holding to a blind faith that

transforms us into living machines. In brief, our people have been converted into politically disfranchised international hirelings [*batraki*], such as they have never been before.[33]

The letters did not reach those to whom they were addressed; instead they found their way to the security organs. The investigation that ensued brought Shaposhnikov under suspicion. He was placed under surveillance and his correspondence opened. He was harassed with all sorts of accusations, although nothing specifically about having disobeyed an order of his superior. It should be pointed out that Pliev had returned from Cuba to the command of the NCMO, and although relations between him and Shaposhnikov were fractious, he never accused Shaposhnikov of insubordination at the time of the Novocherkassk upheaval.

Shaposhnikov fought relentlessly against a push to discharge him from the army, demanding to make his case to higher authorities, up to the Minister of Defense. To no avail: in 1966 he was maneuvered into retirement, ostensibly because of his age (then sixty). After appealing to Brezhnev, he was granted a hearing with officers of the army's political section, who charged him with criticism of the country's leadership, with "freethinking, heterodoxy, and political immaturity."[34] Toward the end of August 1967, upon returning from their dacha, the general and his wife found a team of MVD and KGB agents awaiting them in the courtyard of their apartment house. Upstairs they encountered several people, including a general, who demanded to search their rooms. As readily became apparent, the locks on their door had been broken and a search had already been made. In short order the agents turned up the letters written by "Vissarion" and other compromising documents. Shaposhnikov was charged under Article 70 of the criminal code with engaging in anti-Soviet agitation and propaganda. Persons convicted under this statute were to be deprived of their freedom for six months to seven years, with or without additional exile for a term of two to five years, or by exile for a term of two to five years.[35] After the investigation had dragged on for some time, Shaposhnikov appealed to Iurii Andropov, then head of the KGB, and the charges were dropped. But the general's tribulations were not yet over. He was put on trial, so to speak, by the Rostov party organization and unceremoniously expelled from the CPSU.[36] Looking back on these events, Shaposhnikov lamented that he had been subjected to "moral execution" for more than twenty years. But in December 1988 he was exonerated of having distributed anti-Soviet propaganda and officially rehabilitated. The letter he received from the Chief Military Procurator's office concluded with the sentence: "Only under the conditions of perestroika, the democratization of all dimensions of life of Soviet society, has it become possible to acknowledge that you are innocent."[37]

Siuda

If Shaposhnikov may have been pointed toward a military career by the tales he heard about the soldiering of his great-grandfather and grandfather, perhaps the other figure under review was destined for a life as a rebel by stories about his father's career as a revolutionary. Petr Petrovich Siuda, born in 1937, never knew his father, for he was only twenty-two days old when the elder Petr was arrested, and nine days later he died in prison.[38] Little Petr's father, born to a peasant family in Belorussia, had moved to southern Russia in 1898 at the age of twenty-two. He secured work in a cement factory but was dismissed for defending his fellow workers. This experience led him to join a Social Democratic circle, and in 1903 he joined the Russian Social Democratic Labor Party. Arrested the same year, he escaped confinement, was arrested again in 1904, and escaped again. Active afterward in the underground, he led the Social Democrats of Grozny during the revolution of 1905. Siuda senior continued his political activities in Baku from 1907 to 1918, at some point becoming chairman of an oil-industry party committee. After the February Revolution of 1917, he was elected on the Bolshevik list to the Baku soviet, and during the Civil War was co-opted into the Red leadership. Subsequently appointed a commissar, he successfully carried out the nationalization and restoration of the Maikop oil fields.

We hear of him next as a victim of the purges. In 1937 he came to the defense of a certain Korolev, a party comrade who had been falsely accused and arrested. In turn, Siuda himself was arrested "for direct support and defense of [this] enemy of the people," tortured during interrogation, and executed soon after. Understandably devastated, Petr's mother luckily contrived by way of a son by an earlier marriage to inform Stalin how a comrade in arms of his had perished. Stalin ordered an investigation, and in 1939 the dead man was rehabilitated and his wife given a pension. But four years later Petr's mother, a woman of Cossack origin, was arrested after having been falsely denounced for anti-Soviet agitation. She was sentenced to seven years in prison and served the entire term. Petr spent those years in a series of three orphanages. Because conditions in the institutions were miserable, he frequently ran away. After his mother was released, they experienced grinding poverty and he the stigma of being "the son of a political." In the orphanages the young Siuda had been inculcated with a love of Stalin; but upon learning his father's fate from his mother, as he said, his "idols were smashed." [39]

With such a nightmarish background, little wonder that Petr quit school and left home. As a vagabond he traveled the length and breadth of his country, fathoming its lower depths. He worked episodically in factories, in mines, and in the virgin lands, and served a term in the army as well. Over time he increasingly displayed the foremost trait in his makeup: a stubborn defiance of authority. He participated in strikes, was insubordinate to his military superiors, and resisted pressure to conform to party dictates. Astonishingly, he somehow managed to escape deportation to the Gulag. Although he had come to despise the Stalinist system, his identification with his father made him an admirer of the "authentic" Bolsheviks and the October Revolution. Petr regretted the spotty education he'd had; so, swallowing his pride, he agreed to join the Komsomol in exchange for an opportunity to finish secondary school. After an odyssey lasting something like a decade, Siuda wound up in Novocherkassk in 1961. He secured a job in the assembly shop at NEVZ, and also was enrolled in courses in the factory's technical institute.

He had recently married and his wife was pregnant. His wages came to 120 rubles a month, of which 30 went for the rent on their apartment. Because housing was in short supply, many workers were obliged to secure quarters in the more expensive private market. Similarly, little food was available in the state shops, so people had to purchase in the peasant markets, where prices were relatively high. It was hard to make ends meet, and the announcement of the price rise promised to make things harder.

At the time the strike broke out, Siuda was on the first day of a study leave. For that reason he was not in on the very beginning of the strike, but he turned up some hours later. He also missed out on the June 2 events, for he was arrested very early that morning. Tanks had been introduced to the factory grounds during the night. One of them had blundered into a pylon and caused an explosion, which awakened Siuda. He left home for the factory grounds, and there participated in an angry exchange with an army officer who was pressuring the strikers to return to their jobs. This encounter led to his arrest. Because he had been under surveillance as an unreliable character, when he was taken to the factory director's office, he reports, KGB agents there exclaimed: "Siuda! Glad to see you! We've been waiting!" [40]

Siuda was tried in Rostov, together with six others, in September 1962. The charge against him reads as follows:

> On June 1 he came to the factory, joined the rioters, entered the platform of a truck standing near the factory administration building, whence he put provocative questions to S. N. Elkin, the factory's chief engineer, and incited the crowd to continue the mass disorders.
>
> Standing on the bank of the railroad line, calling on the rioters not to allow the halted train to go on, [he] argued with the factory activists who came to put things in order and restore rail traffic.
>
> In the evening of the same day, Siuda appealed from the top of the [railroad] tunnel to the assembled crowd not to return to work, to go to the City Committee building of the CPSU with provocative demands, proposed the sending of "delegates" to other factories to stop their work. Opposed the police officers who came to the factory to restore order and demanded that they leave. [41]

In his articles Siuda never addressed the indictment systematically. Here and there, though, he conceded much of what he was charged with, while rejecting the tendentious interpretation. Of course there had been a strike, and he had wholeheartedly supported it and striven to keep it going. Needless to say, he took vigorous exception to the characterization of the strike as "mass disorders" and the strikers as "rioters." He admitted having put questions to Elkin, but he genuinely respected the engineer as the only member of the factory administration who had come out to speak to the workers man to man, and had protected him against threatened physical abuse. He had urged the people to go to the city the next day to present their demands to the authorities; but in doing so he had acted as a moderating force, successfully arguing against a proposal to seize the post and telegraph facilities. Plainly, the various charges against Siuda were directed at his exercise of *speech*—he was accused of no unlawful *acts*, let alone violent ones. Nevertheless, he was sentenced to twelve years in a labor camp.

He served less than four years, leaving the camp in July 1966. The terms of most of the imprisoned strikers were commuted at one point or another. In Siuda's case, his mother's appeal to Mikoyan, who had known his father, may have been effective, as had been her appeal to Stalin on behalf of her husband. According to Siuda, many of those released from the camps returned to Novocherkassk, as he did, but a good many of them succumbed to alcoholism or engaged in criminal activity.[42] At some point, Siuda himself reportedly became a heavy drinker.

The turbulence that had marked Siuda's earlier years resumed from the time of his arrest. In jail he was pressured to repent his actions—most others had done so, he was told—but he would not bend. His principled stand did not keep him from sinking into a despair that led him to attempt suicide. Back in Novocherkassk after his release, he worked at Neftemash, a plant that produced oil-drilling machinery. In a rare interval of contentment that lasted two and a half years, he gained technical expertise, enjoyed a good job, and offered significant suggestions for the improvement of plant efficiency. He then ran afoul of a party organizer in the plant who insisted on being named co-author of one of Siuda's proposals. Siuda lost the contest but penned an open letter to the Central Committee and the KGB protesting what had happened. This initiative brought him under close and unremitting KGB surveillance from then on. Besides, he left his job at Neftemash and had great difficulty finding work thereafter. In the meantime, his health seriously deteriorated: he underwent an operation that removed two-thirds of his stomach. After renewed difficulty finding work, he secured a position as an engineer-designer at the Electric Locomotive Engineering Research Institute. He remained a dissenter, refusing to vote in the elections. In 1980 he wrote a letter to Brezhnev, protesting the Soviet intervention in Afghanistan. And when he made common cause with a group of garden-plot holders against the insensitive establishment, he was severely beaten.[43]

In 1980 Siuda learned that his father had not, as he supposed, been fully rehabilitated, and he spent much of the next six years doing the research essential to the restoration of his parent's name. He claims to have written more than 700 letters to various bureaus and authorities in pursuit of his goal. His efforts were endlessly frustrated by people who had the power to help but were disinclined to assist someone scorned as a troublemaker. Driven to despair, in 1983 for the second time he attempted suicide.[44]

In 1987, encouraged by the onset of perestroika, Siuda turned his attention to what he seems to have been the first to call "the Novocherkassk tragedy." His activity from that point through the publication of Nikitina's groundbreaking article has been detailed in Chapter 6. Thereafter he continued what he not unreasonably called his "titanic efforts" to publicize his version of the Novocherkassk tragedy.[45] He believed, among other things, that he might help

prevent a recurrence of anything of the kind. Siuda's testimony figured prominently in the first article on Novocherkassk to appear in the central press, the
account Bespalov and Konovalov published in June 1989 in *Komsomol'skaia
pravda*. He had the satisfaction of seeing many other accounts of the events in
newspapers around the country. He joined with other outraged Novocherkassians in pressing the city government to establish a committee to gather all possible information about the 1962 events. The committee produced two important publications[46] as part of an eventually successful campaign to secure a
reconsideration of the case by the central authorities. The review of the case
had not been completed when, on May 5, 1990, Siuda was found unconscious
in a street near his home, his briefcase gone. He was taken to a hospital, where
he died twenty minutes later.

It was widely assumed that he had been the victim of a political murder.
David Mandel typified this view in the preface to his interview with Siuda: "In
the spring of 1991 [*sic*] Petr was murdered in Novocherkassk, beaten and left to
die in the street. In his briefcase were documents about the 1962 events. The
murder . . . was in all likelihood politically motivated."[47] Nikitina adduced reasons for a categorical denial that he had been murdered. With the Novocherkassk story out in the open, even being discussed in the Supreme Soviet, it
would have been senseless to kill Siuda. Besides, the medical experts had ruled
out a violent assault as a cause of his death.[48]

In an interview, Bespalov fully explained his reasons for disbelieving that
Siuda had been murdered.[49] He could speak with authority, for at that time
Bespalov was campaigning for a seat in the Soviet of Deputies, and Siuda was
assisting him. He sped to Novocherkassk as soon as he received word of Siuda's
death and proceeded directly to the hospital. The doctors and nurses who had
undressed, washed, and examined Siuda's body were just coming off duty. He
interviewed them in their homes before anyone else had a chance to speak to
them. They unanimously agreed that there had been no evidence of gunshots,
clubbing, or any other form of violence. Siuda's wife was not convinced, suspected foul play, and wanted an independent investigation of her husband's
death. A Rostov physician who had had difficulties with the KGB and was
certified by human rights activists as an absolutely reliable expert was brought
in to examine the body. The physician and the activists had a strong interest
in proving that Siuda had been the victim of a political murder, but their efforts to find supporting evidence were fruitless.

According to Bespalov, Siuda's body had been found near a tavern he frequented. The journalist suspected that the briefcase had been picked up by a neighborhood drunk, who expected to find something of value in it. Supporting this assumption is the fact that the briefcase was later found with its contents intact; presumably whoever had taken it threw it away upon finding that it contained only papers. All these considerations count for naught with Siuda's wife, who in June 1997 told me unequivocally that her husband had been killed for political reasons. Having ruled out a murder, Bespalov (and Nikitina) contended that Siuda died of natural causes. Both stressed that his health had been undermined during his years of imprisonment. Additionally, Bespalov pointed to Siuda's poverty-ridden life, while Nikitina viewed the tensions of his last years as a complicating factor. Two-thirds of Siuda's stomach had been removed some time earlier, it should be recalled, and he was severely beaten more than once. Finally, Siuda had become a heavy drinker, and alcohol may have contributed to his death at the age of fifty-three.

In any event, this slight, wiry man with a goatee unquestionably made a mark on history. No serious student of the subject can afford to ignore the first chronicler and tireless propagandist of "the Novocherkassk tragedy."

Chapter 8   Reconsideration and Rehabilitation

The sensational events of the Gorbachev era's middle years were but a prelude to the truly astonishing developments of its last years. No one could have predicted the series of interrelated processes that fed upon each other, gained ever more momentum, and speedily brought what had seemingly been a stable if somewhat troubled Soviet system to a terminal crisis. The loosening of the reins in the perestroika regime unleashed nationalist movements among the non-Russian peoples of the USSR, emboldened the peoples of the satellite states in Eastern Europe to seek independence, and triggered an intensive struggle within the Soviet Union to transform the system by abolishing the Communist party's hegemony.

Nationalist stirrings first appeared in Lithuania, Latvia, and Estonia, which had been annexed pursuant to the Nazi-Soviet pact of 1939. Ukraine, Georgia, and Adzerbaidzhan soon joined in, and agitation soon ensued as well in Kazakhstan, Tadzhikistan, and Kirghizstan. The Baltic republics first declared their national tongues their state languages; soon they proclaimed their sovereignty—that is, the precedence of their own laws over those of the Union; and finally they declared their independence. The other peoples described more or less similar trajectories. The Russian Republic's declaration of sovereignty in June 1990 was of especial importance, for in the next two and one-half months every other Soviet republic followed suit. Of course, the process was resisted by the old guard, and now and then Gorbachev seems to have gone along with their efforts to halt the process forcibly. Two notorious occasions—both resulted in numerous deaths—were the use of troops against demonstrators in Tbilisi in April 1989 and an armed attack on republic installations in Vilnius in January 1990. The attempted coup against Gorbachev in August 1991 was a last-ditch effort of conservative leaders to block a solution of the nationalities question that they could not accept because it went too far toward decentralization of power. This fiasco accelerated the independence drives, and within months the USSR was dead.[1]

The dissolution of the Soviet bloc proceeded in parallel with the dismantling of the Soviet Union. The restive peoples in Eastern Europe sensed new possibilities in Gorbachev's perestroika. Leaders of the opposition in the satellite countries resorted to diverse canny strategies to win greater breathing space and eventually to escape Soviet domination. The Solidarity movement in Poland led the way. In June 1989 the elections it had long sought resulted in an overwhelming victory for the anticommunist forces and the designation of Lech Wałęsa as prime minister. With that the dismantling of the party-state and a move to a market economy by way of "shock therapy" got under way. The Polish example proved infectious, abetted no little by Gorbachev's declaration that he would not intervene to block reforms. In the next seven months Soviet control of the region evaporated as the Berlin wall was torn down and the six remaining Communist regimes in the region were ousted.

A critical juncture in the breakdown of the political structure within the USSR was the convening of the First Congress of People's Deputies on May 25, 1989. Gorbachev had promoted the election of such a body, hoping that an infusion of reform-minded people might help him to overcome the party's resistance to his program of renewal. Although the election law heavily favored party candidates, it also provided opportunities for critics of the status quo to seek a share of the seats. In the event, many important apparatchiki were defeated, while 300 insurgent deputies were elected, among them Andrei Sakharov, Roy Medvedev, and Boris Yeltsin. Gorbachev got much more than he had bargained for, as the critics exploited the freedom of expression they enjoyed in the hall to indict the regime for a wide range of failures and injustices. Sakharov even managed to call for repeal of Article 6 of the Constitution, which gave the CPSU a monopoly of political power. The proceedings of the congress lasted just twelve days, but they were broadcast on television throughout the country and were watched with fascination by an enormous number of people.[2] The broadcasts had the momentous effect, as Martin Malia has suggested, of desacralizing the system.[3] The flood of revelations and denunciations that now poured forth forced the authorities, however reluctantly, to yield one position after another. To be sure, a good deal of zigzagging occurred, as Gorbachev felt obliged to yield to pressures from the KGB, the military, and the party apparatus. But after the failure of the August 1991 coup, the tide could not be stopped. The Communist Party was outlawed in November 1991 and the USSR disestablished the following month.

These tumultuous events are the frame within which the final act in the Novocherkassk saga was played out. The momentous developments then unfolding did not render insignificant the exposure of what had occurred in a southern Russian town in June 1962. As a matter of fact, rather than being relegated to oblivion, Novocherkassk became a cause célèbre, a devastating item in the bill of particulars drawn up against the Soviet regime. To be sure, the Soviet people were shocked to learn that in exchange for neutrality as Germany ravaged Poland, Stalin had secretly conspired with Hitler to subjugate the Baltic countries. Undoubtedly they were revolted by the disclosure that Stalin had ordered the massacre of thousands of Polish officers in the Katyn forest. Still, these were matters in the realm of foreign affairs, and they could be thought of, though not dismissed, as the work of an unspeakably evil figure who had already been discredited. The Novocherkassk events were much closer to home, and they had occurred after Stalin's death. What could be more horrifying than the revelation that the leaders of a state purportedly dedicated to the interests of the working class had ordered the gunning down of workers on strike for better living conditions? When, after the collapse of the Soviet Union, the CPSU was put on trial, a prominent charge against it was the perpetration of the Novocherkassk massacre.[4]

The first report on the Novocherkassk events to appear in the central press was the Bespalov-Konovalov piece published in *Komsomol'skaia pravda* on June 2, 1989. As we saw earlier, it caught the attention of a number of individuals elected to the First Congress of People's Deputies of the USSR, among them A A. Sobchak (later the popular mayor of Leningrad / St. Petersburg). The people of Russia's second city had resoundingly defeated the first secretary of the city's party organization and an alternate Politbiuro member as well to choose Sobchak and other progressives as their delegates. On June 10 Sobchak cited the *Komsomol'skaia pravda* article in support of a request to Gorbachev, the presiding officer. He asked that two items be placed on the agenda: a protest to the procurator general with respect to the trial verdicts and the rehabilitation of the victims.[5] Evidently Gorbachev or his then chief aide, President of the Supreme Soviet A. I. Luk'ianov, referred the matter to the KGB, the Ministry of Defense, and the Procuracy for consideration, but little or no action followed. So on September 26 Sobchak and six other deputies, some from the Rostov region, wrote letters to the heads of those organizations, decrying the inadequacy of the responses. Moving beyond Sobchak's earlier interpellation, they now asked for access to all the relevant documents.[6] Receiving no satisfaction, the seven prodded the organizations again on October 10, but in vain.[7]

Unwilling to let the matter rest, they strove to widen support and secure results by publicizing their concerns. On November 22, V. M. Kalinchenko, a faculty member of the Novocherkassk Polytechnical Institute who had been chosen as a people's deputy, ratcheted up the deputies' demands in an address to a joint session of the Soviet of the Union and the Soviet of Nationalities. Recalling Sobchak's initial request for an investigation, he emphasized the indispensability of an inquiry to determine the entire list of those who had been repressed, to discover the burial places of those who had been killed, and to lay the groundwork for the rehabilitation of the victims, both dead and alive. To that end, he asked the Supreme Soviet to create a commission, headed by Sobchak, to investigate the events; and to ask the heads of the KGB, the Ministry of Defense, and the procurator general to respond to the questions the deputies had sent them.[8] By December 18, arguing that the Novocherkassk events "are agitating wide circles of society," nineteen delegates from the Rostov area to the Second Congress of People's Deputies demanded a Supreme Court–appointed commission to look into the matter and report its findings in the mass media.[9] In the space of six months, critically minded deputies had advanced from respectful queries to major bulwarks of the state to demands that elected representatives under one of their aggressive leaders be assigned the investigatory mission that others were evidently disinclined to undertake.

This demand was not satisfied, at least in part because of a countercampaign waged by military men who had been involved in the Novocherkassk events. On October 18, five generals and five colonels sent Luk'ianov a letter of protest, signed also by thirty other members of the Rostov section of the Soviet Committee of War Veterans. This was not a one-time communication—it mentions an earlier note sent to Luk'ianov directed against the major exposé on Novocherkassk that *Literaturnaia gazeta* had printed on June 21, and others undoubtedly followed. P. P. Falynskov, a tank regiment officer at the time of the Novocherkassk events, had also penned a letter protesting the *Literaturnaia gazeta* article. His was directed to Lt. Col. A. V. Tretetskii, an official in the Chief Military Procuracy, who, as it turned out, would be in charge of the military's review of what had occurred at Novocherkassk.[10] Characteristically, the defenders of the Novocherkassk actions chose to make their case behind the scenes to powerful figures who could pull strings on their behalf. They were unaccustomed to engaging in contests for public favor in the political arena, perhaps considered it beneath their dignity to do so, and, as we shall see, virtually surrendered the public relations contest to their opponents.

Writing out of a sense of aggrieved honor, the war veterans protested against "provocative, sensational reports" in the mass media, which depicted army personnel as "chastisers, capable of shooting at Russian people, at workers who came out to a demonstration." The attack was directed in particular against Roy Medvedev, who had written in the magazine *Druzhba narodov* a brief innocuous sketch—not entirely accurate, though unintentionally so—of what had happened.[11] Identifying themselves as "living witnesses and direct participants in the events," the officers told "how it had been in reality." Offering no word about what had precipitated the strike, they focused on hooliganism and rioting. They falsely claimed that the strikers had repeatedly attempted to seize weapons from the soldiers, and as a result a total of six people were killed. Demanding that Luk'ianov press Medvedev to apologize publicly for what he had written, the officers self-righteously declared: "Soviet soldiers, officers, and generals were not, are not, and never will be chastisers [punitive forces]." Medvedev's "objective is to slander and compromise the armed forces, to undermine the unity of the army and the people, the guarantor of our invincibility."[12]

Despite such agitations, the mounting pressure brought replies of sorts from the key organizations. On November 22, V. A. Kriuchkov, president of the KGB, gave a bit of ground in summarizing the outcome of the trials held after the shooting. But he deceitfully claimed that the agency had no documents on the army's resort to arms, and asserted that a review of the sentences imposed by the courts was not within his agency's competence. A month or so later (Dec. 29), a reply from the Ministry of Defense took the same line with respect to a review. It indicated, however, that the ministry archive possessed a small number of documents, which the petitioners were free to examine. (Unaccountably, they seem not to have availed themselves of this opportunity.) As opposed to these replies, one from the procurator general's office that arrived between the other two (Nov. 27) reported that an investigation, to be made jointly with the KGB, would examine the events and the sentences handed down at the trials.[13]

Seventy-five days later, however, nothing further had issued from the procurator general's office. No wonder that Kalinchenko, frustrated by the apparently persistent inattention of the high-level agencies to the elected deputies' requests, finally appealed to Gorbachev on March 12, 1990, to take appropriate action.[14] Understandably distrustful of agencies that had been deeply implicated in the 1962 events, Kalinchenko and his fellows again pressed for a special commission, one that could be counted on to make an independent examination of the record. Those in authority were not about to surrender control of the sources and their use, but by late 1989, in the face of rising public dissatisfaction, they could no longer get by with obsructionist tactics alone. Unbeknownst to the disgruntled deputies, around the end of 1989 the procurator general of the USSR had assigned the Chief Military Procuracy to examine the circumstances and the consequences of the use of arms by the military forces (both army and internal troops) at Novocherkassk. He also required the Procuracy of the USSR, jointly with the Procuracy of the Russian Republic, to determine the propriety of the convictions of those who had been brought to trial.[15] The investigations proceeded deliberately, and were not completed until mid-1991.

Deputies were impatient for results, and probably addressed further inquiries to the responsible organizations repeatedly. One such letter, written on May 20, 1990, by two people's deputies from Novocherkassk, posed a series of pointed questions:

> What work is being done in the department entrusted you about the "tragic events"? Has a commission been created that could assess the causes that led to the workers' uprising? Who was responsible for the decision to use weapons against a peaceful demonstration? Will those who are guilty be brought to justice? . . . Is the question of establishing the exact number of convicted persons, the rehabilitation of those innocently convicted, and payment of pensions to the families being examined?

They also solicited the attitude of these agencies toward the proposal to build a memorial to the victims of 1962.[16] We have only one reply, that of Minister of Defense Iazov. He provided some interesting details, such as the number of army troops (almost 3,000) that had been concentrated in the city on June 2. In his counterattack on the protesting deputies and the muckraking journalists—it was to be the official position for the next seventeen months—the minister described what had occurred as the necessary and proper response to the work of hooligans engaging in mindless violence. He was either misinformed or blatantly lying when he claimed that the strikers had repeatedly attempted to seize the post and telegraph offices, the state bank, the power station, and the prisons, and that they had tried to wrest the soldiers' weapons from them. In contrast to the Rostov officers, he reported (laconically) that twenty-four persons had been killed and thirty-nine wounded during the restoration of order; but gave greater consideration to the dozens of officers and men who had been struck or injured.[17]

The public contest continued between those who wished to expose and those who wished to conceal or misrepresent the Novocherkassk events. On the one side, investigative reporters took center stage, with the media serving as the showcase for their findings. As earlier indicated, after the Bespalov-Konovalov article was published (June 1989), more than forty pieces appeared, two dozen of them in newspapers with large readerships and others in journals and in pamphlet form. The overwhelming majority were exposés of matters long kept secret and at the same time indictments of those deemed responsible. In contrast, those disposed to justify the shootings and the trial verdicts seemingly published only four items in the same period. Three of the four stemmed from the military community, the fourth from the procurator general's office.[18] While the crusading writers energetically sought new sources of information, their opponents based their briefs largely on the KGB documents produced contemporaneously with the events, which were published only in 1993. True, two of the items reflecting the military's point of view depended in part on information gathered from the beginning of 1990 by the Chief Military Procuracy, but what was leaked generally reinforced the version of the events that the official agencies steadfastly embraced.

The Novocherkassk events became a significant factor in a more comprehensive political war between those who wished to discredit and dismantle the political system and those who wished to protect and perpetuate it. In a reflective article that went beyond reportage, V. Konovalov made explicit what other writers more or less implied: that the search for truth about the Novocherkassk events was integral to the struggle for democracy. No one had consulted the people about the price rises decreed on May 31, 1962; the Novocherkassk workers had no legal way to protest; and when they put themselves outside the law by striking and demonstrating, they were savagely punished. The recent resort to violence against demonstrators in Tbilisi showed, Konovalov asserted, that the old modus operandi remained in force. Parenthetically, the Tbilisi and Vilnius attacks were made much of by many another writer bent on exposing and condemning what had happened at Novocherkassk. The issue, Konovalov concluded, "is one of rights and lawlessness, democracy and its defense, the creation of real laws and their guarantee, true popular rule." Therefore, "so long as the bureaucratic, anti-popular stratum is strong, so long as democracy is limited, there can be no firm safeguard against the recurrence of such tragic events, and their employment in the interests of reactionary forces." [19]

The sentiments of the other side were succinctly expressed in the introduction to an article in a publication of the Ministry of Defense, subtitled "Patriotism and . . . Extremism."

> When you leaf through . . . the past year's numbers of . . . *Literaturnaia gazeta* [and] *Komsomol'skaia pravda*, you [are bound] to conclude that these organs insistently and consistently present readers with a distorted picture of our reality and history. While cloaking themselves with noble strivings in defense of oppressed and insulted nations and peoples, [supposedly] whitening the blemished names of worthy people [and] illuminating hitherto dark pages, in reality they replace patriotism with extremism. . . . The objective of such publications is entirely clear—while promoting "new" thinking and a new way of life, to distort fatherland (and, in the first instance, Soviet) history, to spit and trample upon established traditions and moral values, to blacken the Armed Forces. Frequently the authors of such published materials thus satisfy their petty ambitions and vanity, secure a cheap political authority, [and] court the leaders of "the democratic wave." [20]

The article in *Sovetskaia Rossiia* expounds the view one expects in a Communist organ, but in places it gives the impression of having been written as much in sorrow as in anger. At one point its author, Zh. Kastenenko, remarks: "It is frightful when people are transformed into a mob blinded by hatred and ready to demolish anything in their path." But he strikes an unexpected note when he asserts: "It is frightful when one's own people are fired upon." Affirming that order and respect for the law are necessary in a democratic society, Kastenenko recognizes that no right to strike and demonstrate existed in 1962. These deviations from the official stance, however modest, foreshadowed a radical shift in the next few years in the military's view of the events.

The reform-minded writers succeeded in winning the hearts and minds of the politically interested population on several scores. Certainly the iconoclastic spirit of the times favored the antiestablishment forces. March 14, 1990, saw the passage of an amendment to the Constitution abolishing the monopoly position of the CPSU, and on May 29 the insurgent Boris Yeltsin was elected Speaker of the RSFSR Supreme Soviet. Besides, individuals were sufficiently encouraged by the disclosures that had been appearing in the press to write up their own revealing stories for publication.[21] The liberals made their case with respect to Novocherkassk far more zealously and relentlessly than their opponents. They tracked down a good many persons who had been involved in or affected by the strike and its aftermath. Thus they managed to develop— sometimes stridently—a harrowing image of the events from the bottom up. They reported, often verbatim, the heartrending stories some of these people related, thereby engaging their readers' sympathies, arousing their indignation, and gathering support for their crusade.

Anna Terletskaia told Bespalov, the *Komsomol'skaia pravda* correspondent, about her son's death:

> Gena was fifteen years old. He was enrolled in the food technology secondary school. He fell to a bullet by chance. His friends later told me that when the demonstration began at the gorkom, the school director ordered that none of the students were to be allowed out onto the streets. But the physical education instructor said, "Why lose time?" and led the boys into the yard for a workout. Well, of course the boys ran off. They were interested in watching the goings-on. They watched. . . . They didn't give me the body of my son, indeed none [of the bodies of the slain] were turned over to their relatives. They didn't even turn over for burial the body of the hairdresser who was hit by a stray bullet. Only a year later they called me in to the police station and asked, "Do you know where your son is?" I replied: "If you tell me, I'll know." They told me nothing. They only showed me a batch of watches, to see if Gena's was among them. His watch wasn't there, probably taken at the morgue.[22]

Terletskaia added that she still didn't know where her son was buried.

A letter from Nina Sotnikova to the city soviet movingly bewailed her plight:

> Addressing you is the mother of Sergei Sotnikov, who was convicted and executed for [participation in] the 1962 strike. I ask you to tell me why my son was punished so severely.
>
> His father, also named Sergei Sotnikov, was a party member since 1918, a teacher [and] director of a children's home. When he was taken to the front [where he was killed], I was left with three children. The eldest was ten years old, Serezha four, the youngest nine months. When the evacua-

tion began, a bomb fell on our house. At the time, the eldest was holding the babe in his arms, and both were fatally wounded. . . . The sons buried, I was left alone with Serezha during the occupation. . . . He was my last hope. And it was lost in 1962. I still don't know why my son perished, what he was guilty of. From his youngest years, he was honest and proper, like his father. What kind of a criminal is he?

I am 81 years old. It seems as though I have not lived [*ne zhila na svete*]. My entire family has perished. I beg you to help me learn my son's last words at the trial. Did he remember his home, mother, wife, and two daughters? . . . Help me to find out where his grave is. I haven't long to live. I would like to die in peace.

I am writing poorly, blinded by tears. Help me, you too probably have children.[23]

Nadezhda D'iakonova unburdened her heart in a letter to the editor of *Trud*.

Today is Easter. Through my window [I see] a mass of Novocherkassians heading for the cemetery to place bouquets of crimson tulips on the graves of their loved ones. I go too. But where? Drawn by the flow of people, I go to the town cemetery. Most often I put flowers on my brother's grave. For I don't know where my husband is buried. [The thought gives me, an elderly person, no rest. Twenty-seven years of uncertainty. I don't know how long I will live. But in keeping with the old Russian custom, I would like to have my last resting place alongside my husband.]

On June 2, 1962, my husband, Aleksandr Nikolaevich, as secretary of the party organization in [his] factory's metal products division, conducted a meeting with the workers about the events at NEVZ. Then he was called to a meeting at the gorkom. On the way, he went into a store to buy cigarettes. He exited at the moment when the shooting began. A stray bullet struck him under the left shoulder, and he fell. Together with the slain hairdresser, he was taken to the surgical hospital [where he died].

My husband participated in the Great Patriotic War as a border guard. He managed to survive the war. But to die by a stray bullet in peacetime—that's absurd. Help me. I am tired of uncertainty.[24]

Such stories indicated, among other things, that the shooting orgy had mown down innocent bystanders, including two teenagers, a hairdresser, a Communist worker, and an out-of-town visitor.[25] As for the strikers and demonstrators, the title of a piece in the popular magazine *Rodina*—"They Sought Justice"—harmonized with the premise of many articles, that they had been innocent victims of a war the party-state had waged against the people.[26]

V. Malakhov, a self-described "Old Communist" who had served twenty-seven years in the army and afterward became a jurist, powerfully underscored the point. At the time a cadre officer in a military school, he was one of a group dispatched to Novocherkassk to suppress disorders said to have been fomented by hooligans and extremists. Their superiors repeatedly enjoined them to refrain from asking questions, but he saw no hooligans. Because he was assigned elsewhere in the city, he heard the fusillade from a distance. The next day he saw fire engines removing the blood from the streets; and he bitterly recalled how armed units had driven through the workers' settlements in a "demonstration of the force and power of the people's army, which had meted out punishment to its people." Malakhov had never forgotten the cry of "Fascists!" hurled at the soldiers by a girl; she "had exactly defined our conduct in one word."[27]

That the old guard was determined to hinder in any way possible the campaign to tell the whole truth was brought home anew in an article announcing that photographs produced at the time of the events, and briefly put at the disposal of a documentary filmmaker, had mysteriously disappeared.[28] Fortunately, copies had been made of some of them, and they filled most of a large-format newspaper page. Among them were pictures surreptitiously taken during the June days, with crosses subsequently inscribed on individuals who had been identified as particularly active in the "mass disorders." There were prison photographs as well of the seven who had been condemned to death. Electrifying was a shot of men and women in the front rank of a mass of demonstrators marching toward the city center, holding aloft red banners and portraits of Lenin. This image compelled the viewer to wonder: How could these disciplined proletarian followers of Lenin be characterized as hooligans, criminals, anti-Soviet elements? It is not difficult to guess the identity of those who had sought to keep such evidence from the public.

The article included in a sidebar another revealing item: a signed sample of the pledge exacted from persons who had participated in the grisly, secret burials of those slain on June 2, 1962. It reads: "I, a policeman of the Kamensk Police Department, submit the present document, wherein I pledge to fulfill the government task and to keep it a state secret. If I violate this undertaking, I will be subject to the highest degree of punishment—shooting." Adding impact to the pledge was an accompanying statement by Ol'ga Efremova, who, twenty-nine years after the event, recalled her unsuccessful efforts to learn the whereabouts of the body of her sixteen-year old-son, Anatolii Artiushchenko:

> Well, I went to the police department. They told me at the police depart-
> ment that I should go to the town council building. [I did so.] Secretary
> Sirotin was there. . . . He says: "What do you want?" I reply: "They've
> killed my son, at least give me his body." And he says: "No one was shot
> here. No one killed anyone." A young man came, shut me up, and took
> me to the soldiers. They say: "Well come tomorrow." I came the next day.
> And . . . Sirotin struck [me]. They sent me to the department of nervous
> diseases at the hospital.[29]

The insistent demands of elected representatives, crusading journalists, and
a public outraged by the inhuman withholding of the location of the graves
brought forth at last, in January 1991, the declassification of the relevant information. The Union Procuracy advised the Rostov provincial soviet and the
Novocherkassk city soviet that the bodies had been interred in the hamlet of
Martsevo, near Taganrog; in an old cemetery in the Tarasovskii area; and near
the town of Novoshakhtinsk. The names of those who had been slain were also
revealed to the Rostov soviet, but not made public for some time.[30]

The government agencies did nothing more than reveal the locations in a
general way. The gravesites were unmarked, so it would be no small problem
to find them. That task, plus the recovery of the remains, their transfer to
Novocherkassk, and the provision of a decent burial, was undertaken by the
Novocherkassk Tragedy Foundation (Fond Novocherkasskoi Tragedii). This
organization—it was initially called the Commission and Fund on the Novocherkassk Tragedy—had been established in 1989. It had been created with a
view to gathering all possible information about the June events and their sequel, agitating for a government review of military and court actions, publicizing what had occurred by way of lectures, discussions, and exhibits, securing
the rehabilitation of the victims and compensation for them or their families,
defending before government and social organizations the interests of those
who had suffered, perpetuating the memory of the victims by erecting a monument and holding an annual ceremony on the anniversary of the event, and
raising funds to support its work.[31]

The journalist Irina Mardar' was the first president of the organization. Petr
Siuda was one of the founders of the organization and until his death in May
1990 he zealously supported its work. The other most active members were
Valentina Vodianitskaia, a participant in the strike who had been sentenced to
ten years' imprisonment but was released after four or five years; Tat'iana Bocharova, another journalist, who became the second president; and M. I. Krais-

vetnyi, an archeologist, who was of inestimable importance in recovering the remains of those secretly buried. Persons who had been wounded or imprisoned and their relatives, as well as the kin of those who had been killed, joined or supported the organization, as did other concerned townspeople. From the beginning, Mardar' and her associates had pressured the Novocherkassk town council to endorse and cooperate in their efforts, and they succeeded.

Mardar' asserted that women, moved more by humanitarian than political sentiments, had been in the forefront of the endeavor.[32] No doubt for them the discovery of the whereabouts of the bodies and the desire to give them a proper burial was a primary consideration. Mardar' proved to be an energetic and resourceful leader. She scrupulously collected testimonies from many who had been involved in the events, on both sides, as well as relevant documents both historical and contemporary; and then published a small but valuable collection of these materials.[33] In 1992 she composed a sixty-page pamphlet, *A Chronicle of Unacknowledged Murders*, which presented many new data and reflected a wide range of opinion. Thirty thousand copies of the pamphlet were printed.[34]

On June 2, 1991, the organization was able for the first time to mark the anniversary of the massacre with a notable series of public events. A public meeting on the square featured speeches by representatives of social organizations and participants in the events. A small memorial obelisk, inscribed "June 2, 1962," was unveiled. A screening of documentary films was followed by a meeting with the celebrated General Shaposhnikov. Unveiled, too, was a plaque that had been mounted at the entrance to the electric locomotive factory where the strike had begun. On it were inscribed these words: "Here began the spontaneous initiative of workers driven to despair, which ended June 2, 1962, with a fusillade in the city's central square and further repressions."[35]

The release of information on the burial sites was followed two months later by what can only be described as a bombshell. Well-informed people were aware that the Procuracy General of the USSR and the Chief Military Procuracy were engaged in investigations of the Novocherkassk shootings and the court verdicts. Some complained now and again about the seemingly glacial pace of progress, but it was anticipated that results would ultimately emerge. Did anyone imagine that a break would come from another quarter? A group of people's deputies had called upon the Supreme Court to appoint a commission to review the cases, but there was no indication that the demand had been heeded. Nevertheless, members of the court were evidently moved by the request and decided to undertake a review of their own. Many institutions in the Soviet Union were affected, in some measure, by the fresh winds sweeping through the country. Officials who had reservations about past and present governmental procedures and actions were impelled to voice their thoughts. Indeed, the "new thinking" encouraged in the Gorbachev years undoubtedly prompted more than a few persons to reconsider their own conduct in the past. Among them was L. G. Smirnov, the chief justice of the RSFSR Supreme Court, who had presided over the principal trial of the Novocherkassk strikers. Although, realistically, he had had no choice in the matter, he must have been troubled by the judgments he had rendered in 1962, and perhaps increasingly so in the rapidly changing conditions of recent years.

These suppositions probably explain what happened on March 27, 1991, when, in a striking show of independence, a plenum of the court abrogated the verdicts handed down on August 20, 1962. The seven who had been convicted of banditry and executed were exonerated, on the ground of "absence of criminality in their actions." One of the seven, V. D. Cherepanov, although adjudged innocent of banditry, was not entirely cleared, as he was still held guilty of having broken down the door to the police station in an attempt to liberate arrested strikers.[36] At the same time, the verdicts pertaining to nineteen others who had been convicted of participation in mass disorders were repealed. Surprisingly, this remarkable reversal seems to have been given only passing attention in the press. The court's action was overshadowed by other events of the time: the overwhelming votes for independence in Latvia and Estonia, a nationwide majority vote favoring the transformation of the USSR into a voluntary union, a massive pro-Yeltsin demonstration in Moscow, and the dissolution of the Warsaw Pact.

The procurator general's report was finally completed seven weeks later, in mid-May, and a summary was published in *Pravda* on June 3. A preface seemed to intimate a change in orientation when it referred to "the tragic events in Novocherkassk"—this was the language of Siuda and all those who considered the government culpable. But then it went on to chide publications that had printed pieces "based not on concrete, documented facts, but sometimes on the recollections of eyewitnesses, whose interpretation of what took place . . . is rather subjective." Presumably the report, based on "explanations obtained from former leaders of party, soviet, and law enforcement organs in Novocherkassk and the Rostov region, and from archival documents of the USSR

Ministry of the Interior and the General Staff of the USSR armed forces," was untainted by subjectivity. Accordingly, Procurator General N. S. Trubin, the author of the account, was in a position to describe objectively—to quote the report's title (in slightly altered form)—"How It Was in Novocherkassk in 1962."[37]

A summary account of the strike and demonstration identified as the causes of the strike the more or less simultaneous reduction in wage rates and increase in food prices and the factory manager's boorish response to the workers' expressions of dismay. Genuine grievances there had evidently been, but, it was implied, they could not possibly justify what followed. Angry workers, under the influence of alcohol, rioted and destroyed property. "The organizers and instigators of the disorders" incited the people to confront the military units brought to restore order. They attacked military personnel, overturned vehicles, impeded rail traffic, sought to spread the strike, and attempted (unsuccessfully) to seize the gas depot. With that, countermeasures were taken: tanks sent to the factory grounds, some thirty people arrested, and key institutions in the city secured. On June 2, after the column of demonstrators had crossed the bridge over the Tuzlov River and were marching to the city center, "F. R. Kozlov informed N. S. Khrushchev in Moscow about the situation and requested that the Ministry of Defense order I. A. Pliev, the army commander, to use troops to thwart any possible destructive rioting in the city."

Both MVD and army reinforcements were brought into the city, made combat ready, and assigned to protect government and party buildings. The familiar official view of what followed need not be rehearsed, but the conclusions should be recorded. General Oleshko ordered a warning volley in the square but gave no follow-up order to fire on the crowd. The shooting at the square

> occurred after raging individuals from the crowd fell upon the soldiers and attempted to seize their weapons. The soldiers fired in self-defense and to keep hold of their weapons. . . . Organs of the KGB and the USSR Ministry of the Interior instituted and prosecuted fifty-seven criminal cases in connection with the events in Novocherkassk. A total of 114 persons were convicted, including 7 for banditry and the organization of mass disorders, 82 for participation in mass disorders, and 25 for malicious hooliganism. All the criminal cases have now been reviewed. Forty-six of the persons convicted have been completely rehabilitated in response to protests by procurators about judicial errors that were committed. The sentences of 45 persons were changed in light of improper classifications [of acts com-

mitted] and the severity of the punishments imposed. The Chief Military Prosecutor rightly rejected criminal proceedings instituted in connection with the soldiers' use of weapons during the quelling of the mass disorder, since the investigation disclosed that they had lawfully used their weapons for purposes of defending state property from criminal encroachments and for self-defense.

There is a glaring contradiction between the Supreme Court's abrogation of the verdicts handed down against the strikers "in the absence of criminality in their actions" and the procurator general's justification of the firing upon them. Indeed, the contradiction is apparent in Trubin's own report, which emphasizes drunken, riotous, destructive activity while also speaking, however cursorily, of the reversal of the verdicts in scores of cases and the rehabilitation of those improperly sentenced because of judicial errors and the like. Not unexpectedly, the publication of the Trubin report called forth an uproar. An article on the front page of *Komsomol'skaia pravda* headlined "Is Shooting Permissible?" inquired why the steady progress toward "socialism with a human face" was again and again punctuated by bursts of machine gun fire. The authors were nonplussed by the contention that the people who had been fired upon and those who had done the firing could both be innocent. Besides, was it tolerable to brush aside, as if it were an inconsequential "judicial error," such abominations as the sentence of twelve years in prison imposed upon someone who had hoisted a placard on which he had inscribed the words "Meat, Butter, a Pay Raise"? The article rebutted the report point by point, notably that random shots rather than a sustained barrage had been discharged, that the demonstrators had attempted to seize the soldiers' weapons, and, not least, the categorization of what had been a demonstration as a series of mass disorders.[38]

Yevgeny Yevtushenko vented his rage in a poem directed at the procurator general on the front page of *Literaturnaia gazeta*.[39] Some of its lines read as follows:

> A deep bow to the new verdict
>
>   . . .
>
> Not [from] the procurator general of the Union
> But simply from the generals' Procurator
> That city built on blood——
>   Novocherkassk [where]
> Freedom executed became a gravestone——

But there in sixty-two began
The people's war against the anti-people.
Thus were the people brought to the point
Where self-sacrificing Russian women
Holding children to their breasts
                went against the tanks
Under the bullets of their own country
Tell
                procurator general
Didn't you instantly shudder
When the [loose-leaf] binder pierced
the workers' corpses
                squeezed in the folder
And squirted blood on you
On the gold-embroidered uniform?
                        . . .

Be still
        corpses
You were justly executed
Thanks
        Procurator of the generals
You've described with patriotic heat
And the pedagogical correctness of a point-blank bullet
The criminality of a rebellion against oppression
I will decipher your words
"The authority that shoots is always right"
                        . . .

Terror was white [and] red
We never wearied of fighting against each other
The path is short from the Lena salvo
To the Leninist shootings in the civil war
                        . . .

And even our "thaw" made
Icicles of Novocherkassk blood
How transform hatred into love
A love without machine guns at the ready?
Russia
        You will be great again
If only you renounce great bloodshedding

And [spare] Russia's great women
From clasping their children in a new frightful hour.[40]

Trubin's report must have been made available to the members of the Supreme Soviet of the Russian Federation before it was published, and it was thence that the very first furious response issued. We may surmise that an angry discussion took place, culminating on May 22 in a motion "on the events of June 1962 in Novocherkassk," which was approved by the body and signed by its president, R. I. Khasbulatov. The resolution speaks of the "cruel suppression" of "a peaceful demonstration of workers who requested improvement of their socioeconomic conditions." "Condemning the action of the authorities in accordance with the Declaration of Rights and Freedoms of the Individual Citizen," the Supreme Soviet charged the procurator general to examine within two weeks the criminal trials of those not rehabilitated, to publicize their rehabilitation, and to consider payment to the families of the victims.[41] This resolution marks the adoption by the Supreme Soviet of the viewpoint that Sobchak and a few other deputies had advanced two years earlier and, along with a growing number of their colleagues, had been promoting ever since.

There is no evidence that the procurator general responded in anything like two weeks to the Supreme Soviet's peremptory demand. But the day of reckoning of the Soviet regime was fast approaching. On August 17 a group of top-level members of Gorbachev's government attempted to overthrow the man who had appointed many of them to their posts. Among the conspirators were Kriuchkov, head of the KGB; Iazov, minister of defense; B. K. Pugo, minister of internal affairs; and Luk'ianov, Speaker of the Supreme Soviet of the USSR. Boris Yeltsin, who had been elected president of the RSFSR on June 12, played a leading role in quashing the coup. Gorbachev's power and that of the CPSU had been eroding for some time. With the failure of the coup, the fates of the one and the other were sealed. The reformers seized the helm, and the change in leadership was bound to have an effect on a whole range of matters, including the Novocherkassk question.

On October 10, a plenum of the Supreme Court of the USSR met to reconsider judgments made in the past. Among them was the case of Andrei Amalrik, author of the book *Will the Soviet Union Survive Until 1984?* who now was declared innocent of the charges under which he had been convicted.[42] A reporter observed:

The discussion of a protest by the procurator general of the USSR concerning cases connected with the tragic events of almost thirty years ago in Novocherkassk will undoubtedly be sensational. Quite recently N. S. Trubin publicly declared that the conviction of the "rioters" was in accord with legal norms. Now he is requesting their complete rehabilitation. There can hardly be any doubt as to the outcome of the discussion. Tomorrow at the latest there will be an official acknowledgment of the innocence of more than thirty persons who spent many years in a camp.[43]

Days later (October 18) the Supreme Soviet of the RSFSR passed a detailed law "on the rehabilitation of the victims of political repression," a resolution on its implementation, and another "on the establishment of a memorial day for the victims of political repression."[44] The law's opening lines read:

During the years of Soviet power, millions of people fell victim to the arbitrariness of the totalitarian state. . . . The Supreme Soviet of the RSFSR . . . expresses deep sympathy with the victims of baseless repression, their relatives and loved ones, and declares its steadfast intention to secure real guarantees for the preservation of the legality and rights of the individual. The purpose of the present law is to rehabilitate all victims of political repression . . . in the RSFSR since October 25 (November 7), 1917, the restoration of their civil rights, the elimination of all consequences of arbitrariness, and the provision, so far as feasible at the present time, of compensation for material and moral suffering.

The law further provided for the creation of a commission on rehabilitation that would "guarantee complete access to the archives of courts, military tribunals, procuracies, organs of the KGB, the MVD, and other archives located in the RSFSR."

These statements of intention were not fully implemented with respect to the Novocherkassk case for a good while. On May 22, 1992, the Supreme Soviet of the Russian Federation resolved to secure within two weeks implementation of the law on the rehabilitation of the victims of political oppression with respect to those who had suffered during the June days, and to consider a lump-sum payment to the families of the dead.[45] In August the Ministry of Social Protection announced that the sum awarded would be 25,000 rubles, the amount paid to families of members of the armed forces who died in the line of duty.[46] It must be assumed that serious lapses occurred in the fulfillment of pledges made, and that some petitions submitted to the relevant agencies had been ignored or denied on spurious grounds, or had disappeared in a bureaucratic black hole. A 1995 memorandum, for example, indicates that 15 of the 114 persons convicted had still not been rehabilitated.[47]

In mid-1996, in the course of the presidential election campaign, Yeltsin visited Novocherkassk to garner votes by reminding the residents of the brutality of the party represented by the Communist who was running against him. When the local activists reminded Yeltsin of unfulfilled commitments, he issued an edict on "supplementary measures for the rehabilitation of persons repressed for participation in the events in Novocherkassk in June 1962." It came close to echoing the resolution that the Supreme Soviet had passed on May 22, 1992, in calling upon the Supreme Court to restore to good repute persons not yet rehabilitated and to ensure the application of the earlier law "on the rehabilitation of victims of political repression" to the participants in the June events. In a display of election-year largesse, Yeltsin made fresh promises as well. He agreed to consider raising the pensions of those who had been disabled and to pay compensation to persons who had been wounded. He also supported the erection of a monument to the victims, and pledged to look into funding for a museum to commemorate the Novocherkassk tragedy.[48]

Four years earlier, the Novocherkassk Tragedy Foundation, supported by the city government, had declared June 2, 1992—the thirtieth anniversary of Bloody Saturday—a day of mourning. By then the corpses of the slain, which had been painstakingly recovered and brought to Novocherkassk, were to be interred in a solemn ceremony. Flags were lowered to half-mast and funeral music was beamed by radio to the central square. (Its name had been changed from Lenin Square to the prerevolutionary Ataman Square.) It was recommended that the workers at NEVZ and other plants be given the day off to enable them to attend the scheduled ceremonies. At 9:00 A.M. vehicles bearing twenty coffins containing the remains of the exhumed bodies arrived at the scene of the massacre. The coffins were placed along a barrier, opposite the town hall. Each coffin was attended by relatives of the dead and an honor guard of Cossacks and others. Officials of the Novocherkassk Tragedy Foundation, the city and central administrations, and the Procuracy General addressed the crowd. Relatives of two of the slain and two of those who had been imprisoned also spoke.

After a moment of silence, flowers were laid at the memorial stone. Pallbearers formed a column and, to the accompaniment of a dirge, bore the coffins into the cathedral. Priests performed services for the dead. Relatives of the victims and "sponsors" had set up tables bearing food and drink for the throng. At 4:00 P.M. the coffins were replaced on vehicles for transfer to the cemetery. A woman at the interment, whose mother had been slain there when she was an eleven-month-old infant, sobbed that she was pronouncing the word "Mama" for the first time in thirty years.[49] An hour later, at a press conference, Bocharova spoke about what had been accomplished, problems remaining, and plans for continuing research on the 1962 events. The impressive day-long event that she and her colleagues had staged capped three years of energetic efforts—although it did not mark the end of them.[50]

On the same day, another signal victory was registered for those dedicated to getting out the whole story of the events. A special presidential commission, it was announced, had declassified the (KGB) documents relating to the Novocherkassk events, and intended to make them available to the mass media.[51] Precisely when the declassification procedure was completed and when the media gained access is not clear. The evidence at our disposal suggests it was a matter of eight or nine months. In March 1993, Bocharova published an incisive two-part review of the documents, titled "Under the Head of 'Absolutely Secret,'" in *Novocherkasskie vedemosti*.[52] There may have been other notices of the kind, but without a doubt the 1993 publication of fourteen annotated documents that filled sixty pages of the journal *Istoricheskii arkhiv* was a disclosure of the greatest moment.[53] These items confirmed many if not all of the charges that the advocates of the strikers had been leveling against the authorities. It is not surprising, then, that these documents were introduced as material evidence in the case the post-Soviet government brought against the CPSU in the Constitutional Court. Although the proceedings petered out before definite conclusions were reached, the documents pertaining to Novocherkassk remain an immensely important source on the events of June–September 1962.

Reference has frequently been made in these pages to the full-dress investigation of the Novocherkassk strike and shootings made by the Chief Military Procuracy, commencing at the beginning of 1990 and ending in mid-1991. In charge at first was Lt. Col. A. V. Tretetskii, whose article in the *Voenno-istoricheskii zhurnal* we have had occasion to notice. For one thing, it served as a vehicle to discredit General Shaposhnikov; but its primary purpose was to portray the strike much as the KGB had done, as an orgy of riotous excess, defiance of authority, and willful destruction. Tretetskii alluded to the discredited report of the demonstrators' efforts to seize the state bank, and characterized the shooting on the square as the justified response of individual soldiers to strikers' efforts to grab their weapons. Such a portrayal left no room for doubt as to the appropriateness of the forceful measures taken to restore order and thus ensure the security of persons and property. A key passage in the article quotes approvingly the view of an officer who was on the scene: "Those fundamentally culpable in the deaths of the people . . . were those engaging in hooligan activity, among whom were former convicts. They were the ones who provoked the clash between the demonstrators and the police and soldiers, obliging the latter to fire episodically, and ultimately resulting in the deaths of both the hooligans and other participants in the demonstration."[54] Tretetskii espoused essentially the same point of view in a television interview conducted by Ol'ga Nikitina in May 1992.

At some point in the next months, Tretetskii was replaced as head of the Chief Military Procuracy's investigation by Col. Iu. M. Bagraev. After all, Tretetskii's account of the 1962 eruption was that of the regime that had been discredited and cast out, and it could no longer be sustained. The substitution of Bagraev for Tretetskii signaled a radical shift in the official military position with regard to the Novocherkassk events. Nikitina also interviewed Bagraev on television, in March 1993, and the differences between the two men strike the eye. Tretetskii appears to be a shifty character, for the most part avoiding eye contact with Nikitina and treating the Novocherkassk story as though it were an open-and-shut case. In contrast, Bagraev is urbane, open-minded, reflective, and acutely aware of the complexity of the issues. At one point he remarks with conviction: "History has no need of cosmetics."

The differences between the two are underscored by their investigative procedures. Tretetskii relied exclusively on the testimony of party and KGB officials and of military men devoutly loyal to the Soviet regime. Bagraev's inquiry brought him into contact with some of the same persons, and others of similar convictions. But he understood that a reconstruction grounded on their evidence alone was bound to be one-sided: it was essential to learn what workerparticipants in the strike and demonstration and assorted onlookers had to say. Accordingly, he drew up and distributed a detailed questionnaire that attempted to prod Novocherkassians' memory and elicit comments on a range of matters, some of them controversial (see Appendix C). He and his aides also interviewed former police officers, KGB agents, and military men, who gave testimony in varying degrees at odds with the official line. In mid-1994, when Bagraev aired his findings, the two journalists who had produced the first exposé of the Novocherkassk story in the central press wrote exultantly: "Practically all the conclusions and facts adduced in our journalistic inquiry have been confirmed." The decision to use arms against the "mutinous" demonstrators was made by the Presidium members and party secretaries who had hastily made their way to Novocherkassk, and with Khrushchev's approval. "The fusillade of semi-automatic weapons against the unarmed demonstrators who filled the square before the gorkom was not provoked by armed attacks on soldiers"—they neither threw stones and other things at the soldiers nor attempted to seize their weapons. "The volley was cold-bloodedly prepared and cold-bloodedly executed."[55] Bagraev concluded:

> Deliberately distorting the true picture of what occurred, in all communications, reports, and coded telegrams the responsible persons told only of the "rioting crowd" on the square, accompanied by attacks on the soldiers, who in response "were obliged to resort to arms." However, the investigation has unquestionably established that after the expulsion of intruders from the gorkom, the [assembled people] engaged in no illegal actions, nor any in relation to the soldiers, but they did not want to leave the square, which served as the reason for using arms against them.[56]

Chapter 9   Reflections and Conclusions

Strikes were not specifically banned by law in the Soviet Union, but they were officially regarded as an anachronism, having no relevance for a socialist society, in which the means of production were assertedly owned by and operated in behalf of the working people.[1] Of course, this postulate was fictitious. To be sure, the means of production no longer belonged to capitalist and landowning elites, but long before 1962 it had become evident that the state rather than the people had displaced them. The party-state apparatus produced the plans that shaped the country's economic development, and the populace at large had no part in determining either the allocation of resources or the distribution of the fruits of its labor. Massive trade union organizations existed, of course, but they had long since been co-opted and assigned the task of spurring production rather than defending and promoting the interests of the producers. Moshe Lewin has incisively written of "the re-creation in the postrevolutionary period of an actual proletariat instead of the hoped-for, liberated working class."[2]

This is not to say that the regime was totally indifferent to the welfare of the laboring classes. In the post-Stalin era, an informal social contract of sorts between the workers and the party-state gradually developed. In return for popular acquiescence in the CPSU's hegemony, the regime guaranteed a modest level of goods and services and promised more to come. Some progress in improving living standards had been made before 1962 (although the level for the population at large remained extremely low), and the promise of much more to come was made explicit in the Third Party Program, adopted at the 22nd Party Congress in October 1961. Besides, the workers were independently able to defend their interests to some extent, thanks to a persistent labor shortage and a degree of control they could exercise over the quantity and quality of labor they put in on the shop floor.

Factory managers, under constant pressure to fulfill plans, generally strove

170

as a measure of self-protection to keep plan targets low, and consequently the demands on the workers were not unduly heavy. Besides, the directors tended to tolerate slack work discipline much of the time in order to obtain the workers' cooperation in accelerating the pace of work often required at the end of each month to fulfill the plan. Informal arrangements of the kind negotiated between managers and workers generally made for labor peace and minimized the likelihood of strikes. The wage-adjustment policy that the Kremlin enacted in 1955 required a significantly larger input of labor by the workers if they were to earn the sums they had been paid until then. Because managers and workers had in the past proved adept at blunting or circumventing new policies that disrupted established arrangements, they were generally able to find ways to mitigate the impact of the new decree.[3] Kurochkin's want of suppleness in such matters at NEVZ—recall that he had only recently become manager—undoubtedly contributed to the Novocherkassk crisis.

The NEVZ strikers' slogan—"Meat, Butter, a Pay Raise"—was directed against the recent blows to their well-being struck by the arbitrary alteration of their pay rates and the increase in food prices. Theirs was a demand for limited concessions of a narrowly economic character, essentially the restoration of what they had lost.[4] Because work stoppages were a rarity, the NEVZ strikers had no experience of independent collective action to draw upon for guidance. What they knew of labor actions they had assimilated from films, schoolbooks, and volumes about the revolutionary movement, which glorified the activity of the Bolsheviks. In Leninist thought as it developed in the early twentieth century, trade unionism had a distinctly pejorative connotation; it smacked of moderation, mere reformism, accommodation with rather than repudiation of the existing social order. Although it was not noticed, or at least publicly commented upon, Soviet trade unions—allegedly a higher form of labor organization—represented the ultimate in accommodationism. Therefore, if dissatisfied workers were to battle for their interests, they had to break out of those confining bounds; they would be obliged to resort to an "anachronistic" strike of the kind that unions in capitalist countries often waged, the very "working-class trade union politics" that Lenin had famously castigated in his pamphlet *What Is to Be Done?* But, to repeat, the only independent collective actions with which they had some familiarity were the revolutionary initiatives of the Bolsheviks. Siuda proudly observed that "the workers behaved in accordance with the methods of the revolutionary movement," failing to note the discordance between such methods and the narrow objectives indicated in their signature slogan.[5] Because of their inexperience, the strikers were oblivious of the need to suit the means to the end.

True, they rebuffed the call of one of their number to seize the state bank and post and telegraph offices. But from the outset they evidently strove to make the strike general. They were intent on spreading the stoppage to other plants in the neighborhood, and also hoped (in vain, as it turned out) to send delegations to bring out the workers in other towns. The stopping of a train on two successive days was calculated to spread news of the strike and call forth supporting actions around the country. They engaged in assaults of one kind or another on the governing personnel and the symbols of authority. They spoke insolently to Kurochkin, the plant director; they shouted down and sometimes roughed up the people who tried to rein them in. They drove away police forces and garrison troops sent to bring the disorders under control. They threw bottles and other articles at Basov, the leading party official in the province, and then held him hostage for many hours. They tore down and destroyed portraits of Khrushchev, and speakers heatedly denounced government policies and sometimes the government itself. When they paraded into town holding aloft red banners and portraits of Lenin, they implicitly asserted that they, not those in power, were the true legatees of the revolution.

Such spokesmen for the strikers as Siuda, as well as their supporters more recently, insisted that the strikers were not anti-Soviet, never contemplated overthrowing the government. Undoubtedly, none of them aimed to do away with the Soviet regime. As opposed to their explicit demands, however, the actions of the strikers implicitly challenged those in power. They may have been unaware of the import of their conduct, but to the leaders of the party-state they represented an unmistakable threat. With the means of production state-owned and -operated, any labor stoppage was, ipso facto, subversive of the state's authority. When, to boot, strikers in one enterprise attempted to generalize their action into something like a class struggle, when they engaged in provocative actions that might have had an infectious demonstration effect, those in power were understandably alarmed. It was not so much the demand for meat, butter, and a pay raise as the workers' conduct in support of their demand that had worrisome political implications. How else can one explain the dispatch of a half-dozen of the top party leaders to deal with the troubles at Novocherkassk?

If the Kremlin appears to have been overly sensitive, some recent research may suggest why. Painstaking examination of masses of archival material has revealed that between 1953 and 1964 more than 2,000 antistate or anti-Khrushchev incidents had occurred across the country.[6] They tended to be sporadic, and the great majority of them were diminutive and more or less handily contained by the local authorities. But in the late Khrushchev era (between 1959 and June 1962), a wave of more alarming urban violence directed at the local authorities had erupted in such diverse locales as Temir Tau, Kazakhstan; Krasnodar, in the North Caucasus; Murom and Aleksandrov, in the central industrial region; and Biisk, in the Altai. In several of these cases, military power had been brought into play and caused numerous deaths. Although none of these events approached the Novocherkassk upheaval in extent, in the aggregate they no doubt suggested to those at the top a degree of precariousness that warranted extraordinary measures.[7]

Be that as it may, scenarios other than the bloody suppression of the strike were at least theoretically possible. After all, the leadership made significant concessions in the aftermath of the strike, so it is not unreasonable to suppose—although there can be no certainty on this score—that it might have done so before the showdown, had negotiations been initiated. The workers' insistence on the cancellation of the price increases was certainly an obstacle—it was a delusion to suppose that opposition in one corner of the USSR could compel the party leaders to rescind a decree, promulgated after much soul-searching, that was to be enforced throughout the country. But worker representatives chosen to negotiate could surely have been persuaded that this was a nonnegotiable issue that they might drop in exchange for other desiderata. For example, the restoration of the old work norms might have offset the price increases. But were negotiations conceivable? Arguably they were, if the strikers had not engaged in self-defeating tactics. They played into the hands of the party leaders by parading into the city, where concentrated military power gave the authorities an overwhelming advantage. Rather than the mountain going to Mohammed, they might have waited for Mohammed to come to the mountain. In the industrial zone, their numbers and solidarity made them a force sufficiently formidable to deter the party leaders, on both military and political grounds, from ordering an assault. Could a party ruling in the name of the working class order its armed forces to invade a huge factory, confront a massive insurgent workforce, and impose its will at the cost of incalculable mayhem? A continuation of the strike and fear of leakage of information about it might have put pressure on the authorities to negotiate. Meanwhile, there would have been time for the strikers to choose representatives, form a strike committee, and deliberately formulate both demands and tactics. It should be recalled that Khrushchev had admonished his colleagues, before they left for Novocherkassk, to avoid impulsiveness and eschew resort to arms. Had the strikers held their ground rather than advance into town on Saturday, Mikoyan's preference for restraint and finding a peaceful way out of the impasse would have had a better chance to prevail than Kozlov's more bellicose inclination.

It may be objected that this scenario is excessively sanguine, that even had the workers held their ground, interventions of all sorts might have produced a different outcome. One can be certain that party, Komsomol, and *druzhina* elements would have been hard at work, attempting to discourage and dissuade the strikers, to sow discord and exploit splits in the ranks and undermine the stoppage. Of course, KGB agents could be expected to infiltrate the strikers' community, promote provocations, and seek to behead the movement by seizing its leaders. It might have been possible to seal off the industrial zone, cut off food supplies, and starve the strikers into submission. In the long run, the stratagems available to the authorities could undoubtedly have ground down the strikers. But they surely wished the strike to be terminated quickly. Time, then, was on the strikers' side, and the party leaders might have considered it expedient to negotiate. Obviously, these ruminations have no practical significance, but perhaps they broaden understanding of the range of options at the disposal of the one side and the other.

The terms "strikers" and "workers" have often been used interchangeably in this project, a practice that is misleading because it glosses over important differences in mentality and conduct. Of course, not all the workers at NEVZ or the other enterprises quit work. In each plant a significant percentage of the workforce (probably 10–20%) was affiliated with the party or the Komsomol. While the stresses and strains associated with the outbreak of the strike impelled some members of these groups to make common cause with the strikers, most of them, and especially the party members, opposed the stoppage— but some did so actively and others passively. If the party-Komsomol worker cohort was by no means monolithic, the rest of the workforce was much more variegated. It is impossible to calculate accurately the proportion that *actively* participated in the strike and demonstration, but it was certainly less than half the total. A great many others no doubt sympathized, but for one reason or another did not become personally involved.

Although quantification is out of the question, our scattered data indicate a wide variety of participants in the strike. The student-worker Dement'ev, evidently having in mind Bolshevik tactics in 1917 and their efficacy, mechanically proposed the seizure of the state bank and post and telegraph. Siuda, also a Leninist by inclination, recognized the incomparability of the situations in 1917 and 1962, and consequently argued against this proposal and for a less radical course. Sotnikov, whose father was killed in the Second World War, was a Communist and an exemplary worker, but the double blow of the wage reduction and food price rises impelled him to break away from the party and become one of the most active insurgents. While inveighing against the system, the mature and relatively well educated Korchak behaved rather like a Western labor activist, putting a premium on organization and discipline as the means to achieve limited, realistic ends. A large majority of the strikers appear to have sensed the importance of discipline, and refrained from provocation and violence. Others, although only a tiny minority, inflicted minor injuries on their opponents; and some invaded buildings and vented their rage against the insensitive and unresponsive authorities with mindless destructive activity. A number of these people had criminal records, and alcohol pretty certainly fueled aggressive behavior. The vivid recollection of a female striker cited earlier indicates the presence of anti-Semitic attitudes and conduct reminiscent of the prerevolutionary Black Hundreds in the labor force. Finally, one notes a simple-minded, peasantlike mentality among some of the strikers, who expected salvation through the intervention of some wonderworker, a Voroshilov, a Budenny, or a Mikoyan.

The retrospective thoughts of some key figures on the Novocherkassk events invite attention. In his voluminous memoirs, published under the title *Khrushchev Remembers*, the author remembered nothing whatsoever on the subject. Evidently he was loath to face up to one of the most discreditable events that had occurred on his watch. "The Novocherkassk bloodshed tormented [my father] to the end of his days," Khrushchev's son recently wrote. "He had lived through two wars and seen many deaths, but had never grown used to them. That was probably the reason that he did not write about Novocherkassk in his memoirs. He did not think that he had the right to justify himself, and he could not adopt the position of an indifferent observer."[8] (It may be added that Brezhnev and his colleagues who in 1964 forced Khrushchev from power also felt some remorse, for the following year they reduced the terms of imprisonment of most of those convicted in 1962 by one-half to two-thirds.) Gorbachev pronounced some relevant words in opening a symposium on the Khrushchev years, held on the centennial of the former leader's birth (1994). He and others who had worked with Khrushchev, who identified with him and later became the proponents of perestroika, paid tribute to their deceased comrade while unflinchingly pointing out his flaws and failures. The recently deposed Gorbachev wanted to think, he remarked, that Khrushchev aspired to bring about the reorganization of his country's life peacefully, without the use of force. But, unfortunately, he observed, alluding to the Novocherkassk affair and the suppression of the Hungarian uprising, it turned out otherwise.[9]

Despite official condemnations in the early 1990s of what was done at Novocherkassk in June 1962, and such retrospective regrets as have just been noticed, sentiments of the kind are by no means universal. A notable exponent of continued distortion and cover-up is V. E. Semichastnyi, the head of the KGB at the time of the Novocherkassk massacre. In a 1997 interview he claims, incredibly, to have urged Khrushchev repeatedly to release his agency from eavesdropping and informing activities, and instead to impose these duties on the vast network of party and Komsomol organizations. Specifically on the Novocherkassk events, Semichastnyi reverts more or less to the standard explanations and justifications that he and his agents had advanced in internal communications days and weeks after the strike had been suppressed.[10] For one thing, a large share of the blame for the strike was laid at Kurochkin's door. He had arbitrarily imposed changes in the wage rates, without consultation with the factory union or the people, thereby "of course" provoking "grumbling." Basov had worsened the situation by his haughty manner when he addressed the workers. Semichastnyi asserts that after he was informed of the disturbances, he considered Kurochkin the troublemaker rather than the workers, and was displeased to have his agency drawn into the fray. The plant director had spoken reprehensibly, to be sure, but he made a convenient scapegoat for the party leadership's maladroit management.

Semichastnyi's account of what happened on Saturday is riddled with errors and misrepresentations. He falsely has Mikoyan riding through the city in an automobile, urging the people through a loudspeaker to quiet down, and promising that the troublesome food prices and wage rates would be looked into. Instead of complying with this reasonable proposal, "provocateurs" unleashed a wave of violence against shop windows and automobiles, burst into the gorkom and wrought havoc there, and endeavored to use a direct line to

Moscow to phone Khrushchev. The former KGB chief refers to unsuccessful talks between Kozlov and Mikoyan and worker representatives, neglecting to point out that they (as well as Mikoyan's speech) occurred after the shooting at the gorkom. Not surprisingly, he emphasizes continuing attacks on armored vehicles and, of course, the invasion of the police station and the shooting there, swearing with hand on heart that "even now I cannot say whence the firing came."

Apropos of the shooting at the gorkom, he declares, contrary to abundant evidence: "I must say straightaway that no one in the leadership of the country, the city, or the staff of the North Caucasus Military Organization ordered, or could have ordered, firing upon the people. . . . Possibly a company or platoon commander gave the order to shoot, [when] the forward-pressing crowd almost began to seize a soldier's weapon." Semichastnyi says nothing of the numbers killed and wounded; and, while recalling that some of those arrested had been charged with organizing banditry, omits mention of the execution of seven persons and their subsequent exoneration. While on the one hand he speaks of "the justified anger of the workers," he attributes the disorders to provocateurs who skillfully inflamed them, an (inflated) number of people earlier convicted of crimes and (probably) unruly people of Cossack origin. In the most flagrant falsehood, he flatly denies that the bodies were buried secretly at night, then partially contradicts himself by asserting that (only) some of them were turned over to their families for burial. No doubt Semichastnyi speaks for many others who have an interest in perpetuating old fables. Given the resurgence of the Russian Communist Party, variations on them are likely to be around indefinitely.

In speaking of the Novocherkassk episode as a turning point in the history of modern Russia, Solzhenitsyn explained that it was the first time in decades the people had spoken out; it was "a cry from the soul of a people who could no longer live as they had lived."[11] He may have believed that it foreshadowed the demise of the Soviet regime, but there was little *apparent* support for such an assumption in developments of the decade or so between the Novocherkassk eruption and the time when he penned his remarkable characterization of it. After the collapse of the Soviet regime, many a writer retrospectively designated what had happened at Novocherkassk as a portent of its ultimate fate. As a rule, such pronouncements were stated offhandedly rather than spelled out. It would be simplistic, of course, to suppose that any single occurrence, no matter how grave or sensational, could have produced such a world-historical event as the breakdown of the USSR. But the Novocherkassk eruption did have serious consequences, justifying the belief that it was an early indicator of the much broader complex of phenomena that brought the Soviet Union down.

In addition to the changes implemented in the days and weeks after the massacre (detailed in an earlier chapter), there were long-term consequences. Despite public assertions of party leaders at all levels to the contrary, the price increases had stirred up widespread and intense dissatisfaction, and most prominently at Novocherkassk. It was impossible to ignore such tremors and it was deemed obligatory to avoid a repetition. Therefore, never again from 1962 until the collapse of the Soviet Union did the authorities dare to raise food prices.

To make some headway against the continuing shortages of meat and dairy products, the government began to import large quantities of both animal feed and meat. That a country that had historically exported large quantities of grain was now obliged to import it emphasized more than ever the failure of the Soviet agricultural system. Moreover, the feed-grain imports necessarily increased the cost of production of animal products. Because it was considered politically inadmissible to raise food prices, however, the government was obliged to increase its subsidies to agriculture again and again. "Between 1964 and 1983, prices paid to farmers were raised several times"—in 1965, 1970, and again in 1983—"without a corresponding increase in retail prices, and state revenues were allocated to cover the growing disparities." Between 1965 and 1983, the subsidy on a basket of basic foods multiplied an astounding 15 times, from 3.5 to 54.6 billion rubles, with meat and milk accounting for the lion's share. By 1980, the subsidies consumed 11 percent of the state budget, and three years later, to help cover persisting shortages, the amount of the subsidy was almost doubled.[12] It is not difficult to understand that these expenditures mandated cutbacks in expenditures for other sectors of the economy and affected overall economic growth. Looking backward from the mid-1990s to the late 1970s and early 1980s, Gorbachev ruefully spoke of Soviet agriculture as "a bottomless drain on resources." But "*a noticeable increase on retail food prices was resolutely rejected. The problem was totally divorced from economic considerations, and regarded as a purely political issue. There remained a second option—to increase subsidies from the state budget. But by the early 1980s, they already constituted about 40 billion rubles, and showed a steady tendency to continue growing."[13] The alarm produced by the Novocherkassk eruption had the effect of very seriously unbalancing a Soviet economy that was already beset by multiple difficulties and therefore was a significant contributor to its ultimate collapse.

The regime's way of dealing with labor unrest was also deeply affected by the Novocherkassk events. "As far as is known, no riots on a scale comparable [to those in Novocherkassk in 1962] have occurred in the USSR since then. The Brezhnev leadership . . . took care to be more generous to the workers on the matter of wages than Khrushchev had been."[14] This assertion by a Radio Liberty staff member who kept a close watch on Soviet labor affairs was elaborated by Linda J. Cook: "The Brezhnev regime's responses to labor unrest and organizing initiatives were quite consistent over time: with few exceptions, *mass protests and strikes brought rapid concessions to workers' demands*, while attempts to form independent organizations brought harsh reprisals."[15] Cook's further remarks are decidedly pertinent:

> The [Brezhnev era] leadership took a conciliatory approach to incidents of actual unrest. Ranking party and state officials were typically dispatched to settle strikes. These officials were clearly deputized to make deals on a broad range of labor and social issues and, apparently, to replace managers who had become targets of workers' grievances. . . . Strikes over food shortages brought well-stocked shelves in local stores and very likely contributed to the decision to extend closed distribution of deficit foodstuffs to major enterprises in the early 1980's.[16]

Can there be any doubt that the leadership had assimilated lessons aplenty from the painful Novocherkassk episode?

But there was a price to pay for labor peace. If the relentless growth of agricultural subsidies led to grave distortions in the economy as a whole, the compliant surrender to workers' demands — even though strikes were sporadic and the gains achieved unevenly registered — militated against the rationalization of a technologically backward and highly inefficient industrial economy. Of course, labor relations were by no means the only source of industrial dysfunction. Gertrude Schroeder has provided an excellent, concise analysis of some of the industrial sector's many flaws: "Enterprises bargained with superior agencies for low output targets and maximum allocations of inputs, understated real capabilities and overstated needs, resisted imposition of targets for innovation, hoarded [and grossly wasted] labor and materials . . . and ne-

glected plan targets aimed at improving efficiency and the quality of products."
Such difficulties were compounded by a system of price setting "that reflected
neither scarcities nor utilities, thereby distorting value concepts and depriving
all economic agents of efficient guides to choice."[17]

Because of the accumulation of such irrational habits, an economy that was
supposed to overtake and surpass the world's capitalist countries in productivity and provide the highest standard of living for its peoples, although it made
impressive gains for a while, was unable to sustain the momentum. Instead the
rate of growth proceeded to decline, from 5.2 percent in the 1950s to 4.8 percent in the 1960s to 2.4 percent in the 1970s, thus widening the gap between
the USSR and the world's advanced economies. Given this loss of dynamism,
it would prove impossible simultaneously to modernize its industry, raise living standards, and maintain its status as a superpower.[18] On the matter of living standards, a keen-eyed observer of Soviet life in the late 1970s reported that
the middle class, then numbering over 21 million, had turned pessimistic about
the future.[19] The decline in the delivery of services in the early 1980s sparked
open discontent. After Brezhnev had passed from the scene, the inability of his
long-lived regime to meet its obligations under the social contract provoked
the denunciation of his stewardship as an era of "stagnation," and played a
prominent part in the campaign for perestroika.

Writing early in the Gorbachev era, Paul Kennedy produced a masterly
analysis of the multifold, interlocking problems the Soviet Union then faced.[20]
Naturally, he focused on some of the economic matters touched on here, but
also on developing energy shortages, the imperative to adopt new technologies
and the intractable obstacles to doing so, and demographic problems with serious economic and military implications, such as the declining longevity of
males and rising infant mortality, stemming from the deterioration of health
care. Needless to say, Kennedy addressed military matters as well, noticing how
the arms race put an inordinate burden on the economy as a whole, at the expense of technological modernization in the nonmilitary sectors of the industrial economy and the fulfillment of popular expectations of a better life. The
Soviet economy was further burdened by the USSR's relationship with its
(doubtfully reliable) East European satellites and its assistance to Third World
countries, a facet of its competition on a global scale with the United States.
All told, the USSR appeared to be afflicted with "imperial overstretch"; it
could not possibly fulfill its many commitments, and there were bound to be
dangerous consequences. Although Kennedy cautioned that what he had set

down "does not mean that the USSR is close to collapse," in fact his diagnosis may be read as a perceptive forecast of the breakdown of the USSR, which occurred five or six years later.[21]

In the light of such a broad analysis, the Novocherkassk episode stands out as a significant but not decisive cause of the death of the Soviet Union. One last and by no means unimportant contribution to that end remains to be noted—its impact on the outlook of the population at large. It is impossible to know what proportion of the population knew of the events, how much they knew, and when they knew. Insofar as they learned of it, whether soon after the eruption or when the story began to emerge during the Gorbachev years, the revelations could only have contributed to alienation from and undermining of the post-Stalin order. Evidence has already been presented on the strong impact made by the revelations that began to appear in 1988, and it is worth recording again that the events at Novocherkassk figured prominently in the post-Soviet indictment of the CPSU in the Constitutional Court. Some material has also been adduced on adverse reactions of Novocherkassians when the eruption occurred or soon after, as recalled long afterward by people who at last were emboldened to speak out. Remember the incident recounted earlier, of the young woman who heard a burst of gunfire and cried, "They're shooting!" and her friend retorted, "Are you out of your mind? In our time they don't shoot."[22] For the many who, despite the cover-up, sooner or later became aware of what had happened, it then appeared that Bloody Sunday, 1905, which had long figured as one of the most abominable actions of tsarist Russia, had been replicated by its successor. As Bloody Sunday had radically transformed the way masses of people perceived the tsarist regime, similarly, if less immediately, Bloody Saturday helped to destroy the legitimacy of the Soviet regime.[23]

Appendixes

Appendix A   Bloody Sunday / Bloody Saturday

The tag "Bloody Saturday," immediately applied by witnesses to the fusillade fired in Novocherkassk and later by persons who learned of it, was an obvious reference to what had occurred in St. Petersburg on January 9, 1905. The affiliation of the one event with the other by a section of the public is certainly intelligible, but we may be sure that the public knew little or nothing about the complexities of the background, the immediate causes, and the acting out of Bloody Sunday.[1] If the Soviet people by and large had no interest in verifying the equivalence of the two events, a student of Bloody Saturday cannot avoid making a comparison. To anticipate, the outcome is a mixed picture, displaying both marked differences and striking similarities.[2]

It must be recalled, to begin with, that Russia was at war with Japan in January 1905 and had suffered so many reverses that the regime was substantially discredited. In 1962 the Soviet Union was at peace; its victory in World War II, endlessly celebrated, was fresh in mind and a source of patriotic loyalty.[3] Then, too, the launching in 1957 of the first earth satellite, *Sputnik*, was an indubitable fount of pride. Bloody Sunday occurred in a heavily populated city, the imperial capital, whereas Novocherkassk was a relatively small provincial town, far removed from the Soviet capital, Moscow. Accordingly, there was a large disparity in the number of people involved in the two cases, and the killed and wounded were counted in the hundreds on Bloody Sunday but in scores on Bloody Saturday. Despite the tight censorship enforced by the government, the massacre in St. Petersburg very soon became common knowledge throughout the country, and is generally believed to have touched off the revolution of 1905. The volleys in Novocherkassk were effectively covered up, and produced no such immediate, dramatic sequel. In St. Petersburg a period of labor activism preceded the January fusillade, while in Novocherkassk there had been nothing of the kind.

The tsarist regime, although autocratic, in some circumstances was more permissive than the totalitarian Soviet order. The industrialization of Russia, which began slowly after the emancipation of the serfs in 1861 and gathered momentum during the 1890s, brought into being a numerous working class in the capital and elsewhere. Subject to the starkly exploitative conditions characteristic of the early stages of industrialization, the peasants undergoing transformation into proletarians proved restive. Radical-minded groups who had tried in vain to revolutionize the peasantry discovered in this emerging class a population more open to their message. Sometimes with and sometimes without their instigation, a number of large-scale strikes broke out in the 1890s and the early years of the twentieth century. Government officials worried about the rising threat to social order but were of two minds as to how to cope with it. The Ministry of Finance, an advocate of economic growth and therefore closely aligned with the industrialists, favored repression of labor activity. The Ministry of the Interior, responsible for the maintenance of order, favored some improvement in working conditions through labor legislation. Moreover, it covertly supported an effort, known as Zubatovism after the agent who originated the idea, to draw the workers away from the siren song of the revolutionaries into peaceful and religious-oriented patriotic activities. On the eve of 1905, eleven clubs united in an Assembly of Russian Factory and Mill Workers were functioning in various industrial districts of the capital. Under the leadership of Father G. A. Gapon, the workers in the Assembly gradually broke out of the realm to which they had been relegated by the authorities and began to press for betterment of their lot. The police authorities in the city were pleased by the Assembly's apparent success in channeling the workers' attention away from political opposition into a purely economic struggle.[4] But the further development of this movement was to culminate in Bloody Sunday.

To repeat, nothing remotely like this gradual buildup of worker organization and activity figured in Novocherkassk. After a period in the 1920s when Soviet trade unions more or less actively supported worker interests, the Stalin revolution, beginning in 1928, radically changed their status. Key decisions were increasingly made by the state, the proponents of the unions as active defenders of worker interests were purged, and the unions were transformed into "productionist" organizations—agencies whose principal task was to promote the fulfillment of five-year plans. There was absolutely no chance that the NEVZ union would support, much less lead, a protest against the painful changes in wage norms or the price increases on food.[5]

In the absence of lawful labor activity, obviously there was no possibility that a leader analogous to Father Gapon—and a corps of worker-lieutenants— might emerge and gradually mobilize a mass movement around a carefully composed list of demands. In lieu of a gradual mobilization, the rise of the protest movement in Novocherkassk was precipitous in the extreme. Beginning early in the morning of June 1, it reached its climax a little after noon the next day and petered out twenty-four hours or so after that. Under the circumstances, the demands of the Novocherkassk strikers were rudimentary in comparison with the rather sophisticated platform worked out by the leaders of the movement in the capital. To be sure, things ran far from smoothly for the St. Petersburg organization in the run-up to January 9, but it was a model of order compared with the chaotic sequence of events in Novocherkassk. Finally, given its original sponsorship by the Ministry of the Interior and Gapon's leading role, the demonstration that advanced to Palace Square in St. Petersburg had a decidedly religious character. The protesters carried icons along with portraits of Tsar Nicholas II; they uttered prayers and sang the national anthem, "God Save the Tsar." The Novocherkassk demonstrators emulated their St. Petersburg predecessors in carrying symbols expressive of their deepest loyalties, but the particulars could not have been more different. Instead of the Orthodox faith and the tsar, the red banners and portraits of Lenin bespoke their belief in the promise of the October Revolution.

As for similarities, both Bloody Sunday and Bloody Saturday had their immediate origins in a strike. The stoppage in St. Petersburg began on December 31 at the Putilov Steel Works, a massive plant that employed 12,000 workers. (It will be recalled that the NEVZ workforce numbered 13,000.) At first the strike aimed at nothing more than the reinstatement of four workers who had been peremptorily dismissed, but it then proceeded to expand along two lines. As in Novocherkassk fifty-seven years later, delegations were sent to other industrial enterprises to urge their operatives to quit work, with signal success. By the day of the march to the Winter Palace, almost the entire capital's workforce had been drawn into the strike. Second, as the strike spread, Gapon progressively raised the demands into a full-fledged program, based in good part on a secretly devised scheme he and four of his inner circle had drafted some time before. The petition to be submitted to the tsar included a list of economic desiderata such as the eight-hour day, the legitimization of civil liberties, and equality before the law.[6]

Early in the Putilov strike, a mass of workers gathered at the office of the factory director, S. I. Smirnov, demanding to speak with him. Tension mounted as he at first refused to meet them, then rejected the workers' plea for reinstatement of the dismissed laborers and, making matters worse—recall Kurochkin's recommendation of "*pirozhki* with liver"—voiced some derogatory remarks about the revered leader, Father Gapon.[7]

Days later, the strike having gained wide support, the demands been much broadened, and the authorities shown their disinclination to give ground, the decision was made for a mass parade to the Winter Palace with a petition beseeching the sovereign to come to the aid of his oppressed and devoted subjects. In Novocherkassk, of course, the strikers opted to march to the local headquarters of the CPSU—members of the top leadership had come to the town—to present their demands for relief. In both cases, the authorities were apprised of what was in the wind, and the night before the appointed day deployed large military and police forces.

In St. Petersburg the organizers of the demonstration admonished the participants to "go peacefully and reverently," and anyone who behaved otherwise was rebuked. To accentuate the peaceful character of the procession, women and children were positioned in the first ranks, but were at some point removed to less exposed locations. In Novocherkassk, on the night of June 1 and the following day, the watchwords for the demonstration were discipline, order, the eschewing of forceful activity, and there too women and children led the procession part of the time. Although some members of the radical parties had joined Gapon's movement, they were kept from assuming leadership roles or even pronouncing revolutionary slogans during the January 9 demonstration. Similarly, when on the evening of June 1 the student Iu. Dement'ev called for the seizure of the bank and the post and telegraph offices in the city, he was rebuffed by those who feared the probable consequences of such "rash" actions.

In the one case as in the other, the demonstrators were certain that their peaceful manner was a guarantee against forceful attack. The impressively peaceful tenor of the St. Petersburg demonstration was successfully maintained in the routes of march until the people were fired upon. Absent the religious sentiment of the St. Petersburg procession and the leadership of a Gapon, or any equivalent restraint, the proponents of discipline and order in Novocherkassk did not manage to keep in check the rage of a small minority that produced violence at the police station and the ravaging of the party headquarters.

In the capital, the demonstrators went on a rampage, but only after the shooting broke out at Palace Square.

Not for nothing was St. Petersburg called the "Venice of the North": the city is divided into segments by waterways, not only the Neva River but also tributaries, lesser streams, and canals. In order to reach the Winter Palace from the factory quarters of the city, the demonstrators would have to cross bridges that served as avenues to the city center. The military authorities resolved to block the marchers by massing troops at the key bridges. The same idea was implemented in Novocherkassk, but there the task was easier—the one and only bridge over the Tuzlov River was occupied by tanks. In neither case, however, did the strategy succeed. In St. Petersburg, confrontations at two crossings resulted in the shooting, killing, and wounding of scores of people, but these events did not keep the demonstrators from converging on Palace Square. In at least one sector, large numbers of demonstrators outflanked the troops by crossing on the ice of the frozen Neva. Had the demonstration occurred at any other time but the dead of winter, the military might have succeeded in preventing the workers from reaching the center of the city. The counterpart in Novocherkassk was the bypassing of the Tuzlov bridge by the many demonstrators who scrambled through the shallow river to the other side, but many others marched through and around the tanks on the bridge, whose crews offered no resistance.

At the several places where the St. Petersburg demonstrators approached either bridges or Palace Square, they were met by military forces. Officers in command endeavored to persuade the advancing workers to disperse, but had no more success than if they had tried to stop an incoming tide. At Palace Square, troops with fixed bayonets could not budge the crowd. When the officer in charge threatened to give the order to shoot, demonstrators appealed to his men to disobey. The commander then gave the order to open fire. The people in the square in both St. Petersburg and Novocherkassk at first were shocked, then exploded in anger. Belief in the tsar was shattered not only for those in Palace Square but much more widely. And who can doubt that those involved in the Novocherkassk events, and many more who later heard about them, were shaken in whatever degree of allegiance they may have had to the Soviet regime? The question of who gave the order to fire was debated in the imperial Ministry of the Interior, and it remains a matter of doubt even today with respect to Novocherkassk. In both cases, when official casualty figures were initially released, they were grossly understated. Moreover, and in a way this detail crowns the case here outlined, the Bloody Sunday victims were buried secretly, without notification of the families, "in order to avoid possible demonstrations."[8]

What Walter Sablinsky has written about eyewitness accounts of the shootings in St. Petersburg—"many of which were contradictory, based on rumors, or simply products of the imagination"—holds equally for the recollections of the Novocherkassians. So does his assertion that stories were endlessly repeated and embellished "until the participants themselves were not sure what they had seen with their own eyes."[9] Something of the kind figures in the following instance: A number of children perched in trees near Palace Square to get a better look were among the victims. Many townspeople in Novocherkassk believe that children in trees were killed on June 2, though there is no supporting evidence at all. One of many myths concerning the Novocherkassk events, the story in all probability derives from the unwitting transfer of a matter familiar to Soviet readers from accounts of Bloody Sunday in history textbooks to a different time and place.[10]

Appendix B Leaflet Composed and Distributed by Dissidents, 1977

"Eternal Remembrance . . .
Damnation and Eternal Disgrace"[1]

On the streets of Novocherkassk a multitudinous demonstration is in progress. Over columns of red banners, portraits of Lenin, placards with peaceful slogans. Outwardly similar to a May Day demonstration. But it is not that. It's a popular protest.

On the eve, the Soviet government doubled the price of meat and dairy products. Simultaneously, the wage rates at the largest factory in the city (the electric locomotive works) were reduced by 30 percent. And the workers did not stand for it. They declared a strike, together with their families they went into the street.

Infantry and tanks barred the demonstrators' way to the square at the city center. A lengthy pause. Then submachine guns crackled. They fired at the demonstrators—at children, women, men. Struck by dumdum bullets, people fell and died on the pavement—at the base of the monument to Lenin and all over the surrounding enormous square and the streets adjoining it. This happened twenty years ago [*sic*], on June 2, 1962, in a country that calls itself *socialist*.

And the suppression of this worker action was managed by a group of members of the Central Committee of the Communist Party of the Soviet Union, headed by two members of the Politbiuro, Frol Kozlov and Anastas Mikoyan. The immediate direction of the shooting was assigned to the commander of the North Caucusus Military District, General Pliev, and the first secretary of the Rostov Province CPSU, [A. V.] Basov. They performed this task "brilliantly."

When the pause occurred on the square—and it was caused by the refusal of the soldiers of the local garrison to shoot at unarmed people—Pliev quickly replaced them with non-Russian soldiers from other parts of the province. And they carried out the task set for them. After they had done their dirty work, they were also replaced. Why look at those unarmed peaceful people you've murdered and maimed! Besides, foresightedly, the replacements were not given dumdum bullets, which made it possible subsequently to affirm that the killing on the city streets was accomplished by enemy agents, inasmuch as dumdum bullets are not part of Soviet army equipment.

Neither *Pravda* nor any other Soviet newspaper uttered a word about the Novocherkassk events. And the authorities took steps to prevent news about it [from getting out of] the city, and to squelch rumors within it. Novocherkassk was surrounded by military forces. No one was allowed into or out of the city. Wide-ranging searches and arrests were carried out in the city. They exacted signed pledges of silence [about what had occurred]. They cleared the place of the corpses and wounded. And down to the present, nothing is known of the one or the other. The families of the slain and the wounded were exiled to distant places. A series of trials was carried out. Two of them open (entry with permits!). At one of these trials nine men were judged (all sentenced to death) and two women (each to fifteen years).

And even now there are no exact figures on the number who perished. On the square alone there were 70–80 corpses. How many died or were finished off by their wounds, how many were executed by order of the court, continues to be secret.

These deaths must never be forgotten or forgiven.

We call for the designation of June 2 as a day of remembrance of the victims of despotism, a day of struggle against the bloody official terror.

Signed by B. Bakhmin, E. Bonner, T. Velikanova, Z. Grigorenko, P. Grigorenko, A. Lavut, M. Landa, O. Lukauskaite, N. Meiman, O. Meshko, Iu. Mniukh, A. Polishuk, V. Piatkus, A. Sakharov, F. Serebrov, V. Slepak, V. Turchin, E. Finkelshtein, T. Khodorovich

Appendix C Questionnaire Submitted to Bloody Saturday Participants and Eyewitnesses by the Chief Military Procuracy, 1991–92

For whom and where did the witness work in June 1962?[1] *Preconditions of the disturbances in Novocherkassk:*

Living conditions of the workers and their families in May–June 1962.

What, in [the witness's] opinion, was the cause of the disturbances by the NEVZ workers and the adherence of the Novocherkassk population?

Were these actions organized or spontaneous?

Who was the initiator, the organizer, of the work stoppage, the halting of rail traffic, and the demonstration in the city? With what objective was [all this] done?

Concrete actions of the workers at the factory on June 1 and 2 with respect to the administration, representatives of the state power and the party, and the police.

Worker actions in relation to the First Secretary of the Province Committee of the CPSU, Basov.

What is known about the violation of social order by the workers [and] citizens at the railroad, in the town, at the gorkom, the police station, the bank? Connect these actions with times of day.

The witness's location, his concrete action in each episode of June 1–2, and how it was expressed.

Describe the actions of those engaged in meetings and the servicemen at the party headquarters square. Indicate:

The time when the demonstrators appeared on the square, their intentions and specific actions.

When and with what aims did the demonstrators arrive at the gorkom [and] the local offices of the KGB and MVD.

The situation at the gorkom before the arrival of the demonstrators; were there soldiers, policemen, druzhinniki, and what they were doing in the building?

What were the first acts of the demonstrators, the soldiers, the representatives of the local and party authorities? What were the demands and to whom were they presented, what did they want from the representatives of the authorities?

Were there among the demonstrators drunken individuals who incited violations of social order?

Why did the demonstrators seize the gorkom? Describe in detail the behavior of individual demonstrators, soldiers, and local and party personnel.

What was the aim (time) of the seizure of the building and the demonstrator's action afterward, on the balcony and in the square

The character of the speeches and appeals?

Describe in detail the arrival of General Oleshko, what troops accompanied him, their number, uniforms, weapons, and behavior.

The conduct of Oleshko on the balcony, the character of his speech, his attitude toward the assemblage, [and] his distance from those accompanying him.

Why were store windows and windows of some houses broken in the neighborhood of the gorkom, the local MVD?

How many soldiers were there before the gorkom, the local MVD, and in the buildings? How were they armed, in what uniforms were they dressed (buttons, shoulder straps, etc.)?

Were the demonstrators warned that the soldiers had weapons and would use them?

Why did the soldiers open fire, who gave the command, [who] warned the demonstrators?

How long did the firing last (both length of time and intensity)?

Results of the shooting (how many killed, wounded were seen at the square and at the local KGB? Were there children among them? Their age?

How did the demonstrators behave during the shooting and after it was over; did they return to the scene of the shooting?

Did anyone besides the soldiers engage in shooting, who were they, how were they dressed and armed?

Did you see slain demonstrators (soldiers), when they were taken from the place where they perished? How many were there, their gender, age, character of their injuries?

Were people killed in the evening of June 2, 1962, and the following days? What do you know about that? Source of information?

Where may those who perished be buried? What is known about the wounded and those who are missing?

Thirty years after these tragic events, whom do you consider guilty of what happened, the demonstrators [or] the soldiers? Of what, specifically, are they guilty? Were the demonstrators justified in their behavior, if not, why specifically?

Reference Matter

Notes

Preface and Acknowledgments

1. Appendix A compares Bloody Sunday and Bloody Saturday.

2. Solzhenitsyn, *Gulag Archipelago*, 3:507–14.

3. See his "Open Letter" on the front page of *LG*, June 12, 1991.

4. Continuing interest is attested by the appearance of two fictional accounts of the events: Lebedev, *Rasstrel na ploshchadi*, and Koniukhov, *Komendantskii chas*.

5. Solzhenitsyn, *Gulag Archipelago*, 3:507.

6. Kozlov, *Massovye besporiadki*.

Chapter 1. A Fateful Announcement

1. Tatu, *Power in the Kremlin*, 217–19.

2. One alternative, rationing of the products in short supply, seems not to have been considered, or was rejected out of hand as demeaning for a country representing itself as a superpower. As J. M. Montias has noted, price increases bring demand into balance with supply by cutting out those with less purchasing power, while rationing distributes the burden evenly over the entire population. See his "Economic Conditions and Political Instability," 290.

3. For a cogent background to the riots in East Germany, see Kopstein, *Politics of Economic Decline*, chap. 1, esp. 35f. There an increase in work norms along with increases in food prices amounted to a monthly wage cut of 33%.

4. Schroeder, "Soviet Economy."

5. See Fitzpatrick, *Stalin's Peasants*, chap. 5.

6. Heller and Nekrich, *Utopia in Power*, 547–48.

7. Medvedev, *Khrushchev*, 157.

8. Quoted in Heller and Nekrich, *Utopia in Power*, 547.

9. Nove, *Soviet Economy*, 59. The private plots also produced two-thirds of the potatoes, 40% of the vegetables, and 70% of the eggs (Filtzer, *Soviet Workers and De-Stalinization*, 32).

10. "Iz vospominanii sovetskogo ekonomista akademika E. S. Varga," in *Khrestomatiia po otechestvennoi istorii*, 85. One wonders whether Varga had read Djilas's *New Class*, or whether the two East Europeans had arrived at similar conclusions independently.

11. *Narodnoe khoziastvo SSSR 1962*, 227.

12. *NR*, 173–74.

13. Ibid., 164.

14. Davies, "'Us Against Them.'"

15. *NR*, 159, 168, 173–75; *IA*, 1993, no. 1, pp. 116, 117.

16. *IA*, 1993, no. 1, pp. 113–16; *NR*, 174.

17. *IA*, 1993, no. 1, pp. 112, 115, 116, 118; *NR*, 160, 174, 175.

18. *IA*, 1993, no. 1, pp. 114–17; *NR*, 175.

19. *IA*, 1993, no. 1, pp. 112, 114, 115, 117.

20. Ibid., 114, 116; *NR*, 168.

21. *IA*, 1993, no. 1, p. 112; *NR*, 160, 168, 174, 175.

22. *IA*, 1993, no. 1, pp. 114, 116; *NR*, 160, 168, 174, 175.

23. *IA*, 1993, no. 1, p. 114.

24. Ibid., 112, 118.

25. *NR*, 164.

26. The following sketch of Novocherkassk is based on the article devoted to the town in *Entsiklopedicheskii Slovar'*; Longworth, *Cossacks*; Molchanov and Repnikov, *Novocherkassk*; McNeal, *Tsar and Cossacks*; Dantsev, *Gorod na kholme*.

27. McNeal, *Tsar and Cossacks*, 220.

28. On the strike, see Reichman, "Rostov General Strike."

29. Molchanov and Repnikov, *Novocherkassk*, 64.

30. McNeal, *Tsar and Cossacks*, 128–41.

31. Molchanov and Repnikov, *Novocherkassk*, 80.

32. For an excellent and chilling account of the de-Cossackization campaign, see A. Kozlov, "Razkazachivanie."

33. Longworth, *Cossacks*, 318–19.

34. Sholokhov, *Virgin Soil Upturned*. Sholokhov had been attacked earlier for having portrayed too realistically the brutality with which the Reds at times dealt with the Cossacks during the Civil War. See A. Kozlov, "Razkazachivanie," no. 6.

35. Oskol'kov and Gatashov, "Kollektivizatsiia," 79.

36. Conquest, *Harvest of Sorrow*, 275–77.

37. TsDNI, F81 O22 D73:22; F81 O22 D74:74. On the druzhinniki, see Ritvo, "Totalitarianism Without Coercion."

38. Quoted in Nikitina, "Novocherkassk." References herein will be to the more accessible English translation in *Soviet Law and Government (SLG)*, 30, no. 4. The item just noted occurs on 34–36.

39. Podol'skii, "Ia byl ochevidtsem tragedii," 13.

40. TsDNI, F81 O22 D74:111r–v. It was also noted that there was not a single decent dining hall in the city.

41. TsDNI, F81 O22 D74:71; Kassof, *Soviet Youth Program*, 122–43.

42. TsDNI, F81 O22 D71:2–5.

43. On the educational reform, see DeWitt, "Upheaval in Education." The problem of would-be university students who were required to do factory work for two years was referred to in a report on a party meeting on Aug. 2, 1962 (TsDNI, F9 O1 D2937:107).

44. Nikitina, "Novocherkassk," 36; TsDNI, F81 O12 D72:4.

45. *IA*, 1993, no. 1, pp. 122–23.

46. TsDNI, F81 O22 D47:10r–12v; F9 O1 D2937:106. The playing fields, it was also noted, were poorly maintained.

47. TsDNI, F9 O1 D2936:106–7; Nikitina, "Novocherkassk," 36; *IA*, 1993, no. 1, p. 126.

48. Nikitina, "Novocherkassk," 40. There were also 600 druzhinniki at the plant, many of whom were no doubt Komsomol members.

49. Mardar', *Khronika neob'iavlennogo ubiistva*, 8.

50. Ibid., 36. Apparently the factory's equipment had not been regularly upgraded, for by 1962 it was one of the most technologically backward enterprises (ibid., 5). NEVZ was said to have fulfilled or overfulfilled its production targets in the first five months of 1962 (TsDNI, F81 O22 D73:14, 20; *Znamia kommuny*, May 1, 1962). I suspect that these claims are inflated.

51. Filtzer, *Soviet Workers and De-Stalinization*, 92f. Similar difficulties in East Germany are interestingly detailed in Kopstein, *Politics of Economic Decline*, 1.

52. Nove, *Economic History of the USSR*, 354–59. This proposition is spelled out in detail in Filtzer, *Soviet Workers and De-Stalinization*.

53. Ibid., 102, 116.

54. *Documents of the 22nd Congress*, 5–6, 244; Hosking, *First Socialist Society*, 348–49.

55. In 1965 the average per capita income of industrial worker families was only at the level calculated by Soviet economists as providing minimum subsistence. See Chapman, "Recent Trends," 176.

Chapter 2. June 1: The Strike Begins

1. *IA*, 1993, no. 1, doc. 6.

2. Ibid., 130. Of course, local agents were already at work.

3. Ibid., doc. 1, p. 112. Compare with pp. 122–23 in doc. 6.

4. That is, until the appearance in 1999, after my work had been completed,

of V. A. Kozlov's *Massovye besporiadki*. This volume includes a long, informative chapter, grounded in archival material, on the Novocherkassk upheaval. Kozlov's chapter focuses almost exclusively on the strike itself, Mardar''s *Khronika* less so, inasmuch as she explores various related matters as well.

5. They probably learned of it from the radio or early exposure to the local newspaper, which on June 1 published the complete text of the price increase announcement.

6. The word "liver" was customarily used to refer to the internal organs generally, which cost less than meat. This episode is conspicuous by its absence from the Ivashutin report. There is, however, a reference (p. 123) to Kurochkin's neglect of the workers' needs, and his rude and bureaucratic conduct. Other accounts have Kurochkin recommending "pirozhki with cabbage" rather than liver.

7. Siuda, "Chto zhe togda proiskhodilo?" 2–3.

8. Trotsky, *History of the Russian Revolution*, 1:136–52.

9. In Novocherkassk, many of these individuals became conspicuous and were presently arrested, put on trial, and sentenced to harsh punishments.

10. This insight, derived from my study of the sources, is confirmed by Siuda (*Novocherkassk*, 31).

11. Siuda, "Chto togda proiskhodilo?" 3; Mardar', *Khronika*, 9. This development is also missing from the Ivashutin report. The episode may be conflated there with the subsequent halting of the train and the blowing of its whistle, a matter to be dealt with shortly.

12. Siuda, "Chto togda proiskhodilo?" 3.

13. GVP, 7. The figures given in the KGB report are smaller than those cited in the Chief Military Procuracy's investigation.

14. *IA*, 1993, no. 1, pp. 125–26; Mardar', *Khronika*, 17. A bit of skepticism in regard to this matter is in order. At a meeting of party activists soon afterward, this same Viunen'ko expressed himself at length, sounding like a buffoon, and an inebriated one at that (TsDNI, F81 O22 D71:3–5).

15. Nikitina, "Novocherkassk," 39–40.

16. Karamysheva, "Novocherkassk—62."

17. Mardar', *Khronika*, 17.

18. *IA*, 1993, no. 1, p. 123.

19. He was one of the seven strikers who were tried, sentenced to death, and executed. The information about him is drawn from the procuracy's preliminary investigation preceding the trial, found in GARF, F8131 O31 D93661:130–47.

20. Nikitina, "Oni khoteli naiti pravdu," 27.

21. Siuda, "Chto togda proiskhodilo?" 4. This testimony is especially interesting in that Siuda was arrested and tried for having put angry questions to Elkin on this occasion.

22. Ibid., 4.

23. GVP, 27–28.

24. This according to Iu. V. Rukhman, a KGB official who (at least in the 1990s) sympathized with the strikers. See Nikitina, "Novocherkassk," 43.

25. GVP, 48. Rukhman contends that the disorders might have ended if Basov had behaved thus conciliatorily (ibid., 43).

26. According to the recollection of S. Elkin. See Konovalov and Bespalov, "Novocherkassk, 1962."

27. This version, to which many witnesses testified, is at odds with Ivashutin's account, in which bottles and other items were thrown at Kurochkin (*IA*, no. 1, p. 125).

28. Siuda, "Chto togda proiskhodilo?" 4.

29. GVP, 17, 20, 22.

30. Siuda, "Chto togda proiskhodilo?" 4. Siuda, erroneously, has this event occurring before Basov's arrival rather than after it.

31. Mardar′, *Khronika*, 16–17.

32. Nikitina, "Novocherkassk," 44.

33. A KGB agent reported that Siuda urged the crowd to maintain order and refrain from damaging factory equipment (GVP, 49).

34. When he arrived at NEVZ at 5:00 A.M. he was arrested.

35. *IA*, 1993, no. 1, p. 126.

36. Phillips, "Message in a Bottle"; Transchel, "Under the Influence." These works deal with an earlier period of Soviet history, but there is no reason to doubt that what they describe persisted through the later decades. On drunkenness during work hours at NEVZ: TsDNI, F901 O1 D2936:27.

37. One who so testified was S. E. Elkin: GVP, 14.

38. Ibid., 24–25.	39. Ibid., 23–24.
40. Ibid., 16.	41. Mardar′, *Khronika*, 9.
42. Yelin, "Massacre of Workers."	43. GARF, F8131 O31 D93661:19–20.

44. Extended testimony on what their units were subjected to when they were sent to NEVZ is set down by two officers in Mardar′, *Khronika*, 15–16.

45. GVP, 19, 37, 20, 22, 21, 33. The simultaneous appearance of workers who exemplified disciplined behavior and others who engaged in "hooliganism" echoes a division manifest in Russia in the early years of the twentieth century. Some workers had resorted to "excesses"—violence and vandalism—during the revolution of 1905, but it was only during a general strike of July 1914 that the term "hooliganism" came into use. The Russian Social Democrats endeavored to eliminate this kind of thing, which they considered dangerous and self-destructive; but it tended to crop up whenever and wherever labor was involved in intense conflicts. See Neuberger, *Hooliganism*, 255ff.

46. Konovalov, "Listen, Understand, Forgive?" 29; Nikitina, "Oni khoteli naiti pravdu," 26–27.

47. This according to a then young engineer who observed the action. Interview, Rostov, July 1997.

48. *Rasskaz o pochetnom shakhtere*, 26–27.

49. Tompson, *Khrushchev*, 18, 49.

50. Ibid., 84.

51. Burlatsky, *Khrushchev and the First Soviet Spring*, 2, 72, 85.

52. Adzhubei, *Te desiat' let*, 183.

53. Kramer, "New Evidence on Soviet Decision-Making," 366–69. The notes compiled by Vladimir Malin, head of the General Department of the Central Committee, are appended to the article. Kramer's account is supplemented by information he extracted from other recently declassified materials.

54. The quotations are taken from the Malin notes (ibid., 390).

55. Ibid., 369, 371–72. Khrushchev gives a more detailed account of Mikoyan's stance, remarking that his colleague was so upset that he threatened suicide. See *Khrushchev Remembers: The Glasnost Tapes*, 122–23. I have left out of the account the impact of the Suez crisis, which coincided with the Hungarian uprising and served as an added incentive to act decisively in Hungary.

56. Siuda, *Novocherkassk*, 32.

57. *Khrushchev Remembers: The Glasnost Tapes*, 125.

58. Adzhubei, *Te desiat' let*, 281.

59. GVP, 30.

60. Mardar', *Khronika*, 29; Konovalov and Bespalov, "Novocherkassk, 1962"; Nikitina, "Novocherkassk," 42.

61. GVP, 45.

62. Ibid., 42–43, 45.

63. Ibid., 11, 59–60.

64. Podol'skii, "Ia byl ochevidtsem tragedii," 11.

65. GVP, 44–45.   66. GVP, 44.

67. *IA*, 1993, no. 1, p. 130.   68. Ibid., 113.

69. According to one source (GVP, 8), the entire group arrived on June 1, but another (*IA*, 1990, no. 3, notes 10 and 11) states that several of them arrived on June 2.

70. GVP, 34. Whether the incident occurred or not, it correctly reflects Pliev's position, and it points up the tension that sometimes appeared between the political and military sectors of the government.

71. Quoted in Nikitina, "Novocherkassk," 43.

72. It is quoted in Mardar', *Khronika*, 18–19, and Nikitina, "Novocherkassk," 45. It was *officially* made public in an article by Iu. Bagraev and V. Pavliutkin in *Krasnaia zvezda*, Oct. 7, 1995.

73. GVP, 35–36.

74. Ibid., 43. In a recently published posthumous memoir, Mikoyan retrospectively described Kozlov as "an unintelligent person of pro-Stalinist inclination, a reactionary, a careerist and, moreover, an unscrupulous one." Mikoian, *Tak bylo*, p. 609.

75. Burlatsky, *Khrushchev and the First Soviet Spring*, 78. Mikoyan claims to have urged Khrushchev (in vain) to designate one person rather than Kozlov and himself to deal with the trouble at Novocherkassk. Mikoian, *Tak bylo*, p. 610.

76. GVP, 46. Possibly his claim was a retrospective effort at self-vindication, but there is oblique support for the claim in Michel Tatu's observations, made in a different context, that Shepilov, a younger man not implicated in Stalin's bloody purges, had most scathingly denounced members of the so-called antiparty group for their connivance in those crimes. He also seems to have been sensitive to what the foreign press wrote about the Soviet Union. See Tatu, *Power in the Kremlin*, 163, 197–99.

77. GVP, 43.

78. His message was deemed so important that it was reprinted in all the central newspapers the following day, and on June 4 in the Novocherkassk daily, *Znamia kommuny*.

79. The word *odergyvat'* is translated "to slap down" in Tatu, *Power in the Kremlin*, 219n.

Chapter 3. June 2: Bloody Saturday

1. GVP, 52–53, 26–27.
2. GVP, 65–67.
3. GVP, 67.
4. GVP, 52.
5. Nikitina, "Novocherkassk," 45–46.
6. GVP, 66–68.
7. Mardar', *Khronika*, 30.
8. Ibid., 29–30.
9. GVP, 53.

10. GVP, 44, 54–55. Mikoyan wrote of his work in the area in *V nachale dvadtsatykh*.

11. GVP, 61, 97.

12. GVP, 75.

13. Tretetskii, "Novocherkassk," 73; Mardar', *Khronika*, 31–32. A KGB colonel jumped from the second floor at the rear of the building and injured his foot so seriously that it had to be amputated.

14. Mardar', *Khronika*, 32. No further information is available on Shelepin's activity.

15. *IA*, 1993, no. 1, p. 126.

16. GVP, 69, 107, 63, 97.

17. Mardar', *Khronika*, 31–32; GVP, 59.

18. GVP, 97, 98.

19. Nikitina, "Novocherkassk," 48–49, 51. He was subsequently expelled from the party.

20. GARF, F8131 O31 D93661:152–53. In the investigation that preceded her trial, she denied having said this. In her tirade from the balcony, she claimed that she too had been beaten, a nearby person asserted, but he could see no evidence of bruises (GVP, 72).

21. GVP, 78, 81.

22. GVP, 85.

23. This according to a witness in the preliminary investigation: GARF, F8131 O31 D93661:150.

24. GVP, 76–90 and 161, deals with the events at the police station. Most of the testimony was collected in the early 1990s, but that of Repkin and Azizov from the record of a trial held in June 1962. Some additional details are given in Bagraev and Pavliutkin, "Novocherkassk, 1962-I."

25. GVP, 77.

26. Ibid.

27. Mikoian, *Tak bylo*, pp. 610–11.

28. GVP, 98.

29. Minutes later, no clashes having occurred, he was told to have his men withdraw. We shall return to this curious sequence anon.

30. GVP, 97–98, 94, 99.

31. GVP, 95, 98, 104, 126, 132. Col. A. A. Tiurin, the commander of a detached battalion of MVD troops, expressed a discordant view: that after the building had been cleared, disorders in the square increased, with demonstrators pushing and kicking soldiers in the stomach (GVP, 93). Significantly, he made this statement on June 5, just days after the shooting, when what was to be the (fraudulent) official version of the events was being concocted.

32. GVP, 95, 100.

33. Ibid., 104.

34. Ibid., 100. Marshal S. M. Budenny, a cavalry commander and hero during the Civil War, had been born in the Don region, and he returned there to live after that conflict ended. He was thought to be partial to the region's people and to have high-level influence.

35. GVP, 96. I have found no corroborating evidence on this point, but it should not be dismissed out of hand.

36. GVP, 95, 101, 111. One who was there later testified that he looked at his watch just then, and it read 12:32.

37. GVP, 107.
38. Nikitina, "Novocherkassk," 54; *KD*, 12.
39. GVP, 105, 106, 108, 109, 110, 132, 134–35.
40. GVP, 131–32; Mardar', *Khronika*, 38–39.
41. GVP, 130, 127, 126, 113, 107, 111.   42. GVP, 113–14, 112.
43. GVP, 101, 111, 113, 124, 130.   44. Nikitina, "Novocherkassk," 53.
45. *KD*, 12–13.   46. GVP, 114, 132, 103, 112, 125, 101.
47. Malakhov, "Novocherkassk: Iun' 1962. Svidetel'stvo kadrovogo ofitsera."
48. GVP, 114, 95; *KD*, 11.
49. But two persons, one a soldier and the other an individual who was a youth at the time, reported isolated attempts to seize a soldier's weapon: GVP, 64; *KD*, 12.
50. *IA*, 1993, no. 1, pp. 127, 131.
51. Mardar', *Khronika*, 40, cites an eyewitness account. A recent article suggests that the number who perished was at least twenty-six and possibly as many as thirty: Kraisvetnyi, "Novocherkassk—62."
52. GVP, 106, 109, 131.
53. *KD*, 12–13; Siuda thought it was an open question ("Sbornik," 21).
54. GVP, 127.
55. *IA*, 1993, no. 1, p. 131. Judging by these data, young people were disproportionately represented in the crowd.
56. Interview with M. I. Kraisvetnyi, July 1997.
57. *KD*, 13.
58. GVP, 166.
59. GVP, 98, 100, 102, 104–5.
60. GVP, 99, 120, 121, 124, 126. The reporter Iu. Bespalov quoted A. N. Ladilov, the deputy head of a Rostov military school, as saying he had heard a second command, but Ladilov's testimony to the Military Procuracy is vague on the point. Bespalov, "Streliat' mozhno?" 1; GVP, 99.
61. GVP, 129.
62. GVP, 21.
63. GVP, 130, 131, 133. More on probable firing from the procuracy building in a moment.
64. GVP, 96.
65. GVP, 98.
66. GVP, 122–23. No other witness told of seeing what Chetverikin described.
67. GVP, 136–37.   68. GVP, 127.
69. GVP, 98, 105.   70. GVP, 132–35.
71. GVP, 135–36. Unaccountably, Tiurin places the time of the shooting some forty minutes later than two other witnesses.

72. Obviously, such a plan would have had to be contrived before the morning of June 2, with the understanding that it would be put into effect should conditions require it.

73. Siuda, "Versiia dlia issledovatelia," 21; Mardar', *Khronika*, 38–39.

74. GVP, 137–38. The kind of covert operation portrayed here was unlikely to have been committed to paper.

75. Bagraev and Pavliutkin, "Novocherkassk, 1962-I." The authors pungently remark that journalists often criticize the military for carrying out its orders, while the political authorities who give the orders escape censure.

76. Lt. Col. Tretetskii had been in charge of the investigation at first, and it is possible that elements of his draft, which took a different tack, were inadvertently incorporated into the final summary, with neither Bagraev nor one of his assistants noticing the inconsistency. The contrasting views of Tretetskii and Bagraev are treated in Chapter 8.

Chapter 4. After the Massacre

1. Mardar', *Khronika*, 33. She mistakenly believed there was only one source on this episode, that of the (doubtfully reliable) head of the Rostov KGB, Iu. P. Tupchenko. Not firsthand testimony, much of it seems to be derived from Kozlov's radio speech delivered on June 3. The speech is printed in *IA*, 1993, no. 1, pp. 118–22.

2. GARF, F8131 O31 D93661:109–13. During the preliminary investigation, the Komsomol members denounced what they had done and testified against Mokrousov.

3. Antonov's account appears in Nikitina, "Dni zatmeniia," *Komsomolets*, June 22, 1988.

4. Mikoyan's speech survived only thanks to a tape recording made by a Novocherkassk resident. It was subsequently lost, but before then part of its content was printed twice, first in *Novocherkasskie vedemosti*, May 4–10, 1991, and again in Mardar', *Khronika*, 52–53.

5. *IA*, 1993, no. 1, pp. 118–22.

6. GARF, F8131 O31 D93661:111.

7. "S magnitofonnoi lenty: Golos iz proshlogo," *Novocherkasskie vedemosti*, May 10, 1991.

8. The indictment (*IA*, 1990, no. 3, p. 154) cursorily states the formal charge. The preliminary investigation record provides colorful details: GARF, F8131 O31 D93661:112.

9. Siuda, "Sbornik," 78. In another hearsay account, Tupchenko had him saying, "Among us only Iurka Gagarin and Manka the cafeteria manager live well": Mardar', *Khronika*, 33.

10. Nekrasov, *Who Can Be Happy and Free in Russia?* 87–88.

11. Field, *Rebels in the Name of the Tsar*, 31–111.

12. Ibid., 39–40.   13. Ibid., 46, 69.

14. Ibid., 52, 47–48.   15. Ibid., 40, 51, 67; *KD*, 22.

16. Field, *Rebels in the Name of the Tsar*, 48.

17. Tretetskii, "Novocherkassk," 73.

18. Field, *Rebels in the Name of the Tsar*, 60, 51.

19. *KD*, 7.

20. Anguished people who besieged the building in hopes of locating a missing relative had been barred from entering: Mardar', *Khronika*, 41; GVP, 145.

21. *IA*, 1993, no. 1, p. 127; Mardar', *Khronika*, 52; Nikitina, "Novocherkassk," 55.

22. Mardar', *Khronika*, 42–44. There is a great deal of detail on the slain and the burials in GVP, 138–66.

23. *IA*, 1993, no. 1, pp. 121, 135. On June 4, Kozlov, Mikoyan, and Polianskii also attended a meeting of the city's party committee, at which Kozlov spoke; his remarks were not recorded. TsDNI, F81 O22 D71.

24. Malakhov, "Novocherkassk."

25. GARF, F8131 O31 D98326:15. The man who made this "insolent" response was arrested, tried, and sentenced to a long prison term. Many persons in Novocherkassk characterized the shootings of unarmed people on Bloody Saturday as a fascist act.

26. *IA*, 1993, no. 1, p. 127.

27. Much later, Mikoyan was often quoted as having said something very similar. *KD*, 7, 8. A sidebar in a national newspaper attributed to Mikoyan the words: "We, together with Nikita Sergeevich Khrushchev, decided that we would resort to any measures necessary to restore order": *Sobesdnik*, June 23, 1992. Nothing like this statement appears in the portion of Mikoyan's speech that has survived, and I believe that who said what has been confused in some minds.

28. The small turnout at a meeting held at NEVZ on June 12 is perhaps an indication of who was really isolated. Maksimova, "Imena zhertv Novocherkasskogo rasstrela."

29. Bespalov, "Novocherkassk, 1962."

30. The agent, Iu. V. Rukhman, imparted this information in a television interview, a copy of which I have had an opportunity to see.

31. Mikoian, *Tak bylo*, p. 610.

32. Khrushchev's speech (or, more likely, a relevant portion of it) was also broadcast in Novocherkassk after the massacre. GARF, F81319 O31 D93661:12. On June 4, Semichastnyi reported to Khrushchev reactions to the speech, mostly positive. *NR*, 166–69.

33. GVP, 115–17. Complicating an already complex situation is the role attributed to the minister of defense, A. R. Malinovskii. Perhaps because Pliev had proved reluctant to resort to force, Kozlov reportedly asked Khrushchev to have Malinovskii order the commander of the NCMO to use his troops "to thwart any possible destructive activity in the city." This occurred either shortly after the demonstrators crossed the Tuzlov or immediately after the Moscow leaders fled from the gorkom. Tretetskii, "Novocherkassk," 70; Trubin, "Kak eto bylo." See also Mardar', *Khronika*, 31.

34. Tretetskii, "Novocherkassk," 72; Mardar', *Khronika*, 50.

35. Reports of unrest in neighboring towns—"anti-Soviet" graffiti and leaflets—prompted Kozlov to send Kirilenko to Rostov, Shelepin to Taganrog, and Polianskii to Shakhty to keep sparks from bursting into flames. Mardar', *Khronika*, 51–52.

36. Iaroshenko, "Pamiat' khranit," 8.

37. Podol'skii, "Eto bylo," 11.

38. *KD*, 15–16.

39. Mardar', *Khronika*, 51.

40. GARF, F81319 031 D9366:250. Mardar' (*Khronika*, 52) reports the same slogan elsewhere, suggesting that it had considerable appeal. Although it served a good agitational purpose, the slogan was of course inaccurate: people fared much better under Khrushchev than under Stalin.

41. *KD*, 8.

42. *IA*, 1993, no. 1, p. 128. As regards the curfew, an item in *Znamia kommuny*, July 27, announced that persons under sixteen years of age were not to be on the streets from 9:00 P.M. to 6:00 A.M. in the summer and from 8:00 P.M. in the winter unless accompanied by a parent.

43. At the Aug. 13 meeting of the oblast party committee where Kurochkin was expelled, a report on the results of an inquiry stated: "Comrade Kurochkin managed the enterprise unsatisfactorily, visited the departments very infrequently, did not rely on the party and economic activists . . . did not always take into account the opinions and recommendations of the party committee, neglected the everyday needs and cultural requirements of the workers, [and] permitted bureaucratic, soulless relations with the people": TsDNI, F9 O1 D2936:28, 31. Material of this sort, along with criticism of Novocherkassk party officials, is printed in *IA*, 1993, no. 4, p. 176.

44. *IA*, 1993, no. 1, pp. 128, 136; TsDNI, F81 O22 D72:4–6.

45. On Oleshko, see GVP, 118–19. Pliev's role in Cuba receives a good deal of attention in Fursenko and Naftali, *"One Hell of a Gamble,"* esp. 192. According to the authors (193), Pliev had "caught Khrushchev's eye by effectively carrying out the awful duty of putting down the riots at Novocherkassk." In my judgment, Defense

Minister Malinovskii, under whom Pliev had served in Hungary and Manchuria (ibid., 272), is more likely to have chosen him for the Cuban assignment. Some time afterward, Pliev resumed command of the NCMO.

46. According to knowledgeable Novocherkassians with whom I spoke in 1998.

47. On storming, its causes and consequences, see Filtzer, *Soviet Workers and De-Stalinization*, 19–22.

48. TsDNI, F9 01 D2936:28–31. Deficiencies were reported for other Novocherkassk factories as well.

49. Cited in Nikitina, "Novocherkassk," 40.

50. Although evidence is lacking, some adjustment favorable to the workers may have been made. At any rate, after the 1953 riots in Berlin, "the [work] norms quickly returned to the status quo ante": Kopstein, *Politics of Economic Decline*, 37.

51. "O dal'neishem uluchshenii." Undoubtedly the document was widely distributed within the party ranks right away, but it was published only the following year.

52. *IA*, 1993, no. 4, pp. 163–68. See also 161–62. Another document in the same series indicated that many Soviet individuals influenced by Liberty and Free Russia broadcasts were sending anonymous letters to these foreign radio stations, a practice that had to be stopped. Ibid., 170.

Chapter 5. The Trial

1. I was aware of an eight-volume record of the trial, but my efforts to gain access in two successive years were fruitless. Nevertheless, it is possible to say a good deal about the proceedings on the basis of KGB records produced contemporaneously with the events, published in *IA*, 1993, no. 4, pp. 145–60. At least equally important is the record of the preliminary investigation, found in GARF, F131 O32 D93661. This record is invaluable, because investigations of the kind invariably foreshadow the substance of the trial (Feiffer, *Justice in Moscow*, 86). The point is corroborated in this instance by KGB Vice President Ivashutin and USSR Procurator Rudenko, who said after the trial that "the witnesses fully confirmed the testimony they had given in the preliminary investigation" (*IA*, 1993, no. 4, p. 174).

2. Berman, *Soviet Criminal Law and Procedure*.

3. Feiffer, *Justice in Moscow*, 16.

4. See arts. 4, 11, 12, 14, 16, 46, and 51 of the Criminal Code in Berman, *Soviet Criminal Law and Procedure*.

5. For a detailed examination of party intervention in criminal trials, see Solomon, "Soviet Politicians and Criminal Prosecutions."

6. Berman, *Soviet Criminal Law and Procedure*, 119–23.

7. On a visit to Novocherkassk in October 1998, I attempted to track down

the defense attorneys, whose names were listed in *KD*, 23. I was told by a lawyer who had participated in one of the lesser trials that all but one of the defense attorneys were no longer living. That one, S. S. Oganesev, who had made a brief statement critical of the trial (Bespalov and Konovalov, "Novocherkassk, 1962"), was too ill to see me. The lawyer with whom I spoke was evasive, but I had the distinct impression that he and in all likelihood the entire complement of advocates had been appointed rather than chosen by the accused.

8. Kaminskaya, *Final Judgment*, 13–15.

9. Mardar', *Khronika*, 57.

10. *IA*, 1993, no. 4, p. 145.

11. According to one of the people's assessors, the question of broadcasting the trial was discussed but rejected (Nikitina, "Novocherkassk," 58). During the main trial the local newspaper, *Znamia kommuny*, devoted an extraordinary amount of coverage to the new Soviet achievements in space by the cosmonauts A. G. Nikolaev and P. P. Popovich, which were hailed as "the triumph of communism." In a wonderful display of "uneven development," most of the other columns focused on the urgent need to bring in the harvest.

12. *IA*, 1993, no. 4, p. 145.   13. *KD*, 13.

14. *IA*, 1993, no, 4, pp. 174–76.   15. Ibid., 173–75.

16. The indictment is presented ibid., 145–60.

17. Smirnov had served in 1945–46 as the USSR's deputy chief prosecutor at the Nuremberg war crimes trials. In 1961 he was head of the Soviet delegation to the Second United Nations Congress on Crime Prevention and the Treatment of Criminals. In 1966 he presided at the trial of the dissidents Andrei Siniavskii and Iulii Daniel' (Institute of Study of the USSR, *Prominent Personalities*).

18. Nikitina, "Novocherkassk," 58–59. This exchange points up the fictional character of the statute in the Code of Criminal Procedure (art. 15) that asserts the equality of the judge and the assessors. In fact, as Kaminskaya contends, because the assessors lacked legal training, "they were endowed with powers they were incapable of exercising." Rather than genuine participants, they were dependent on the judge, who practically always had his way: Kaminskaya, *Final Judgment*, 15, 55–56.

19. GARF, F8131 O31 D93661:161. Not surprisingly, the indictment fails to mention his outstanding record. Sotnikov's father, by the way, had died at the front in 1943.

20. "The multitude of articles in the general press and in legal journals," observed Walter D. Conner, "attest to the epidemic nature of employee theft." See his "Workers, Politics, and Class Consciousness," 324.

21. Burlatsky, *Khrushchev and the First Soviet Spring*, 223.

22. Tsukanov, *Rasstrel v Novocherkasske*, 17–18.

23. Bespalov and Konovalov, "Novocherkassk, 1962."

24. *IA*, 1993, no. 4, pp. 154–60.

25. GARF, F8131 O31 D93661:69, 79, 80, 82, 109, 111, 132–34, 177.

26. The names of the witnesses and their political affiliations are given in the record of the preliminary investigation, ibid., 52–56.

27. Information on Korchak is found in GARF, F8131 O31 D93661:130–35. Quite a bit of it was published in Kruglinskaia, "Poslednee leto Andreia Korchaka."

28. Extracts from several of the confessions may be found in the indictment: *IA*, 1993, no. 4, pp. 146–49.

29. IA, 1993, no. 4, p. 173.; TsDNI, F81 O22 D73:28.; GARF, F8131 O31 D98327:25.

30. GARF, F8131 O31 D98327:25.

31. Conquest, *Great Terror*, 147.

32. Kaminskaya, *Final Judgment*, 132. See also Conquest, *Great Terror*, chap. 5.

33. The verdicts are printed in *KD*, 23–30.

34. Much later, an engineer wrote that there was no danger at all of an explosion: Siuda, "Sbornik," 59.

35. *IA*, 1993, no. 4, pp. 173, 174, 176; TsDNI, F81 O22 D73:44.

36. *IA*, 1993, no. 4, pp. 173–75.

37. TsDNI, F9 O22 D73:20–41; F9 O22 D71:32–48.

38. Tucker and Cohen, *Great Purge Trial*, 586.

39. Mardar', *Khronika*, 52.

Chapter 6. Anatomy of a Cover-Up

1. Siuda, *Novocherkassk*, 32; *IA*, 1993, no. 1, p. 130.

2. *IA*, 1993, no. 1, p. 130.

3. NA, State Department file 761.00/10–1962: A-550 (Oct. 10, 1962).

4. GVP, 114, 123.

5. One of these pledges is reproduced in Chapter 8.

6. Konovalov, "Listen, Understand, Forgive?" 28–29; Siuda, "Sbornik," 24–25; GVP, 108, 128; Bocharova, "Pod grifom 'sovershenno sekretno,'" *Novocherkasskie vedemosti*, Mar. 19.

7. Aleksei Adzhubei, Khrushchev's son-in-law and the editor of *Izvestiia*, wrote long after the events that Khrushchev and other leaders "tried to forget about the Novocherkassk events as soon as possible. None of the journalists dared to begin a detailed investigation. . . . We were taught for a long time to see nothing and hear nothing. And consequently to know nothing" (*Te desiat' let*, 282).

8. *NR*, 165.

9. Richmond, "'Eye of the State,'" 584–85.

10. Solzhenitsyn, *Gulag Archipelago*, 3:507. Roy Medvedev seems to have been led astray on this point by Solzhenitsyn. See his *Khrushchev*, 171.

11. According to M. Mondich, a Radio Liberty staff member, the information in the *Telegraph* article came from members of the Soviet delegation to the International Youth Festival in Helsinki. Open Society Archive, Budapest, Radio Liberty files, no. 1413, "Iun′skie sobytiia 1962 goda," 3. I am grateful to the librarian of the Open Society Archive for making available to me a collection of Radio Liberty materials on the Novocherkassk events.

12. NA, State Department files 761.00/7–2762 (July 27, 1962); 761.00/862 (Aug. 10, 1962); 861.181/8/1462 (Aug. 14, 1962).

13. Ibid., 761.00/7–2762 (July 27, 1962); 761.00/8–1762 (Aug. 17, 1962).

14. Phone conversation with Bassow, January 1997.

15. Bassow discusses his expulsion in *Moscow Correspondents*, 214–21.

16. Open Society Archive, Radio Liberty files, pxc 14, no. 1338 (Sept. 13, 1962).

17. Ibid., no. 1359, "The Truth About Novocherkassk."

18. Boiter, "When the Kettle Boils Over," 36–38.

19. McCauley mentions the Boiter article (3n) but tells nothing of its substance. Elsewhere (251) she writes: "We have not dealt with the occasional reports of strikes that reach the west because the unofficial strike has not formed part of the usual pattern of labor disputes since the twenties, and the occasional walk-out or slowdown is not particularly significant."

20. Solzhenitsyn, *Gulag Archipelago*, 3:507–14.

21. Kolasky, *Two Years in Soviet Ukraine*, 191–92.

22. Holubenko, "Soviet Working Class," 12–13.

23. Nikitina, "Novocherkassk," 34; Solzhenitsyn, *Gulag Archipelago*, 3:507.

24. Haynes and Semyonova, *Workers Against the Gulag*, 76–81.

25. The names are not given in the pamphlet, but nineteen are appended to an abridged version of the leaflet in Belotserkovskii, *Iz portativnogo gulaga rossiiskoi emigratsii*, 48–49. It is reproduced in Appendix B.

26. Reddaway, *Uncensored Russia*, 127–30.

27. Grigorenko, *Memoirs*, 272, 279–86. He reproduces (284–85) an interesting bit of the conversation he had with his interrogator.

28. Roy Medvedev noticed it in his *Khrushchev*, 171. This work was published in a Russian edition as well in the United States, but not in Russia. Geoffrey Hosking, no dissident, also noticed it in *First Socialist Society*, 389–90. One of the more substantial treatments of these years is Heller and Nekrich, *Utopia in Power*, 592–96. Editions in Russian and French had appeared in Paris in 1982.

29. Quoted in Tarasulo, *Gorbachev and Glasnost*, xxi.

30. White, *Gorbachev in Power*, chap. 3.

31. Siuda's biography is sketched in Chapter 7. Elements of it alluded to in this chapter are drawn from an interview conducted by David Mandel in 1988, published in Russian as Siuda, *Novocherkassk*, and in English as "Survival and Resistance: A Soviet Family's Story," chap. 1 in Mandel's *Rabotyagi*.

32. Siuda, "Novocherkasskaia tragediia," *24 Chasa*; "Chto zhe togda proiskhodilo?" and "Versiia dlia issledovatelia," *KD*, 3–5, 20–21; "Novocherkasskaia tragediia," *Karta*. The last item, published posthumously, was made available by Siuda's widow. The lengthiest of the articles, it may have been written first and served as the template for the other pieces. Of course, Siuda's answers to Mandel's questions about the strike are also significant.

33. Siuda, "Novocherkasskaia tragediia," *24 Chasa*, 10.

34. Siuda, "Sbornik," 24–25, 61. The "Sbornik" is a collection of Siuda's unpublished papers compiled in 1989. I am deeply indebted to Iurii Bespalov for giving me access to these materials.

35. His writings came into the hands of a *Manchester Guardian* correspondent, Jonathan Steele, with results treated farther along; and the sociologist David Mandel, who went to Novocherkassk to interview Siuda. I have been unable to locate samizdat copies of his works or his publications in the outlets mentioned, but it is safe to say that their contents were very similar to what came out in the articles he later published.

36. Siuda, "Sbornik," 45–47.

37. Ibid., 44–45.

38. The letter, dated May 1988, appears ibid., 45–46.

39. Ibid., 48.

40. Ibid., 46–49.

41. Nikitina, "Dni zatmeniia, dni prozreniia."

42. Nikitina, "Novocherkassk," 33.

43. Interview with Nikitina, Rostov-on-Don, July 1997.

44. Bespalov wrote about this incident in "Novocherkassk 1962: Kak deviat' let."

45. She later learned of eight files in the province's MVD archive, but was told she would never gain access to them.

46. The piece was reprinted in the Novocherkassk newspaper, *Znamia kommuny*, and many copies of the article were distributed at NEVZ (Siuda, "Sbornik").

47. Ibid., 49–56.

48. Ibid., 56.

49. Nikitina, "Dni zatmeniia, dni prozreniia," *Komsomolets*, June 2, 1990. She had meanwhile brought out an important two-part article in an unofficial organ, *Don*: "Novocherkassk: Khronika tragedii."

50. BBC Current Affairs Unit, CARIS Talk, no. 66/68. This item, found in the

Radio Liberty file on Novocherkassk, Open Society Archive, may have been used by that organization as well.

51. Bespalov, "Novocherkassk 1962: Kak deviat' let."

52. As Bespalov wrote in "Novocherkassk 1962," *KP*, June 3, 1990, 2, the authors received scores of letters from readers, mostly confirming the story and adding details or making corrections; a few denounced them for foisting a "fabrication" on the public.

53. The following account is based on my interview in October 1998 with Kalinchenko, at present a professor at the Novocherkassk Polytechnical Institute. Siuda depicts Kalinchenko as initially reticent ("Sbornik," 86, 89–90).

54. *Izvestiia*, June 11, 1989, p. 7. What followed is treated in Chapter 8.

55. Fomin and Shchekochikhin, "Togda v Novocherkasske"; Bespalov, "Novocherkassk"; Kruglinskaia, "Poslednee leto Andreia Korchaka"; Volkov, "Novocherkassk."

56. Nikitina, "Novocherkassk," 33.

57. Zhukov, "Russia's Archives."

58. "Novocherkasskaia tragediia, 1962," *IA*, 1993, no. 1, 110–36; no. 4, 145–77. The publication may have been facilitated by Rudolf Pikhoia, who was simultaneously the editor of the journal and the head of the Russian Archival Service (Rosarkhiv).

Chapter 7. Shaposhnikov and Siuda

1. Mikhail Arkhipov published an informative though rather hagiographic fifteen-part biography of Shaposhnikov, based on extensive conversations with the general, titled "Sud'ba opal'nogo generala," in the newspaper *Raionnye vesti*, Apr. 22–July 27, 1995. Shaposhnikov's brief account of his family background was published after his death as "Ne okazhis' pered faktom zabveniia." An accompanying column by Liudmila Karamysheva provides some additional biographical details.

2. Somewhat later, in 1962, Defense Minister A. R. Malinovskii published three articles and then a book on military strategy, which stressed that "rockets and atomic armaments were only a part of a country's defense equipment and that all other defense sectors must be strengthened as well": Tatu, *Power in the Kremlin*, 217.

3. Arkhipov, "Sud'ba opal'nogo generala," pt. 3, May 5, 1995.

4. Bespalov and Konovalov, "Novocherkassk, 1962"; Fomin and Shchekochikhin, "Togda v Novocherkasske"; Shaposhnikov, "Novocherkassk—62"; GVP, 29–31; Arkhipov, "Sud'ba opal'nogo generala," pt. 2, Apr. 25, 1995.

5. Shaposhnikov, "Novocherkassk—62."

6. Arkhipov, "Sud'ba opal'nogo generala." Shaposhnikov's story found its

way into the U.S. press in 1990. After interviewing the general, David Remnick included his account in a long dispatch on Novocherkassk, published in the *Washington Post*, Dec. 18, 1990. Much the same material is included in Remnick's *Lenin's Tomb*, 414–19.

7. As indicated by, among others, Tupchenko in GVP, 48.

8. *IA*, 1993, no. 1, p. 135, nn. 10, 11.

9. Nikitina, "Novocherkassk," 37–38.

10. Interview with the general's daughter, Nina Matveena Shaposhnikova, June 1997. This is something of a puzzle, because passages from the diary were cited in the 1989 *LG* article.

11. GVP, 31.

12. Ibid., 30.

13. Shaposhnikov's reference to a "first meeting" with the two is puzzling, for he nowhere mentions a second.

14. GVP, 36.

15. GVP, 30.

16. GVP, 36.

17. GVP, 29–31.

18. Quoted in Tretetskii, "Novocherkassk," 76.

19. Ibid., 75. This matter is repeated in GVP, 41.

20. Tretetskii, "Novocherkassk," 75.

21. Shaposhnikov, "Ten' na tragediiu," 5–6.

22. Siuda, "Novocherkasskaia tragediia," *24 Chasa*, and his other articles as well. There is an obvious disparity between what the two say, but in one case as in the other the soldiers were essentially unarmed.

23. This order has not come to light.

24. According to A. S. Antonov, a soldier who was there. Nikitina, "Dni zatmeniia, dni prozreniia," *Komsomolets*, June 22, 1988.

25. It was at that point, Shaposhnikov claimed, that he had ordered the tanks' weapons disarmed, their hatches opened, and the vehicles to remain in place. GVP, 52–53.

26. Ibid., 40. As opposed to Mikheev's count, Shaposhnikov says there were six or seven tanks on the bridge (ibid., 53). Mikheev's number is more credible.

27. Arkhipov, "Sud'ba opal'nogo generala," pt. 2, Apr. 25, 1995.

28. Shaposhnikov, "Ten' na tragediiu," 6.

29. Solzhenitsyn, *Gulag Archipelago*, 3:510. Shaposhnikov's daughter told me unequivocally that her father was not acquainted with Solzhenitsyn's work.

30. Arkhipov, "Sud'ba opal'nogo generala," pt. 2, Apr. 25, 1995.

31. Two weeks after the event, Lenin had recorded "the toll of Bloody Sunday": Thousands of "unarmed workers, women and children . . . were killed and wounded" by the army. "The tsar's henchmen and their European flunkies say: 'We

have taught them a lesson. . . . ' Yes, it was a great lesson, one the Russian proletariat will not forget": Lenin, *Polnoe sobranie sochinenii*, 201.

32. The following statement is emblematic: "The most important indication of the socialist army's character is that it expresses and defends the interests of the laboring classes, above all the [industrial] working class. As opposed to the imperialist army, which serves the interests of the exploitative minority, the socialist army is the army of the working people": Volkogonov et al., *Voina i armiia*, 345.

33. *LG*, June 21, 1989, p. 13.

34. Arkhipov, "Sud'ba opal'nogo generala," pt. 12, June 24, 1995. An interesting document detailing the KGB investigation and its findings is in GARF, F8131 O36 D1808.

35. The article elaborates: "for the purpose of subverting or weakening Soviet authority . . . or circulating for the same purpose slanderous fabrications which defame the Soviet state and social system, or preparing or keeping, for the same purpose, literature of such content": Berman, *Soviet Criminal Law and Procedure*, 180.

36. Parts of this story, as told by Shaposhnikov, first appeared in the 1989 interview in *LG*, and at much greater length in Arkhipov, "Sud'ba opal'nogo generala," pts. 5–14, May 11–July 22, 1995.

37. *LG*, June 21, 1989, p. 13.

38. Information about Siuda and his family is drawn largely from an interview with Siuda conducted in Novocherkassk by David Mandel in 1988 and published in his *Rabotyagi*.

39. Ibid., 23.

40. Siuda, "Novocherkasskaia tragediia," *Karta*, 18; Mandel, *Rabotyagi*, 36.

41. Siuda, "Sbornik," 15–21   42. Mandel, *Rabotyagi*, 38–39, 41.

43. Ibid., 38–44.   44. Ibid., 44–45.

45. Siuda, "Sbornik," 49.

46. A collection of relevant documents: "Novocherkassk—1962," *KD*; and Mardar''s 60-page *Khronika*, the most considerable account of the events published through 1998.

47. Mandel, *Rabotyagi*, 15.

48. Nikitina, "Dni zatmeniia, dni prozreniia," *Komsomolets*, June 2, 1990.

49. Interview with Bespalov, June 1997.

Chapter 8. Reconsideration and Rehabilitation

1. On the unsuccessful efforts to work out a new Union treaty, see Miller, *Mikhail Gorbachev and the End of Soviet Power*, chap. 11.

2. Some 200 million people tuned in daily to watch the "riveting" spectacle of deputies attacking "the sacred cows and enthroned dogmas": Mickewicz, *Changing*

Channels, 83–91. This volume recounts in an excitingly intimate way the large role of television in the last years of the USSR.

3. See the excellent chap. 12 of Malia, *Soviet Tragedy*.

4. See Kozlov, *Arkhivy kremlia*, 52–53. The documents on Novocherkassk are those that had been published in *IA*, 1993, nos. 1 and 4.

5. *Izvestiia*, June 11, 1989, p. 7.

6. This letter and related documents are printed in *KD*, 30–33.

7. The Novocherkassk deputy V. M. Kalinchenko referred to the lack of response to these efforts on the floor of the Congress: ibid., 31.

8. Ibid.

9. Ibid., 33.

10. Tretetskii, "Novocherkassk," 75.

11. The same material is printed in Medvedev's more accessible *Khrushchev*, 171.

12. *KD*, 22–33. Charges against the armed forces were apt to touch a nerve in the wake of the disastrous Afghanistan adventure. The last Soviet troops had been withdrawn in February 1989.

13. Ibid., 31–33. The letter from the Ministry of Defense, signed by M. Moiseev and printed in *KD*, foreshadows the longer and more informative one by the minister, Gen. D. T. Iazov, which was published nine months later in *LG*, Sept. 12, 1990, p. 2.

14. *KD*, 33.

15. GVP, 1.

16. This document is appended to Nikitina, "Novocherkassk," 60–62, together with two evasive replies from the KGB and the MVD.

17. *LG*, Sept. 12, 1990, p. 2. It is worth noting that the liberal journal rather than the Ministry of Defense published Iazov's letter. V. K. Fomin, one of the deputies who had posed the questions, was also an *LG* correspondent.

18. The Iazov letter in *LG*, Sept. 12, 1990, p. 2; Tretetskii, "Novocherkassk"; Kastanenko, "Za gran'iu razuma"; Trubin, "Kak eto bylo."

19. Konovalov, "Listen, Understand, Forgive?" 29.

20. Tretetskii, "Novocherkassk," 68.

21. Podol'skii, "Ia byl ochevidtsem tragedii"; Malakhov, "Novocherkassk."

22. Bespalov, "Novocherkassk, 1962," *KP*, May 3, 1990, p, 2.

23. "Kakoi zhe on prestupnik?" *Novocherkasskie vedemosti*," May 4–10, 1991, p. 5. This page presents other relevant material as well.

24. Dmitriev, "Novocherkassk." The bracketed sentences at the end of the first paragraph are taken from a longer version of this letter in *KD*, 13.

25. Isaev, "Black Day in Novocherkassk," 64. Also GVP, 159.

26. Nikitina, "Oni khoteli naiti pravdu," 98.

27. Malakhov, "Novocherkassk," 3.

28. Volkov, "Novocherkassk."

29. Ibid.

30. Bespalov, "Novocherkassk: Poslednaia taina?" 4; "Rasskrecheny mesta za-khorenenii," *Izvestiia* (evening ed.), Jan. 25, 1991, p. 1.

31. Regulations of the Fond Novocherkasskoi Tragedii (FNT), (1992). The group worked toward these ends from the first, but its goals and procedures were formalized in 1992.

32. Interview with Mardar', June 1997.

33. *KD*, 1990, no. 2.

34. Mardar', *Khronika*.

35. Isaev, "Zemliaki pomnit ikh," *Trud*, June 4, 1991.

36. Kruglinskaia, "Poslednee leto Andreia Korchaka."

37. Trubin, "Kak eto bylo." The English translation in *Soviet Law and Government* should be used with caution.

38. Poltaev and Bespalov, "Streliat' mozhno?"

39. Evtushenko, "Otkrytoe pis'mo." Quoted by permission of the poet.

40. At least two other poems memorialized the Novocherkassk massacre: Iu. Minkin, "Ekho shest'desiat vtorogo," *Donskaia rech'*, June 2, 1992; and V. Vasilenko, "Rekviem," published in a collection of his work (Novocherkassk, 1994).

41. *Rossiiskaia gazeta*, June 2, 1991, 4.

42. He had died in exile some years earlier.

43. Rosanov, "Gor'koe torzhestvo."

44. *Vedemosti s"ezda narodnykh deputatov RSFSR i Verkhovnogo Soveta RSFSR*, no. 44, pp. 1690–97.

45. Open Society Archive, Radio Free Europe Research Institute, "Russia and CIS Today," no. 58320, June 2, 1992.

46. A copy of the document is in the archive of the FNT.

47. From the procurator general's office to the head of the President's Commission on Pardons, Nov. 2, 1995, FNT papers.

48. *Sobranie zakonodatel'stva Rossiiskoi Federatsii*, no. 24 (May 10, 1996), 5826–27. These promises have mostly been unfulfilled.

49. Interview with Valentina Vodianitskaia, June 1987.

50. Unpublished agenda for the day of mourning, in possession of the FNT.

51. Open Society Archive, Radio Free Europe Research Institute, "Russia and the CIS Today," no. 58320, June 2, 1962.

52. Mar. 19, 1993, p. 3; Mar. 26, 1993, p. 9.

53. Bocharova, "Novocherkasskaia tragediia—1962"; *IA*, 1993, nos. 1 and 4.

54. Tretetskii, "Novocherkassk," 73.

55. Bespalov and Konovalov, "Postavlena tochka." I have not succeeded in

finding where Bagraev's remarks were published in full, but they were certainly based on the summary of his investigation's findings completed in 1994. The summary, on which I have drawn heavily, has not appeared in print.

56. GVP, 137.

Chapter 9. Reflections and Conclusions

1. Pravda, "Spontaneous Workers' Activities," 350.

2. Lewin, "Concluding Remarks," 383.

3. Filtzer, *Soviet Workers and De-Stalinization*, esp. chaps. 1 and 6.

4. Further demands, economic and perhaps even political, might have been formulated if the strike had not ended so swiftly. "Strictly political demands come only after a revolt has gained momentum": Montias, "Economic Conditions," 285.

5. Mandel, *Rabotyagi*, 31–33. The primitive character of the NEVZ strike made it akin to the cotton workers' strike at Teikovo in 1932 and contrasts sharply with the sophisticated organization and tactics of the Donbass coal miners' strike in 1989. See Rossman, "Teikovo Cotton Workers' Strike"; Friedgut and Siegelbaum, *Soviet Miners' Strike*. The observation of two distinguished labor historians is decidedly relevant: "The regime co-opted those who might have become labor's leaders and punished those who might have formed oppositions." Siegelbaum and Suny, *Making Workers Soviet*, 26.

6. Burds, "Urban Riots."

7. These and other disorders are treated in Kozlov, *Massovye besporiadki*. Besides, a youth riot involving several thousand persons had occurred in 1957 in Khrestivka, Stalino oblast. See Kuromiya, *Freedom and Terror in the Donbas*, 325–26.

8. Sergei Khrushchev, *Nikita Khrushchev*, 501. Adzhubei believed that his father-in-law had drawn some lessons from the event, and quoted him as saying that "to express dissatisfaction is an inalienable right of people" (*Te desiat' let*, 282–83).

9. N. S. Khrushchev, 5.

10. For the interview, see "Utrennii chai v 'Pravde piat': Otvety na voprosy redaktsii Vladimir Semichastnyi," *Pravda-5*, Nov. 11, 1997. Compare what follows with an excerpt from Semichastny's report to the party leaders on July 13, 1962:

> A group of criminal-hooligan and self-seeking elements provoked disorder, taking advantage of the justified grievances of some workers with the factory administration on questions of the organization of work and the living conditions of the workers, the revision of norms and pay for various kinds of productive work, and also the existence of incorrect and even soulless attitudes of some of the factory leaders to the needs and requirements of the workers. (*IA*, 1993, no. 4, p. 145)

11. Solzhenitsyn, *Gulag Archipelago*, 3:507.

12. Cook, *Soviet Social Contract*, 58–60. By the 1980s one-third of the coun-

try's hard currency earnings was spent to import grain and food: Schroeder, "Soviet Economy."

13. Gorbachev, *Zhizn' i reformy*, 1:197 (italics mine). Gorbachev's hand-wringing on the question of continued growth was justified. In 1986 the subsidy on meat and dairy products alone came to 50 billion rubles: Teague, *Solidarity and the Soviet Worker*, 345.

14. Teague, *Solidarity and the Soviet Worker*, 39.

15. Cook, *Soviet Social Contract*, 74 (italics mine).

16. Ibid.; Gidwitz, "Labor Unrest." Kozlov, *Massovye besporiadki*, speaks repeatedly of the "crisis" that beset the last Khrushchev years and the corrective "compromise," involving better provisioning, that the Brezhnev regime made with the populace.

17. Schroeder, "Soviet Economy," 5–6.

18. Ibid., 6–10.

19. Bushnell, "'New Soviet Man.'"

20. Kennedy, *Rise and Fall of the Great Powers*, 488–514.

21. Ibid., 513.

22. GVP, 107.

23. A Rostov historian ludicrously remarked in 1997 that in all the capitalist countries, including the United States, antigovernment actions are routinely suppressed by armed forces, and such deeds are hardly noticed. He continued, obtusely: "The sharp reaction of the press and popular opinion to [the Novocherkassk events] is to be explained [only] by the circumstance that the USSR was from the beginning a worker-peasant, popular state, which extended all rights to the working masses": Kislitsyn, "Chto proizoshlo v Novocherkasske?" 324.

Appendix A. Bloody Sunday / Bloody Saturday

1. What was known undoubtedly stemmed from the account presented in the virtual Soviet bible, composed under Stalin's direction, *History of the Communist Party of the Soviet Union (Bolsheviks)*, or one of its many derivatives. The key lines read:

> On January 9, 1905, the workers marched to the Winter Palace. . . . [Nicholas II] gave orders to fire upon the unarmed workers. That day over a thousand workers were killed and more than two thousand wounded. . . . The streets of St. Petersburg ran with workers' blood. . . . The fearful news of the tsar's crime spread far and wide. The whole working class, the whole country was stirred by indignation and abhorrence. There was not a town where the workers did not strike in protest against the tsar's villainous act and did not put forward political demands. . . . Revolution in Russia had begun. (58)

2. The data on Bloody Sunday here adduced are mostly drawn from Sablinsky's excellent *Road to Bloody Sunday*.

3. See Tumarkin, *Living and the Dead*.

4. Sablinsky, *Road to Bloody Sunday*, 200–201.

5. A useful account of the evolution of labor conditions and organizations in the USSR appears in McCauley, *Labor Disputes in Soviet Russia*, chaps. 2 and 3.

6. The petition is reproduced in Sablinsky, *Road to Bloody Sunday*, 344–49.

7. Ibid., 159–60.

8. Ibid., 265–67.

9. Ibid., 262.

10. See, for example, Pankratova, *History of the USSR*, 3:44. It is worth noting that, according to his mother, the present-day political figure Gen. Aleksandr Lebed, who was born in Novocherkassk, witnessed the shooting from a nearby tree: Ladnyi, "35 let."

Appendix B. Leaflet Composed and Distributed by Dissidents, 1977

1. Belotserkovskii, *Iz portativnogo gulaga rossiiskoi emigratsii*, 48–49.

Appendix C. Questionnaire Submitted to Bloody Saturday Participants and Eyewitnesses by the Chief Military Procuracy, 1991–92

1. This document was found among papers of the Fond Novocherkasskoi Tragedii.

Bibliography

Manuscript Materials

Fond Novocherkasskoi Tragedii, Novocherkassk.

Glavnaia Voennaia Prokuratura. "O Novocherkasskikh sobytiiakh, 1962 goda." Moscow, 1994.

Gosudarstvennaia Arkhiv Rossiiskoi Federatsii, Moscow. F8131.

National Archives, Washington, D.C. State Department files 761.

Open Society Archive, Budapest. Materials in Radio Free Europe files relating to the Novocherkassk events.

Siuda, P. P. "Sbornik materialov po delu o Novocherkasskoi tragedii, 01--03 iun'ia 1962 goda." Novocherkassk, 1989.

Tsentralyi Arkhiv Noveishee Istorii, Rostov-on-Don. F9, F81.

Newspapers

Izvestiia
Komsomol'skaia pravda
Literaturnaia gazeta
Novocherkasskie vedemosti
Pravda
Sobesdnik
Trud
Znamia kommuny (Novocherkassk)

Documentary Films

Kak eto bylo. Moscow, 1998. (Television broadcast, Oct. 25, 1998.)

Novocherkassk 1962 god. Rostov-on-Don, 1992.

Novocherkasskaia tragediia: 30 let spustia. Rostov-on-Don, 1991.

Novocherkassk 62. Letopisets Rossii, no. 3. Rostov-on-Don, 1992.

Interviews

Iurii Bespalov, Tat'iana Bocharova, Vladimir Kalinchenko, Mikhail Kraisvetnyi, Irina Mardar', Ol'ga Nikitina, Nina Shaposhnikova, Valentina Vodianitskaia

Published Primary and Secondary Sources

Adzhubei, A. *Te desiat' let*. Moscow, 1989.

Andrle, Vladimir. *A Social History of Twentieth Century Russia*. London, 1994.

Arkhipov, Mikhail. "Sud'ba opal'nogo generala." *Raionnye vesti*, Apr. 22–July 27, 1994.

Bagraev, Iu., and V. Pavliutkin. "Novocherkassk, 1962-I: Tragediia na ploshchadi." *Krasnaia zvezda*, Oct. 7, 1995.

Bassow, Whitman. *The Moscow Correspondents: Reporting on Russia from the Revolution to Glasnost*. New York, 1989.

Belotserkovskii, Vadim. *Iz portativnogo gulaga rossiiskoi emigratsii: Sbornik statei*. Munich, 1983.

Berman, Harold J. *Justice in the USSR: An Interpretation of Soviet Law*. Cambridge, Mass., 1966.

———, ed. *Soviet Criminal Law and Procedure: The RSFSR Codes*. Trans. Harold J. Berman and James W. Spindler. Cambridge, Mass., 1966.

Bespalov, Iu. "Novocherkassk—1962." *Komsomol'skaia pravda*, June 3, 1990.

———. "Novocherkassk 1962: Kak deviat' let nazad my pisali stat'iu voshedshuiu v istorii." *Moskovskii komsomolets*, South weekly ed., June 6–13, 1997.

———. "Novocherkassk: Poslednaia taina?" *Komsomol'skaia pravda*, Jan. 18, 1991.

———. "Streliat' mozhno?" *Komsomol'skaia pravda*, June 8, 1991.

Bespalov, Iu., and V. Konovalov. "Novocherkassk, 1962." *Komsomol'skaia pravda*, July 2, 1989.

———. "Postavlena tochka v rassledovanii Novocherkasskikh sobytiiakh 1962 goda." *Izvestiia*, June 4, 1992.

Bocharova, T. "Pod grifom 'sovershenno sekretno.'" *Novocherkasskie vedomosti*, Mar. 19 and 26, 1993.

Boiter, Albert. "When the Kettle Boils Over." *Problems of Communism*, January–February 1964.

Burds, Jeffrey. "Urban Riots in the Late Khrushchev Era: Patterns and Perspectives." Paper presented to the 30th Annual Convention of the American Association for the Advancement of Slavic Studies, Boca Raton, Fla., Sept. 25, 1998.

Burlatsky, Fedor. *Khrushchev and the First Soviet Spring*. London, 1991.

Bushnell, John. "The 'New Soviet Man' Turns Pessimist." In *The Soviet Union Since*

Stalin, ed. Stephen F. Cohen, Alexander Rabinowitch, and Robert Sharlet. Bloomington, 1980.

Chapman, Janet. "Recent Trends in the Soviet Industrial Wage Structure." In *Industrial Labor in the USSR*, ed. Arcadius Kahan and Blair Ruble. New York, 1979.

Conner, Walter D. "Workers, Politics, and Class Consciousness." In *Industrial Labor in the USSR*, ed. Arcadius Kahan and Blair Ruble. New York, 1979.

Conquest, Robert. *The Great Terror: Stalin's Purge of the Thirties.* New York, 1968.

———. *Harvest of Sorrow.* New York, 1986.

———. *The Industrial Workers in the USSR.* New York, 1967.

Cook, Linda J. *The Soviet Social Contract and Why It Failed: Welfare Policy and Workers' Politics from Brezhnev to Yeltsin.* Cambridge, Mass., 1993.

Dantsev, A. A. *Gorod na kholme.* Novocherkassk, 1993.

Davies, R. W. *Soviet History in the Yeltsin Era.* New York, 1997.

Davies, Sarah. "'Us Against Them': Social Identity in Soviet Russia, 1934–41." *Russian Review* 56 (1997): 70–89.

Davis, Natalie Zemon. "The Rites of Violence." In Davis, *Society and Culture in Early Modern France: Eight Essays.* Stanford, 1975.

DeWitt, Nicholas. "Upheaval in Education." *Problems of Communism*, January–February 1959.

Djilas, Milovan. *The New Class.* New York, 1957.

Dmitriev, Iu. "Novocherkassk: Ekho tragedii." *Trud*, Oct. 28, 1990.

Documents of the 22nd Congress of the CPSU. Vol. I. New York, 1961.

Donnelly, Christopher. *Red Banner: The Soviet Military System in Peace and War.* Coulsdon, Surrey, 1988.

Entsiklopedicheskii Slovar'. Moscow, 1897.

Evtushenko, E. "Otkrytoe pis'mo general'nomu prokuroru SSSR." *Literaturnaia gazeta*, June 12, 1991.

Feiffer, George. *Justice in Moscow.* New York, 1964.

Field, Daniel. *Rebels in the Name of the Tsar.* New York, 1976.

Filtzer, Donald. *Soviet Workers and De-Stalinization: The Consolidation of the Modern System of Soviet Production Relations.* Cambridge, 1992.

Fitzpatrick, Sheila. *Stalin's Peasants: Resistance and Survival in the Russian Village After Collectivization.* New York, 1994.

Fomin, V., and Iu. Shchekochikhin. "Togda v Novocherkasske." *Literaturnaia Gazeta*, June 21, 1989.

"Fotografii ischezli pri nevyiasnennykh obstoiatel'stvakh." *Komsomol'skaia pravda*, Apr. 27, 1991.

Friedgut, Theodore H., and Lewis H. Siegelbaum. *The Soviet Miners' Strike, July*

1989: Perestroika from Below. Carl Beck Papers in Russian and East European Studies, no. 804. Pittsburgh, 1990.

Fursenko, Aleksandr, and Timothy Naftali. *"One Hell of a Gamble": Khrushchev, Castro, and Kennedy, 1958–1964.* New York, 1997.

Getty, Arch. "Russian Archives: Is the Door Half Open or Half Closed?" *Perspectives,* May–June 1996.

Gidwitz, Betsy. "Labor Unrest in the Soviet Union." *Problems of Communism,* November–December 1982.

Gill, Graeme. *The Rules of the Communist Party of the Soviet Union.* Armonk, N.Y., 1988.

Goldman, Marshall I. *U.S.S.R. in Crisis: The Failure of an Economic System.* New York, 1983.

Gorbachev, Mikhail. *Zhizn' i reformy.* 2 vols. Moscow, 1995. English translation: *Memoirs.* New York, 1996.

Grigorenko, Petr. *Memoirs.* Trans. Thomas P. Whitney. New York and London, 1982.

Haynes, Viktor, and Olga Semyonova, eds. *Workers Against the Gulag: The New Opposition in the Soviet Union.* London, 1979.

Heller, Mikhail, and Aleksandr Nekrich. *Utopia in Power: History of the Soviet Union from 1917 to the Present.* Trans. Phyllis B. Carlos. New York, 1986.

History of the Communist Party of the Soviet Union (Bolsheviks). Moscow, 1939.

Holubenko, M. "The Soviet Working Class, Discontent and Opposition." *Critique,* Spring 1975.

Hosking, Geoffrey. *The First Socialist Society: A History of the Soviet Union from Within.* Cambridge, Mass., 1985.

Iaroshenko, O. "Pamiat' khranit." *Krytyi dvor,* 1990, no. 2.

Institute of Study of the USSR. *Prominent Personalities in the USSR.* Metuchen, N.J., 1968.

Isaev, A. "Black Day in Novocherkassk." *Soviet Law and Government* 30, no. 4 (1992). First published as "Chernyi den' v Novocherkasske." *Trud,* June 1, 1991.

———. "Zemliaki pomnit ikh." *Trud,* June 4, 1991.

Kahan, Arcadius. *Essays and Studies of the Soviet and East European Economies.* Newtonville, Mass., 1991.

Kaminskaya, Dina. *Final Judgment: My Life as a Soviet Defense Attorney.* Trans. Michael Glenny. New York, 1982.

Karamysheva, Liudmila. "Novocherkassk—62: Vragov ne vizhu." *Komsomol'skaia pravda,* June 23, 1994.

Kassof, Allen. *The Soviet Youth Program: Regimentation and Rebellion.* Cambridge, Mass., 1965.

Kastanenko, Zh. "Za gran'iu razuma." *Sovetskaia Rossiia,* Feb. 1, 1991.

Kennedy, Paul. *The Rise and Fall of the Great Powers: Economic Change and Military Conflict from 1500 to 2000*. New York, 1987.

Khrestomatiia po otechestvennoi istorii (1946–1995). Moscow, 1996.

Khrushchev, N. S. *Khrushchev Remembers: The Glasnost Tapes*. Trans. Jerrold Schechter and Vyacheslav V. Luchkov. Boston, 1990.

———. *Khrushchev Remembers: The Last Testament*. Trans. and ed. Strobe Talbott. Boston, 1974.

———. "Miting sovetskoi i kubinskoi molodezha v Kremle: Vystuplenie Tovarishcha N. S. Khrushcheva." *Pravda*, June 3, 1962.

Khrushchev, Sergei. *Nikita Khrushchev and the Creation of a Superpower*. University Park, Pa., 2000.

Kislitsyn, S. A. "Chto proizoshlo v Novocherkasske v 1962?" In *Donskaia istoriia v voprosakh i otvetov*, ed. E. N. Dumilov and S. A. Kislitsyn. Rostov-on-Don, 1997.

Kolasky, John. *Two Years in Soviet Ukraine: A Canadian's Personal Account of Russian Oppression and the Growing Opposition*. Toronto, 1972.

Koniukhov, V. *Komendantskii chas*. Rostov-on-Don, 1998.

Konovalov, V. "Listen, Understand, Forgive?" *Soviet Law and Government* 30, no. 4 (1992). First published as "Uslyshat', poniat', prostit'?" *Rodina*, 1980, no. 3.

Konovalov, V., and Iu. Bespalov. "Novocherkassk, 1962." *Komsomol'skaia pravda*, June 2, 1989.

Kopstein, Jeffrey. *The Politics of Economic Decline in East Germany, 1945–1989*. Chapel Hill, 1997.

Kozlov, A. "Razkazachivanie." *Rodina*, 1990, nos. 6 and 7.

Kozlov, V. A. *Massovye besporiadki v SSSR pri Khrushcheve i Brezhneve (1953–nachalo 1980-kh godov)*. Novosibirsk, 1999.

———, ed. *Arkhivy kremlia i staroi ploshchadi: Dokumenty po "Delu KPSS."* Novosibirsk, 1995.

Kraisvetnyi, M. "Novocherkassk—62; novye podrobnosty." *Donskie oblastnye vedemosty*, May 28, 1998.

Kramer, Mark. "New Evidence on Soviet Decision-Making and the 1956 Polish and Hungarian Crises." *Cold War International History Project Bulletin*, Winter 1996–97.

Kruglinskaia, I. "Poslednee leto Andreia Korchaka." *Izvestiia*, Mar. 30, 1991.

Kuchkova, O. "V korridorakh vlasti." *Komsomol'skaia pravda*, Jan. 14, 1990.

Kulawig, Erik. *Tretten historier om ulydige russere, Folkelig modstand regimet under Khrustjov, 1953–1964* [Thirteen Stories About Disobedient Russians: Popular Resistance to the Khrushchev Regime (1953–64)]. Odense, Denmark, 1999.

Kurkov, V. "Novocherkassk, 1962." *Gudok*, Nov. 14, 1990.

Kuromiya, Hiroaki. *Freedom and Terror in the Donbas: A Ukrainian-Russian Borderland, 1870s–1990s*. New York, 1998.

Ladnyi, V. "35 let tomu nazad v Novocherkasske podorozhalo miaso . . ." *Komsomol'skaia pravda*, June 3, 1997.

Lebedev, I. *Rasstrel na ploshchadi*. Moscow, 1997.

Lenin, V. I. *Polnoe sobranie sochinenii*. 5th ed. Vol. 9. Moscow, 1960.

Lewin, Moshe. "Concluding Remarks." In *Making Workers Soviet: Power, Class, and Identity*, ed. Lewis H. Siegelbaum and Ronald Grigor Suny. Ithaca, 1994.

Longworth, Philip. *The Cossacks*. London, 1969.

Makarevskii, V. "O prem'ere N. S. Khrushcheve, marshale G. K. Zhukove i generale I. A. Plieve." *Mirovaia ekonomika i mezhdunarodnye otnosheniia*, 1994, nos. 8–9.

Maksimova, E. "Imena zhertv Novocherkasskogo rasstrela." *Izvestiia*, June 5, 1992.

Malakhov, V. "Novocherkassk: Iun' 1962. Svidetel'stvo kadrovogo ofitsera prinimavshego uchastie v podavlenii 'bunta.'" *Izvestiia*, May 18, 1991.

Malia, Martin. *The Soviet Tragedy: A History of Socialism in Russia, 1917–1991*. New York, 1994.

Mandel, David. *Rabotyagi: Perestroika and After Viewed from Below: Interviews with Former Soviet Workers*. New York, 1994.

Mannteufel, Ingo. "Der 'Blutsamstag' in der Sowjetunion." *Osteuropa* 48, no. 7 (July 1998).

Mardar', Irina. *Khronika neob'iavlennogo ubiistva*. Novocherkassk, 1992.

McCauley, Martin. *Khrushchev and the Development of Soviet Agriculture: The Virgin Land Programme, 1953–1964*. New York, 1976.

McCauley, Mary. *Labor Disputes in Soviet Russia, 1957–1965*. Oxford, 1969.

McNeal, Robert H. *Tsar and Cossacks, 1895–1914*. New York, 1987.

Medvedev, Roy. *Khrushchev*. Trans. Brian Pearce. Garden City, N.Y., 1983.

Melancon, Michael. "New Findings on the Lena Goldfield Massacre: Voices from the Lena." Paper presented to the Southern Conference on Slavic Studies, Asheville, N.C., March 1998.

———. "The Ninth Circle: The Lena Goldfield Massacre of 4 April 1912." *Slavic Review* 53, no. 3 (1994).

Mickewicz, Ellen. *Changing Channels: Television and the Struggle for Power in Russia*. New York, 1997.

[Mikoian, A.] "S magnitofonnoi lenty: Golosa iz proshlogo." *Novocherkasskie vedemosti*, May 4–10, 1991.

———. *Tak bylo: Razmyshleniia o mimnuvshem*. Moscow, 1999.

———. *V nachale dvadtsatykh . . .* Moscow, 1975.

Miller, John. *Mikhail Gorbachev and the End of Soviet Power*. New York, 1993.

Molchanov, P. I., and I. G. Repnikov. *Novocherkassk: Istoricheskii-kraevedcheskii ocherk*. Rostov-on-Don, 1985.

Montias, J. M. "Economic Conditions and Political Instability in Communist Countries: Observations on Strikes, Riots, and Other Disturbances." *Studies in Comparative Communism* 13, no. 4 (Winter 1980).

Narodnoe khoziaistvo SSSR 1962. Moscow, 1963.

Nekrasov, Nicholas. *Who Can Be Happy and Free in Russia?* Trans. Juliet M. Soskice. New York, 1917.

Neuberger, Joan. *Hooliganism: Crime, Culture, and Power in St. Petersburg, 1900–1914.* Berkeley, 1993.

Nikitina, Ol'ga. "Dni zatmeniia, dni prozreniia." *Komsomolets*, June 22, 1988.

———. "Dni zatmeniia, dni prozreniia." *Komsomolets*, June 2, 1990.

———. "Novocherkassk: Chronicle of a Tragedy." *Soviet Law and Government* 30, no. 4 (1992). First published as "Novocherkassk: Khronika tragedii." *Don*, 1990, nos. 8 and 9.

———. "Oni khoteli naiti pravdu." *Rodina*, 1990, no. 3.

Nove, Alec. *An Economic History of the USSR.* New York, 1962.

———. *The Soviet Economy.* Rev. ed. New York, 1965.

"Novocherkasskaia tragediia, 1962." *Istoricheskii arkhiv*, 1993, nos. 1 and 4.

N. S. Khrushchev (1894–1971): Materialy nauchnoi konferentsii posviashchennoi 100-letiiu so dnia rozhdeniia N. S. Khrushcheva. Moscow, 1994.

"Ob'ediniaites' vokrug Khrista–Bol'sheviki povysli tseny." In *Neizvestnaia Rossiia XX vek*, vol. 3. Moscow, 1993.

"Obrashchenie TsKPSS i Soveta Ministrov SSSR ko vsem rabochim i rabotnikam, i kolkhoznikam i kolkhoznitsam, rabochim i rabotnikam sovkhozov, sovetskoi intelligentsii, ko vsem sovetskomu narodu." *Izvestiia*, June 1, 1962.

"O dal'neishem uluchshenii bytovogo obsluzhivanii naseleniia." *Spravochnik partiinogo rabotnika*, 4th ed. Moscow, 1963.

Oskol'kov, E. N., and V. V. Gatashov. "Kollektivizatsiia sel'skogo khoziaistva v severo-kavkazkom krae." In *Agrarnaia politika kommunisticheskoi partii na Donu i Severnom Kavkaze (1920–1939).* Rostov-on-Don, 1988.

Pankratova, A. M. *A History of the USSR.* 3 vols. Moscow, 1947–48.

Phillips, Laura. "Message in a Bottle: Working-Class Culture and the Struggle for Revolutionary Legitimacy." *Russian Review* 56, no. 1 (January 1997).

Podol'skii, S. "Eto bylo, bylo . . ." *Krytyi dvor*, 1990, no. 2.

———. "Ia byl ochevidtsem tragedii." *Literaturnaia gazeta*, Oct. 31, 1990.

Poltaev, G., and Iu. Bespalov. "Streliat' mozhno?" *Komsomol'skaia Pravda*, June 8, 1991.

"Poslednaia zhertva Novocherkasskoi boini." *Kazach'ia volia*, 1992, no. 1.

Pravda, Alex. "Spontaneous Workers' Activities in the Soviet Union." In *Industrial Labor in the Soviet Union*, ed. Arcadius Kahan and Blair Ruble. New York, 1979.

Rasskaz o pochetnom shakhtere: N. S. Khrushchev v Donbasse. Stalino, 1961.

"Rasskrecheny mesta zakhoronenii." *Izvestiia*, evening ed., Jan. 18, 1991.

Reddaway, Peter, ed. *Uncensored Russia*. New York, 1972.

Reichman, Henry. "The Rostov General Strike of 1902." *Russian History* 9, pt. 1 (1982): 67–85.

Remnick, David. *Lenin's Tomb: The Last Days of the Soviet Empire*. New York, 1993.

Richmond, Steven. "'The Eye of the State': An Interview with Soviet Chief Censor Vladimir Solodin." *Russian Review* 56, no. 4 (October 1997).

Ritvo, Herbert. "Totalitarianism Without Coercion." *Problems of Communism*, November–December 1960.

Rosanov, A. "Gor'koe torzhestvo." *Literaturnaia gazeta*, Oct. 9, 1991.

Rossman, Jeffrey J. "The Teikovo Cotton Workers' Strike of April 1932: Class, Gender, and Identity Politics in Stalin's Russia." *Russian Review* 56, no. 1 (January 1997).

Rudé, George. *The Crowd in History, 1730–1848*. New York, 1964.

Sablinsky, Walter. *The Road to Bloody Sunday: Father Gapon and the St. Petersburg Massacre of 1905*. Princeton, 1976.

Schroeder, Gertrude. "The Soviet Economy and the Fate of the USSR." In *The Collapse of the Soviet Union*, ed. Mark Kramer. Boulder: Westview, forthcoming.

[Semichastnyi, V. E.] "Utrennyi chai v 'Pravde Piat': Otvety na voprosy redaktsii: Vladimir Semichastnyi." *Pravda 5*, Nov. 20, 1997.

Shaposhnikov, M. K. "Ne okazhis' pered faktom zabveniia." *Semeinaia khronika*, Feb. 27, 1997.

———. "Novocherkassk—62: Diktatura bezzakoniia." *Sobesednik*, June 23, 1992.

———. "Ten' na tragediiu." *Literaturnaia gazeta*, June 4, 1991.

Sholokhov, Mikhail. *Virgin Soil Upturned*. Moscow, 1932.

Siegelbaum, Lewis H., and Ronald Grigor Suny, eds. *Making Workers Soviet: Power, Class, and Identity*. Ithaca, 1994.

Siuda, P. P. "Chto togda proiskhodilo?" *Krytyi dvor*, 1990, no. 2.

———. *Novocherkassk, 1–3 iun'ia 1962 g.: Zabastovka i rasstrel: Na osnove svidetel'stv ochevidtsev i interviu s P. P. Siuda*. Moscow, 1992. Citations are to the English translation, chap. 1 in David Mandel, *Rabotyagi: Perestroika and After Viewed from Below: Interviews with Former Soviet Workers*. New York, 1994.

———. "Novocherkasskaia tragediia." *24 Chasa*, no. 1 (August 1989).

———. "Novocherkasskaia tragediia." *Karta*, 1993, no. 1.

———. "Versiia dlia issledovatelia." *Krytyi dvor*, 1990, no. 2.

Sobranie zakonodatel'stva Rossiiskoi Federatsii. No. 24, May 10, 1996.

Solomon, Peter. "Soviet Politicians and Criminal Prosecutions: The Logic of Party Intervention." In *Cracks in the Monolith: Party Politics in the Brezhnev Era*, ed. James R. Millar. Armonk, N.Y., 1992.

Solzhenitsyn, Aleksandr I. *The Gulag Archipelago: An Experiment in Literary Investigation.* 3 vols. New York, 1974–78.

Spravochnik partiinogo rabotnika. 4th ed. Moscow, 1963.

Steele, Jonathan. "A Sausage Roll That Sparked a Massacre." *Manchester Guardian,* July 15, 1988.

Stepanov, Boris. "Propusk proveriali trizhdy . . ." *Krytyi dvor,* 1990, no. 2.

Tarasulo, Isaac J. *Gorbachev and Glasnost: Viewpoints from the Soviet Press.* Wilmington, Del., 1989.

Tatu, Michel. *Power in the Kremlin from Khrushchev to Kosygin.* Trans. Helen Katel. London, 1969.

Teague, Elizabeth. *Solidarity and the Soviet Worker: The Impact of the Polish Events of 1980 on Soviet Internal Politics.* London, 1988.

Tompson, William J. *Khrushchev: A Political Life.* London, 1995.

Transchel, Katherine S. "Under the Influence: Drinking, Temperance, and Cultural Revolution in Russia, 1900–1932." Ph.D. dissertation, University of North Carolina, Chapel Hill, 1996.

Tretetskii, A. V. "Novocherkassk: Iun' 1962 goda." *Voenno-istoricheskii zhurnal,* 1991, no. 1.

Trotsky, Leon. *History of the Russian Revolution.* 3 vols. New York, 1936.

Trubin, N. "Kak eto bylo." *Pravda,* June 3, 1991. English translation in *Soviet Law and Government* 30, no. 4 (1992).

Tsukanov, A. *Rasstrel v Novocherkasske: Tragediia prodolzhaetsia.* Volgograd, 1990.

Tucker, Robert C., and Stephen Cohen, eds. *The Great Purge Trial.* New York, 1965.

Tumarkin, Nina. *The Living and the Dead: The Rise and Fall of the Cult of World War II in Russia.* New York, 1994.

Ugolovnyi kodeks R.S.F.S.R. ofitsial'nyi tekst s izmeneniiami na 1 Avgusta 1962 g.: S prilozheniem po stateino-sistematizirovannykh materialov. Moscow, 1962.

Vedomosti s"ezda narodnykh deputatov RSFSR i Verkhovnogo Soveta RSFSR. No. 44, Oct. 19, 1991.

Volkogonov, D. A., et al., eds. *Voina i armiia.* Moscow, 1977.

Volkov, O. "Novocherkassk, 2 iun'ia 1962." *Komsomol'skaia pravda,* Apr. 27. 1991.

White, Stephen. *Gorbachev in Power.* Cambridge and New York, 1990.

Wynn, Charters. *Workers, Strikes, and Pogroms: The Donbass-Dnepr Bend in Late Imperial Russia, 1870–1905.* Princeton, 1992.

Yelin, E. "The Massacre of Workers at Novocherkassk: A Chapter in the History of the Working Class in the USSR." *Ukrainian Review,* 1984, no. 2.

Zelnik, Reginald. *Law and Disorder on the Narova River.* Berkeley, 1995.

Zhukov, Y. N. "Russia's Archives: Opportunities and Restrictions." *Perspective* 8, no. 3 (January–February 1998).

Index

235